ABOUT THIS PUBLICATION

FOR SERVICE ASSISTANCE

Customer Service Department
704.898.0770

North Carolina General Statues is published by The Muliti-Media Group of Greater Charlotte in Charlotte, North Carolina. Copyright 2015 by the Multi-Media Group of Greater Charlotte. This book or parts thereof may not be reproduced in any form, stored in a retrieval system, or transmitted in any form by any means—electronic, mechanical, photocopy, recording or otherwise—without prior written permission of the publisher, except as provided by United States of America copyright law.

The records required by U.S. Code 2257(a) through (c) and the pertinent regulations 28 C.F.R. Cli. 1, Part 75 with respect to this publication and all materials associated with such records are maintained by The Multi-Media Group of Greater Charlotte, Publisher and available for review by Attorney General.

www.visionbooks.org

Copyright © 2015 by MMGGC
All rights reserved!

TID: 4989348
ISBN (10) digit: 1502304767
ISBN (13) digit: 978-1502304766

123-4-56789-01238-Paperback
123-4-56789-01238-Hardback

First Edition

090520140547

Printed in the United States of America

2015 EDITION

# North Carolina Criminal Law And Procedure-Pamphlet # 5

# Printed In conjunction with the Administration of the Courts

North Carolina Criminal Law and Procedure
Pamphlet Reference Guide

| Chapters | Pamphlet |
|---|---|
| Chapter 1 Civil Procedure | 1 |
| Chapter 1 Civil Procedure (Continue) | 2 |
| Chapter 1A Rules of Civil Procedure | 2 |
| Chapter 1B Contribution. | 2 |
| Chapter 1C Enforcement of Judgments. | 2 |
| Chapter 1D Punitive Damages. | 2 |
| Chapter 1E Eastern Band of Cherokee Indians. | 2 |
| Chapter 1F North Carolina Uniform Interstate Depositions and Discovery Act. | 2 |
| Chapter 2 - Clerk of Superior Court [Repealed and Transferred.] | 3 |
| Chapter 3 - Commissioners of Affidavits and Deeds [Repealed.] | 3 |
| Chapter 4 - Common Law | 3 |
| Chapter 5 - Contempt [Repealed.] | 3 |
| Chapter 5A - Contempt | 3 |
| Chapter 6 - Liability for Court Costs | 3 |
| Chapter 7 - Courts [Repealed and Transferred.] | 3 |
| Chapter 7A – Judicial Department | 3 |
| Chapter 7A – Continuation (Judicial Department) | 4 |
| Chapter 7A – Continuation (Judicial Department) | 5 |
| Chapter 7B - Juvenile Code | 5 |
| Chapter 8 - Evidence | 6 |
| Chapter 8A - Interpreters for Deaf Persons [Recodified.] | 6 |
| Chapter 8B - Interpreters for Deaf Persons | 6 |
| Chapter 8C - Evidence Code | 6 |
| Chapter 9 - Jurors | 6 |
| Chapter 10 - Notaries [Repealed.] | 6 |
| Chapter 10A - Notaries [Recodified.] | 6 |
| Chapter 10B - Notaries | 6 |
| Chapter 11 - Oaths | 6 |
| Chapter 12 - Statutory Construction | 6 |
| Chapter 13 - Citizenship Restored | 6 |
| Chapter 14 - Criminal Law | 7 |
| Chapter 14 –Criminal Law (Continuation) | 8 |
| Chapter 15 - Criminal Procedure | 9 |
| Chapter 15A - Criminal Procedure Act (Continuation) | 10 |
| Chapter 15A - Criminal Procedure Act (Continuation) | 11 |
| Chapter 15B - Victims Compensation | 11 |
| Chapter 15C - Address Confidentiality Program | 11 |
| Chapter 16 - Gaming Contracts and Futures | 11 |
| Chapter 17 - Habeas Corpus | 11 |

| | |
|---|---|
| Chapter 17A - Law-Enforcement Officers [Recodified.] | 11 |
| Chapter 17B - North Carolina Criminal Justice Education and Training System [Recodified.]  Chapter 17C - North Carolina Criminal Justice Education and Training Standards Commission | 11 |
| | 11 |
| Chapter 17D - North Carolina Justice Academy | 11 |
| Chapter 17E - North Carolina Sheriffs' Education and Training Standards Commission | 11 |
| Chapter 18 - Regulation of Intoxicating Liquors [Repealed.] | 12 |
| Chapter 18A - Regulation of Intoxicating Liquors [Repealed.] | 12 |
| Chapter 18B - Regulation of Alcoholic Beverages | 12 |
| Chapter 18C - North Carolina State Lottery | 12 |
| Chapter 19 - Offenses against Public Morals | 12 |
| Chapter 19A - Protection of Animals | 12 |
| Chapter 20 - Motor Vehicles | 13 |
| Chapter 20 - Motor Vehicles (Continuation) | 14 |
| Chapter 20 - Motor Vehicles (Continuation) | 15 |
| Chapter 20 - Motor Vehicles (Continuation) | 16 |
| Chapter 21 - Bills of Lading | 17 |
| Chapter 22 - Contracts Requiring Writing | 17 |
| Chapter 22A - Signatures | 17 |
| Chapter 22B - Contracts Against Public Policy | 17 |
| Chapter 22C - Payments to Subcontractors | 17 |
| Chapter 23 - Debtor and Creditor | 17 |
| Chapter 24 – Interest | 17 |
| Chapter 25 – Uniform Commercial Code | 18 |
| Chapter 25 – Uniform Commercial Code (Continuation) | 19 |
| Chapter 25A – Retail Installment Sales Act | 20 |
| Chapter 25B - Credit | 20 |
| Chapter 25C - Sales of Artwork | 20 |
| Chapter 26 - Suretyship | 20 |
| Chapter 27 - Warehouse Receipts [Repealed.] | 20 |
| Chapter 28 - Administration [Repealed.] | 20 |
| Chapter 28A - Administration of Decedents' Estates | 20 |
| Chapter 28B - Estates of Absentees in Military Service | 20 |
| Chapter 28C - Estates of Missing Persons | 20 |
| Chapter 29 - Intestate Succession | 21 |
| Chapter 30 - Surviving Spouses | 21 |
| Chapter 31 - Wills | 21 |
| Chapter 31A - Acts Barring Property Rights | 21 |
| Chapter 31B - Renunciation of Property and Renunciation of Fiduciary Powers Act | 21 |
| Chapter 31C - Uniform Disposition of Community Property Rights at Death Act | 21 |
| Chapter 32 - Fiduciaries | 21 |
| Chapter 32A - Powers of Attorney | 21 |
| Chapter 33 - Guardian and Ward [Repealed and Recodified.] | 21 |

| | |
|---|---|
| Chapter 33A - North Carolina Uniform Transfers to Minors Act | 21 |
| Chapter 33B - North Carolina Uniform Custodial Trust Act | 21 |
| Chapter 34 - Veterans' Guardianship Act | 22 |
| Chapter 35 - Sterilization Procedures | 22 |
| Chapter 35A - Incompetency and Guardianship | 22 |
| Chapter 36 - Trusts and Trustees [Repealed.] | 22 |
| Chapter 36A - Trusts and Trustees | 22 |
| Chapter 36B - Uniform Management of Institutional Funds Act [Repealed.] | 22 |
| Chapter 36C - North Carolina Uniform Trust Code | 22 |
| Chapter 36D - North Carolina Community Third Party Trusts, Pooled Trusts | 23 |
| Chapter 36E - Uniform Prudent Management of Institutional Funds Act | 23 |
| Chapter 37 - Allocation of Principal and Income [Repealed.] | 23 |
| Chapter 37A - Uniform Principal and Income Act | 23 |
| Chapter 38 - Boundaries | 23 |
| Chapter 38A - Landowner Liability | 23 |
| Chapter 39 - Conveyances | 23 |
| Chapter 39A - Transfer Fee Covenants Prohibited | 23 |
| Chapter 40 - Eminent Domain [Repealed.] | 23 |
| Chapter 40A - Eminent Domain | 23 |
| Chapter 41 - Estates | 23 |
| Chapter 41A - State Fair Housing Act | 23 |
| Chapter 42 - Landlord and Tenant | 23 |
| Chapter 42A - Vacation Rental Act | 23 |
| Chapter 43 - Land Registration | 23 |
| Chapter 44 - Liens | 24 |
| Chapter 44A - Statutory Liens and Charges | 24 |
| Chapter 45 - Mortgages and Deeds of Trust | 24 |
| Chapter 45A - Good Funds Settlement Act | 24 |
| Chapter 46 - Partition | 24 |
| Chapter 47 - Probate and Registration | 25 |
| Chapter 47A - Unit Ownership | 25 |
| Chapter 47B - Real Property Marketable Title Act | 25 |
| Chapter 47C - North Carolina Condominium Act | 25 |
| Chapter 47D - Notice of Settlement Act [Expired.] | 25 |
| Chapter 47E - Residential Property Disclosure Act | 25 |
| Chapter 47F - North Carolina Planned Community Act | 25 |
| Chapter 47G - Option to Purchase Contracts | 25 |
| Chapter 47H - Contracts for Deed | 25 |
| Chapter 48 - Adoptions | 26 |
| Chapter 48A - Minors | 26 |
| Chapter 49 - Bastardy | 26 |
| Chapter 49A - Rights of Children | 26 |
| Chapter 50 - Divorce and Alimony | 26 |
| Chapter 50A - Uniform Child-Custody Jurisdiction and | |

| | |
|---|---|
| Enforcement Act | 26 |
| Chapter 50B - Domestic Violence | 26 |
| Chapter 50C - Civil No-Contact Orders | 26 |
| Chapter 51 - Marriage | 26 |
| Chapter 52 - Powers and Liabilities of Married Persons | 27 |
| Chapter 52A - Uniform Reciprocal Enforcement of Support Act [Repealed.] | 27 |
| Chapter 52B - Uniform Premarital Agreement Act | 27 |
| Chapter 52C - Uniform Interstate Family Support Act | 27 |
| Chapter 53 - Banks | 27 |
| Chapter 53A - Business Development Corporations and North Carolina Capital Resource Corporations | 28 |
| Chapter 53B - Financial Privacy Act | 28 |
| Chapter 54 - Cooperative Organizations | 28 |
| Chapter 54A - Capital Stock Savings and Loan Associations [Repealed.] | 28 |
| Chapter 54B - Savings and Loan Associations | 29 |
| Chapter 54C - Savings Banks | 29 |
| Chapter 55 - North Carolina Business Corporation Act | 30 |
| Chapter 55A - North Carolina Nonprofit Corporation Act | 31 |
| Chapter 55B - Professional Corporation Act | 31 |
| Chapter 55C - Foreign Trade Zones | 31 |
| Chapter 55D - Filings, Names, and Registered Agents for Corporations, Nonprofit Corporations, and Partnerships | 31 |
| Chapter 56 - Electric, Telegraph and Power Companies [Repealed.] | 31 |
| Chapter 57 - Hospital, Medical and Dental Service Corporations [Recodified.] | 31 |
| Chapter 57A - Health Maintenance Organization Act [Recodified.] | 31 |
| Chapter 57B - Health Maintenance Organization Act [Recodified.] | 31 |
| Chapter 57C - North Carolina Limited Liability Company Act. | 31 |
| Chapter 58 - Insurance. | 32 |
| Chapter 58 - Insurance (Continuation) | 33 |
| Chapter 58 - Insurance (Continuation) | 34 |
| Chapter 58 - Insurance (Continuation) | 35 |
| Chapter 58 - Insurance (Continuation) | 36 |
| Chapter 58 - Insurance (Continuation) | 37 |
| Chapter 58 - Insurance (Continuation) | 38 |
| Chapter 58A - North Carolina Health Insurance Trust Commission [Recodified.] | 38 |
| Chapter 59 - Partnership. | 39 |
| Chapter 59B - Uniform Unincorporated Nonprofit Association Act. | 39 |
| Chapter 60 - Railroads and Other Carriers [Repealed and Transferred.] | 39 |
| Chapter 61 - Religious Societies | 39 |
| Chapter 62 - Public Utilities | 39 |

| | |
|---|---|
| Chapter 62 - Public Utilities (Continuation) | 40 |
| Chapter 62A - Public Safety Telephone Service And Wireless Telephone Service | 40 |
| Chapter 63 - Aeronautics | 40 |
| Chapter 63A - North Carolina Global TransPark Authority | 40 |
| Chapter 64 - Aliens | 40 |
| Chapter 65 – Cemeteries | 40 |
| Chapter 66 - Commerce and Business | 41 |
| Chapter 67 - Dogs | 41 |
| Chapter 68 - Fences and Stock Law | 41 |
| Chapter 69 - Fire Protection | 41 |
| Chapter 70 - Indian Antiquities, Archaeological Resources and Unmarked Human Skeletal Remains Protection | 42 |
| Chapter 71 - Indians [Repealed.] | 42 |
| Chapter 71A - Indians | 42 |
| Chapter 72 - Inns, Hotels and Restaurants | 42 |
| Chapter 73 - Mills | 42 |
| Chapter 74 - Mines and Quarries | 42 |
| Chapter 74A - Company Police [Repealed.] | 42 |
| Chapter 74B - Private Protective Services Act [Repealed.] | 42 |
| Chapter 74C - Private Protective Services | 42 |
| Chapter 74D - Alarm Systems | 42 |
| Chapter 74E - Company Police Act | 42 |
| Chapter 74F - Locksmith Licensing Act | 42 |
| Chapter 74G - Campus Police Act | 42 |
| Chapter 75 - Monopolies, Trusts and Consumer Protection | 42 |
| Chapter 75A - Boating and Water Safety | 43 |
| Chapter 75B - Discrimination in Business | 43 |
| Chapter 75C - Motion Picture Fair Competition Act | 43 |
| Chapter 75D - Racketeer Influenced and Corrupt Organizations | 43 |
| Chapter 75E - Unlawful Activities in Connection With Certain Corporate Transactions | 43 |
| Chapter 76 - Navigation | 43 |
| Chapter 76A - Navigation and Pilotage Commissions | 43 |
| Chapter 77 - Rivers, Creeks, and Coastal Waters | 43 |
| Chapter 78 - Securities Law [Repealed.] | 43 |
| Chapter 78A - North Carolina Securities Act | 43 |
| Chapter 78B - Tender Offer Disclosure Act [Repealed.] | 43 |
| Chapter 78C - Investment Advisers | 43 |
| Chapter 78D - Commodities Act | 43 |
| Chapter 79 - Strays [Repealed.] | 43 |
| Chapter 80 - Trademarks, Brands, etc. | 44 |
| Chapter 81 - Weights and Measures [Recodified.] | 44 |
| Chapter 81A - Weights and Measures Act of 1975. | 44 |
| Chapter 82 - Wrecks [Repealed.] | 44 |
| Chapter 83 - Architects [Recodified.] | 44 |

| | |
|---|---|
| Chapter 83A - Architects | 44 |
| Chapter 84 - Attorneys-at-Law | 44 |
| Chapter 84A - Foreign Legal Consultants | 44 |
| Chapter 85 - Auctions and Auctioneers [Repealed.] | 44 |
| Chapter 85A - Bail Bondsmen and Runners [Recodified.] | 44 |
| Chapter 85B - Auctions and Auctioneers | 44 |
| Chapter 85C - Bail Bondsmen and Runners [Recodified.] | 44 |
| Chapter 86 - Barbers [Recodified.] | 44 |
| Chapter 86A - Barbers | 44 |
| Chapter 87 - Contractors | 44 |
| Chapter 88 - Cosmetic Art [Repealed.] | 44 |
| Chapter 88A - Electrolysis Practice Act | 44 |
| Chapter 88B - Cosmetic Art | 45 |
| Chapter 89 - Engineering and Land Surveying [Recodified.] | 45 |
| Chapter 89A - Landscape Architects | 45 |
| Chapter 89B - Foresters | 45 |
| Chapter 89C - Engineering and Land Surveying | 45 |
| Chapter 89D - Landscape Contractors | 45 |
| Chapter 89E - Geologists Licensing Act | 45 |
| Chapter 89F - North Carolina Soil Scientist Licensing Act | 45 |
| Chapter 89G - Irrigation Contractors | 45 |
| Chapter 90 - Medicine and Allied Occupations | 45 |
| Chapter 90 - Medicine and Allied Occupations (Continuation) | 46 |
| Chapter 90 - Medicine and Allied Occupations (Continuation) | 47 |
| Chapter 90 - Medicine and Allied Occupations (Continuation) | 48 |
| Chapter 90A - Sanitarians and Water and Wastewater Treatment Facility Operators | 48 |
| Chapter 90B - Social Worker Certification and Licensure Act | 48 |
| Chapter 90C - North Carolina Recreational Therapy Licensure Act | 48 |
| Chapter 90D - Interpreters and Transliterators | 48 |
| Chapter 91 - Pawnbrokers [Repealed.] | 48 |
| Chapter 91A - Pawnbrokers Modernization Act of 1989 | 48 |
| Chapter 92 - Photographers [Deleted.] | 48 |
| Chapter 93 - Certified Public Accountants | 48 |
| Chapter 93A - Real Estate License Law | 49 |
| Chapter 93B - Occupational Licensing Boards | 49 |
| Chapter 93C - Watchmakers [Repealed.] | 49 |
| Chapter 93D - North Carolina State Hearing Aid Dealers and Fitters Board. | 49 |
| Chapter 93E - North Carolina Appraisers Act | 49 |
| Chapter 94 - Apprenticeship | 49 |
| Chapter 95 - Department of Labor and Labor Regulations | 49 |
| Chapter 95 - Department of Labor and Labor Regulations (Continuation) | 50 |
| Chapter 96 - Employment Security | 50 |
| Chapter 97 - Workers' Compensation Act | 50 |
| Chapter 97 - Workers' Compensation Act (Continuation) | 51 |

| | |
|---|---|
| Chapter 98 - Burnt and Lost Records | 51 |
| Chapter 99 - Libel and Slander | 51 |
| Chapter 99A - Civil Remedies for Criminal Actions | 51 |
| Chapter 99B - Products Liability | 51 |
| Chapter 99C - Actions Relating to Winter Sports Safety and Accidents | 51 |
| Chapter 99D - Civil Rights | 51 |
| Chapter 99E - Special Liability Provisions | 51 |
| Chapter 100 - Monuments, Memorials and Parks | 51 |
| Chapter 101 - Names of Persons | 51 |
| Chapter 102 - Official Survey Base | 51 |
| Chapter 103 - Sundays, Holidays and Special Days | 51 |
| Chapter 104 - United States Lands | 51 |
| Chapter 104A - Degrees of Kinship | 51 |
| Chapter 104B - Hurricanes or Other Acts of Nature | 51 |
| Chapter 104C - Atomic Energy, Radioactivity and Ionizing Radiation [Repealed and Recodified.] | 51 |
| Chapter 104D - Southern States Energy Compact | 51 |
| Chapter 104E - North Carolina Radiation Protection Act | 51 |
| Chapter 104F - Southeast Interstate Low-Level Radioactive Waste Management Compact [Repealed] | 51 |
| Chapter 104G - North Carolina Low-Level Radioactive Waste Management Authority Act of 1987 [Repealed] | 51 |
| Chapter 105 - Taxation | 51 |
| Chapter 105 - Taxation (Continuation) | 52 |
| Chapter 105 - Taxation (Continuation) | 53 |
| Chapter 105 - Taxation (Continuation) | 54 |
| Chapter 105A - Setoff Debt Collection Act | 55 |
| Chapter 105B - Defaulted Student Loan Recovery Act | 55 |
| Chapter 106 - Agriculture | 55 |
| Chapter 106 - Agriculture (Continue) | 56 |
| Chapter 106 - Agriculture (Continue) | 57 |
| Chapter 107 - Agricultural Development Districts [Repealed.] | 57 |
| Chapter 108 - Social Services [Repealed and Recodified.] | 57 |
| Chapter 108A - Social Services | 57 |
| Chapter 108B - Community Action Programs | 58 |
| Chapter 108C Medicaid and Health Choice Provider Requirements. | 58 |
| Chapter 108D Medicaid Managed Care for Behavioral Health Services. | 58 |
| Chapter 109 - Bonds [Recodified.] | 58 |
| Chapter 110 - Child Welfare | 58 |
| Chapter 111 - Aid to the Blind | 58 |
| Chapter 112 - Confederate Homes and Pensions [Repealed.] | 58 |
| Chapter 113 - Conservation and Development | 58 |
| Chapter 113 - Conservation and Development (Continuation) | 59 |

| | |
|---|---|
| Chapter 113A - Pollution Control and Environment | 59 |
| Chapter 113A - Pollution Control and Environment (Continuation) | 60 |
| Chapter 113B - North Carolina Energy Policy Act of 1975 | 60 |
| Chapter 114 - Department of Justice | 60 |
| Chapter 115 - Elementary and Secondary Education [Repealed.] | 60 |
| Chapter 115A - Community Colleges, Technical Institutes, and Industrial Education Centers [Repealed.] | 60 |
| Chapter 115B - Tuition and Fee Waivers | 60 |
| Chapter 115C - Elementary and Secondary Education | 60 |
| Chapter 115C - Elementary and Secondary Education (Continuation) | 61 |
| Chapter 115C - Elementary and Secondary Education (Continuation) | 62 |
| Chapter 115C - Elementary and Secondary Education (Continuation) | 63 |
| Chapter 115D - Community Colleges | 63 |
| Chapter 115E - Private Educational Facilities Finance Act [Recodified] | 63 |
| Chapter 116 - Higher Education | 63 |
| Chapter 116 - Higher Education (Continuation) | 63 |
| Chapter 116A - Escheats and Abandoned Property [Repealed.] | 64 |
| Chapter 116B - Escheats and Abandoned Property | 64 |
| Chapter 116C - Continuum of Education Programs | 64 |
| Chapter 116D - Higher Education Bonds | 64 |
| Chapter 116E -Education Longitudinal Data System | 64 |
| Chapter 117 - Electrification | 64 |
| Chapter 118 - Firemen's and Rescue Squad Workers' Relief and Pension Funds [Recodified.] | 64 |
| Chapter 118A - Firemen's Death Benefit Act [Repealed.] | 64 |
| Chapter 118B - Members of a Rescue Squad Death Benefit Act [Repealed.] | 64 |
| Chapter 119 - Gasoline and Oil Inspection and Regulation | 64 |
| Chapter 120 - General Assembly | 65 |
| Chapter 120 - General Assembly (Continuation) | 66 |
| Chapter 120 - General Assembly (Continuation) | 67 |
| Chapter 120C - Lobbying | 67 |
| Chapter 121 - Archives and History | 67 |
| Chapter 122 - Hospitals for the Mentally Disordered [Repealed.] | 67 |
| Chapter 122A - North Carolina Housing Finance Agency | 67 |
| Chapter 122B - North Carolina Agricultural Facilities Finance Act [Repealed.] | 67 |
| Chapter 122C - Mental Health, Developmental Disabilities, and Substance Abuse Act of 1985 | 67 |
| Chapter 122C - Mental Health, Developmental Disabilities, and Substance Abuse Act of 1985 (Continuation) | 68 |

| | |
|---|---|
| Chapter 122D - North Carolina Agricultural Finance Act | 68 |
| Chapter 122E - North Carolina Housing Trust and Oil Overcharge Act | 68 |
| Chapter 123 - Impeachment | 69 |
| Chapter 123A - Industrial Development [Repealed.] | 69 |
| Chapter 124 - Internal Improvements | 69 |
| Chapter 125 - Libraries | 69 |
| Chapter 126 - State Personnel System | 69 |
| Chapter 127 - Militia [Repealed.] | 69 |
| Chapter 127A - Militia | 69 |
| Chapter 127B - Military Affairs | 69 |
| Chapter 127C - Advisory Commission on Military Affairs | 69 |
| Chapter 128 - Offices and Public Officers | 69 |
| Chapter 128 - Offices and Public Officers (Continuation) | 70 |
| Chapter 129 - Public Buildings and Grounds | 70 |
| Chapter 130 - Public Health [Repealed.] | 70 |
| Chapter 130A - Public Health | 70 |
| Chapter 130A - Public Health (Continuation) | 71 |
| Chapter 130A - Public Health (Continuation) | 72 |
| Chapter 130B - Hazardous Waste Management Commission [Repealed.] | 72 |
| Chapter 131 - Public Hospitals [Repealed.] | 72 |
| Chapter 131A - Health Care Facilities Finance Act | 72 |
| Chapter 131B - Licensing of Ambulatory Surgical Facilities [Repealed.] | 72 |
| Chapter 131C - Charitable Solicitation Licensure Act [Repealed.] | 72 |
| Chapter 131D - Inspection and Licensing of Facilities | 72 |
| Chapter 131E - Health Care Facilities and Services | 72 |
| Chapter 131E - Health Care Facilities and Services (Continuation) | 73 |
| Chapter 131F - Solicitation of Contributions | 73 |
| Chapter 132 - Public Records | 73 |
| Chapter 133 - Public Works | 74 |
| Chapter 134 - Youth Development [Recodified.] | 74 |
| Chapter 134A - Youth Services [Repealed.] | 74 |
| Chapter 135 - Retirement System for Teachers and State Employees; Social Security; Health Insurance Program for Children | 74 |
| Chapter 135 - Retirement System for Teachers and State Employees; Social Security; Health Insurance Program for Children | 75 |
| Chapter 136 - Transportation | 75 |
| Chapter 136 - Transportation (Continuation) | 76 |
| Chapter 137 - Rural Rehabilitation [Repealed.] | 76 |
| Chapter 138 - Salaries, Fees and Allowances | 76 |
| Chapter 138A - State Government Ethics Act | 76 |

| | |
|---|---|
| Chapter 139 - Soil and Water Conservation Districts | 76 |
| Chapter 140 - State Art Museum; Symphony and Art Societies | 76 |
| Chapter 140A - State Awards System | 76 |
| Chapter 141 - State Boundaries | 76 |
| Chapter 142 - State Debt | 76 |
| Chapter 143 - State Departments, Institutions, and Commissions | 77 |
| Chapter 143 - State Departments, Institutions, and Commissions (Continuation) | 78 |
| Chapter 143 - State Departments, Institutions, and Commissions (Continuation) | 79 |
| Chapter 143 - State Departments, Institutions, and Commissions (Continuation) | 80 |
| Chapter 143A - State Government Reorganization | 80 |
| Chapter 143B - Executive Organization Act of 1973 | 80 |
| Chapter 143B - Executive Organization Act of 1973 (Continuation) | 81 |
| Chapter 143B - Executive Organization Act of 1973 (Continuation) | 82 |
| Chapter 143C - State Budget Act | 83 |
| Chapter 143D - The State Governmental Accountability and Internal Control Act | 83 |
| Chapter 144 - State Flag, Official Governmental Flags, Motto, and Colors | 83 |
| Chapter 145 - State Symbols and Other Official Adoptions. | 83 |
| Chapter 146 - State Lands | 83 |
| Chapter 147 - State Officers | 83 |
| Chapter 148 - State Prison System | 84 |
| Chapter 149 - State Song and Toast | 84 |
| Chapter 150 - Uniform Revocation of Licenses [Repealed.] | 84 |
| Chapter 150A - Administrative Procedure Act [Recodified.] | 84 |
| Chapter 150B - Administrative Procedure Act | 84 |
| Chapter 151 - Constables [Repealed.] | 84 |
| Chapter 152 - Coroners | 84 |
| Chapter 152A - County Medical Examiner [Repealed.] | 84 |
| Chapter 152A - County Medical Examiner [Repealed.] (Continuation) | 85 |
| Chapter 153 - Counties and County Commissioners [Repealed.] | 85 |
| Chapter 153A - Counties | 85 |
| Chapter 153B - Mountain Resources Planning Act | 85 |
| Chapter 153C - Uwharrie Regional Resources Act | 85 |
| Chapter 154 - County Surveyor [Repealed.] | 85 |
| Chapter 155 - County Treasurer [Repealed.] | 85 |
| Chapter 156 - Drainage | 85 |

| | |
|---|---|
| Chapter 156 – Drainage (Continuation) | 86 |
| Chapter 157 - Housing Authorities and Projects | 86 |
| Chapter 157A - Historic Properties Commissions [Transferred.] | 86 |
| Chapter 158 - Local Development | 86 |
| Chapter 159 - Local Government Finance | 86 |
| Chapter 159 - Local Government Finance (Continuation) | 87 |
| Chapter 159A - Pollution Abatement and Industrial Facilities Financing Act [Unconstitutional.] | 87 |
| Chapter 159B - Joint Municipal Electric Power and Energy Act | 87 |
| Chapter 159C - Industrial and Pollution Control Facilities Financing Act | 87 |
| Chapter 159D - The North Carolina Capital Facilities Financing Act | 87 |
| Chapter 159E - Registered Public Obligations Act | 87 |
| Chapter 159F - North Carolina Energy Development Authority [Repealed.] | 87 |
| Chapter 159G - Water Infrastructure | 87 |
| Chapter 159H - [Reserved.] | 87 |
| Chapter 159I - Solid Waste Management Loan Program and Local Government Special Obligation Bonds | 87 |
| Chapter 160 - Municipal Corporations [Repealed And Transferred.] | 87 |
| Chapter 160A - Cities and Towns | 88 |
| Chapter 160A - Cities and Towns (Continuation) | 89 |
| Chapter 160B - Consolidated City-County Act | 89 |
| Chapter 160C - Baseball Park Districts [Repealed.] | 90 |
| Chapter 161 - Register of Deeds | 90 |
| Chapter 162 - Sheriff | 90 |
| Chapter 162A - Water and Sewer Systems | 90 |
| Chapter 162B Continuity of Local Government in Emergency. | 90 |
| Chapter 163 Elections and Election Laws. | 90 |
| Chapter 163 Elections and Election Laws. (Continuation) | 91 |
| Chapter 164 Concerning the General Statutes of North Carolina. | 92 |
| Chapter 165 Veterans. | 92 |
| Chapter 166 Civil Preparedness Agencies [Repealed.] | 92 |
| Chapter 166A North Carolina Emergency Management Act. | 92 |
| Chapter 167 State Civil Air Patrol [Repealed.] | 92 |
| Chapter 168 Persons with Disabilities. | 92 |
| Chapter 168A Persons With Disabilities Protection Act. | 92 |

SUBCHAPTER XIII. SENTENCING SERVICES PROGRAM.

Article 61.

Sentencing Services Program.

§ 7A-770. Purpose.

This Article shall be known and may be cited as the "Sentencing Services Act." The purpose of this Article is to establish a statewide sentencing services program that will provide the judicial system with information that will assist that system in imposing sentences that make the most effective use of available resources. In furtherance of this purpose, this Article provides for the following:

(1)     Establishment of local programs that can provide judges and other court officials with information about local correctional programs that are appropriate for offenders who require a comprehensive sentencing plan that combines punishment, control, and rehabilitation services.

(2)     Increased opportunities for certain felons to make restitution to victims of crime through financial reimbursement or community service.

(3)     Local involvement in the development of sentencing services to assure that they are specifically designed to meet local needs.

(4)     Effective use of available community corrections programs by advising judges and other court officials of the offenders most suited for a particular program. (1983, c. 909, s. 1; 1991, c. 566, ss. 2, 3; 1999-306, s. 1.)

§ 7A-771. Definitions.

As used in this Article:

(1)     Recodified as subdivision (3b) by Session Laws 1999-306, s. 1, effective January 1, 2000.

(2)     Recodified as subdivision (3a) by Session Laws 1999-306, s. 1, effective January 1, 2000.

(2a)    "Director" means the Director of Indigent Defense Services.

(3)     Repealed by Session Laws 1999-306, s. 1, effective January 1, 2000.

(3a)    "Sentencing plan" means a plan presented in writing to the sentencing judge which provides a detailed assessment and description of the offender's background, including available information about past criminal activity, a matching of the specific offender's needs with available resources, and, if appropriate, the program's recommendations regarding an intermediate sentence.

(3b)    "Sentencing services program" means an agency or State-run office within the superior court district which shall (i) prepare sentencing plans; (ii) arrange or contract with public and private agencies for necessary services for offenders; and (iii) assist offenders in initially obtaining services ordered as part of a sentence entered pursuant to a sentencing plan, if the assistance is not available otherwise.

(4)     Repealed by Session Laws 1991, c. 566, s. 4.

(4a)    "Superior court district" means a superior court district established by G.S. 7A-41 for those districts consisting of one or more entire counties, and otherwise means the applicable set of districts as that term is defined in G.S. 7A-41.1.

(5)     Repealed by Session Laws 1999-306, s. 1, effective January 1, 2000. (1983, c. 909, s. 1; 1989, c. 770, s. 58; 1991, c. 566, ss. 2, 4; 1993 (Reg. Sess., 1994), c. 767, s. 14; 1995, c. 324, s. 21.9(c); 1997-57, s. 5; 1999-306, s. 1; 2002-126, s. 14.7(d).)


§ 7A-772.  Allocation of funds.

(a)     The Director may award grants in accordance with the policies established by this Article and in accordance with any laws made for that purpose, including appropriations acts and provisions in appropriations acts, and adopt regulations for the implementation, operation, and monitoring of sentencing services programs. Sentencing services programs that are grantees shall use the funds exclusively to develop a sentencing services program that provides sentencing information to judges and other court officials. Grants shall be awarded by the Director to agencies whose comprehensive program plans promise best to meet the goals set forth herein. The Director shall consider the plan required by G.S. 7A-774 in making funding decisions. If a senior resident superior court judge has not formally endorsed the plan, the Director shall consider that fact in making grant decisions, but the Director may, if appropriate, award grants to a program in which the judge has not endorsed the plan as submitted.

(b) The Director may establish local sentencing services programs and appoint those staff as the Director deems necessary. These personnel may serve as full-time or part-time State employees or may be hired on a contractual basis when determined appropriate by the director. Contracts entered under the authority of this subsection shall be exempt from the competitive bidding procedures under Chapter 143 of the General Statutes. The Office of Indigent Defense Services shall adopt rules necessary and appropriate for the administration of the program. Funds appropriated by the General Assembly for the establishment and maintenance of sentencing services programs under this Article shall be administered by the Office of Indigent Defense Services. (1983, c. 909, s. 1; 1991, c. 566, ss. 2, 5; 1995, c. 324, s. 21.9(d); 1999-306, s. 1; 2002-126, s. 14.7(e).)

§ 7A-773. Responsibilities of a sentencing services program.

A sentencing services program shall be responsible for:

(1) Identifying offenders who:

a. Are charged with or have been offered a plea by the State for a felony offense for which the class of offense and prior record level authorize the court to impose an active punishment, but do not require that it do so;

b. Have a high risk of committing future crimes without appropriate sanctions and interventions; and

c. Would benefit from the preparation of an intensive and comprehensive sentencing plan of the type prepared by sentencing services programs.

(2) Preparing detailed sentencing services plans requested pursuant to G.S. 7A-773.1 for presentation to the sentencing judge.

(3) Contracting or arranging with public or private agencies for services described in the sentencing plan.

(4) Repealed by Session Laws 1999-306, s. 1. (1983, c. 909, s. 1; 1991, c. 566, s. 2; 1993 (Reg. Sess., 1994), c. 767, s. 15; 1995, c. 324, s. 21.9(e); 1999-306, s. 1.)

§ 7A-773.1. Who may request plans; disposition of plans; contents of plans.

(a) A judge presiding over a case in which the offender meets the criteria set forth in G.S. 7A-773(1) may request, at any time prior to the imposition of sentence, that the sentencing services program provide a sentencing plan. The court may also request, at any time prior to the imposition of sentence, that the program provide a sentencing plan in misdemeanor cases in which the class of offense is Class A1 or Class 1 and the prior conviction level is Level III, if the court determines that the preparation of such a plan is in the interest of justice. In addition, in cases in which the offender meets the criteria set forth in G.S. 7A-773, the defendant or a prosecutor, at any time before the court has accepted a guilty plea or received a guilty verdict, may request that the program provide a plan. However, prior to an adjudication of guilt, a defendant may decline to participate in the preparation of a plan within a reasonable time after the request is made. In that case, no plan shall be prepared or presented to the court by the sentencing services program prior to an adjudication of guilt. A defendant's decision not to participate shall be made in writing and filed with the court. The comprehensive sentencing services program plan prepared pursuant to G.S. 7A-774 shall define what constitutes a reasonable time within the meaning of this subsection.

(b) Any sentencing plan prepared by a sentencing services program shall be presented to the court, the defendant, and the State in an appropriate manner.

(c) Sentencing plans prepared by sentencing services programs may include recommendations for use of any treatment or correctional resources available, unless the sentencing court instructs otherwise. Sentencing plans that identify an offender's needs for education, treatment, control, or other services shall, to the extent feasible, also identify resources to meet those needs. Plans may report that no intermediate punishment is appropriate under the circumstances of the case.

(d) To the extent allowed by law, the sentencing services program shall develop procedures to ensure that the program staff may work with offenders before a plea is entered. To that end, information obtained in the course of preparing a sentencing plan may not be used by the State for any purpose at trial and is subject to the provisions of G.S. 15A-1333. (1999-306, s. 1; 2000-67, s. 15.9(b).)

§ 7A-774. Requirements for a comprehensive sentencing services program plan.

Agencies applying for grants shall prepare a comprehensive sentencing services program plan for the development, implementation, operation, and improvement of a sentencing services program for the superior court district, as prescribed by the Director. The plan shall be updated annually and shall be submitted to the senior resident superior court judge for the superior court district for the judge's advice and written endorsement. The plan shall then be forwarded to the Director for approval. The plan shall include:

(1) Goals and objectives of the sentencing services program.

(2) Specification of the kinds or categories of offenders for whom the programs will provide sentencing information to the courts.

(3) Proposed procedures for the identification of appropriate offenders to comply with the plan and the criteria in G.S. 7A-773(1).

(4) Procedures for preparing and presenting plans to the court.

(4a) Strategies for ensuring that judges and court officials who are possible referral sources use the program's services in appropriate cases.

(5) Procedures for obtaining services from existing public or private agencies, and a detailed budget for staff, contracted services, and all other costs.

(6) to (8). Repealed by Session Laws 1999-306, s. 1. (1983, c. 909, s. 1; 1991, c. 566, ss. 2, 7; 1999-306, s. 1.)

§ 7A-775. Sentencing services board.

(a) Each sentencing services program shall establish a sentencing services board to provide direction and assistance to the sentencing services program in the implementation and evaluation of the plan. Sentencing services boards may be organized as nonprofit corporations under Chapter 55A of the General Statutes. The sentencing services board shall consist of not less than 12 members, and shall include, insofar as possible, judges, district attorneys, attorneys, social workers, law-enforcement officers, probation officers, and other interested persons. The sentencing services board shall meet on a regular basis, and its duties include, but are not limited to, the following:

(1)     Preparation and submission of the sentencing services program plan to the senior resident superior court judge and the Director annually, as provided in G.S. 7A-772(a);

(1a)    Development of an annual budget for the program;

(2)     Hiring, firing, and evaluation of program personnel;

(3)     Selection of board members;

(4)     Arranging for an annual financial audit.

(5)     Development of procedures for contracting for services.

(b)     If the board serves as an advisory board to a sentencing services program located in a local or State agency, the board's duties do not include budgeting and personnel decisions. (1983, c. 909, s. 1; 1991, c. 566, ss. 2, 6; 1999-306, s. 1; 2006-203, s. 11; 2006-264, s. 1(a).)

§ 7A-776. Limitation on use of funds.

Funds provided for use under the provisions of this Article shall not be used for the operating costs, construction, or any other costs associated with local jail confinement, or for any purpose other than the operation of a sentencing services program that complies with this Article. (1983, c. 909, s. 1; 1991, c. 566, s. 2; 1999-306, s. 1.)

§ 7A-777. Evaluation.

The Director shall evaluate each sentencing services program on an annual basis to determine the degree to which the program effectively meets the needs of the courts in its judicial district by providing them with sentencing information. In conducting the evaluation, the Director shall consider the goals and objectives established in the program's plan, as well as the extent to which the program is able to ensure that the offenders served by the plan meet the criteria established in G.S. 7A-773(1). (1983, c. 909, s. 1; 1991, c. 566, ss. 2, 7; 1999-306, s. 1.)

§§ 7A-778 through 7A-789. Reserved for future codification purposes.

SUBCHAPTER XIV. DRUG TREATMENT COURTS.

Article 62.

North Carolina Drug Treatment Court Act.

§ 7A-790. Short title.

This Article shall be known and may be cited as the "North Carolina Drug Treatment Court Act of 1995". (1995, c. 507, s. 21.6(a); 1998-23, s. 9; 1998-212, s. 16.15(a).)

§ 7A-791. Purpose.

The General Assembly recognizes that a critical need exists in this State for judicial programs that will reduce the incidence of alcohol and other drug abuse or dependence and crimes, including the offense of driving while impaired, delinquent acts, and child abuse and neglect committed as a result of alcohol and other drug abuse or dependence, and child abuse and neglect where alcohol and other drug abuse or dependence are significant factors in the child abuse and neglect. It is the intent of the General Assembly by this Article to create a program to facilitate the creation of local drug treatment court programs and driving while impaired (DWI) treatment court programs. (1995, c. 507, s. 21.6(a); 1998-23, s. 9; 1998-212, s. 16.15(a), (b); 2001-424, s. 22.8(a); 2009-451, s. 15.11.)

§ 7A-792. Goals.

The goals of the drug treatment court programs funded under this Article include the following:

(1) To reduce alcoholism and other drug dependencies among adult and juvenile offenders and defendants and among respondents in juvenile petitions for abuse, neglect, or both;

(2) To reduce criminal and delinquent recidivism and the incidence of child abuse and neglect;

(3) To reduce the aclohol-related and other drug-related court workload;

(4) To increase the personal, familial, and societal accountability of adult and juvenile offenders and defendants and respondents in juvenile petitions for abuse, neglect, or both; and

(5) To promote effective interaction and use of resources among criminal and juvenile justice personnel, child protective services personnel, and community agencies. (1995, c. 507, s. 21.6(a); 1998-23, s. 9; 1998-212, s. 16.15(a); 2001-424, s. 22.8(b).)

§ 7A-793. Establishment of Program.

The North Carolina Drug Treatment Court Program is established in the Administrative Office of the Courts to facilitate the creation and funding of local drug treatment court programs. The Director of the Administrative Office of the Courts shall provide any necessary staff for planning, organizing, and administering the program. Local drug treatment court programs funded pursuant to this Article shall be operated consistently with the guidelines adopted pursuant to G.S. 7A-795. Local drug treatment court programs established and funded pursuant to this Article may consist of adult drug treatment court programs, juvenile drug treatment court programs, family drug treatment court programs, or any combination of these programs. (1995, c. 507, s. 21.6(a); 1998-23, s. 9; 1998-212, s. 16.15(a), (c); 2001-424, s. 22.8(c).)

§ 7A-794. Fund administration.

The Drug Treatment Court Program Fund is created in the Administrative Office of the Courts and is administered by the Director of the Administrative Office of the Courts in consultation with the State Drug Treatment Court Advisory Committee. (1995, c. 507, s. 21.6(a); 1998-23, s. 9; 1998-212, s. 16.15(a), (d); 2007-393, s. 12.)

§ 7A-795. State Drug Treatment Court Advisory Committee.

The State Drug Treatment Court Advisory Committee is established to develop and recommend to the Director of the Administrative Office of the Courts guidelines for the drug treatment court program and to monitor local programs wherever they are implemented. The Committee shall be chaired by the Director or the Director's designee and shall consist of not less than seven members appointed by the Director and broadly representative of the courts, law enforcement, corrections, juvenile justice, child protective services, and substance abuse treatment communities. In developing guidelines, the Advisory Committee shall consider the Substance Abuse and the Courts Action Plan and other recommendations of the Substance Abuse and the Courts State Task Force. (1995, c. 507, s. 21.6(a); 1998-23, s. 9; 1998-212, s. 16.15(a), (e); 2001-424, s. 22.8(d).)

§ 7A-796. Local drug treatment court management committee.

Each judicial district choosing to establish a drug treatment court shall form a local drug treatment court management committee, which shall be comprised to assure representation appropriate to the type or types of drug treatment court operations to be conducted in the district and shall consist of persons appointed by the senior resident superior court judge with the concurrence of the chief district court judge and the district attorney for that district, chosen from the following list:

(1) A judge of the superior court;

(2) A judge of the district court;

(3) A district attorney or assistant district attorney;

(4) A public defender or assistant public defender in judicial districts served by a public defender;

(5) An attorney representing a county department of social services within the district;

(6) A representative of the guardian ad litem;

(7) A member of the private criminal defense bar;

(8) A member of the private bar who represents respondents in department of social services juvenile matters;

(9) A clerk of superior court;

(10) The trial court administrator in judicial districts served by a trial court administrator;

(11) The director or member of the child welfare services division of a county department of social services within the district;

(12) The chief juvenile court counselor for the district;

(13) A probation officer;

(14) A local law enforcement officer;

(15) A representative of the local school administrative unit;

(16) A representative of the local community college;

(17) A representative of the treatment providers;

(18) A representative of the area mental health program;

(19) Any local drug treatment coordinator; and

(20) Any other persons selected by the local management committee.

The local drug treatment court management committee shall develop local guidelines and procedures, not inconsistent with the State guidelines, that are necessary for the operation and evaluation of the local drug treatment court. (1995, c. 507, s. 21.6(a); 1998-23, s. 9; 1998-212, s. 16.15(a), (f); 2001-424, s. 22.8(e); 2008-187, s. 4.)

§ 7A-797. Eligible population; drug treatment court procedures.

The Director of the Administrative Office of the Courts, in conjunction with the State Drug Treatment Court Advisory Committee, shall develop criteria for eligibility and other procedural and substantive guidelines for drug treatment court operation. (1995, c. 507, s. 21.6(a); 1998-212, s. 16.15(a).)

§ 7A-798: Repealed by Session Laws 2007-393, s. 13, effective October 1, 2007.

§ 7A-799. Treatment not guaranteed.

Nothing contained in this Article shall confer a right or an expectation of a right to treatment for a defendant or offender within the criminal or juvenile justice system or a respondent in a juvenile petition for abuse, neglect, or both. (1995, c. 507, s. 21.6(a); 1998-23, s. 9; 1998-212, s. 16.15(a); 2001-424, s. 22.8(f).)

§ 7A-800. Payment of costs of treatment program.

Each defendant, offender, or respondent in a juvenile petition for abuse, neglect, or both, who receives treatment under a local drug treatment court program shall contribute to the cost of the alcohol and other drug abuse or dependency treatment received in the drug treatment court program, based upon guidelines developed by the local drug treatment court management committee. (1995, c. 507, s. 21.6(a); 1998-23, s. 9; 1998-212, s. 16.15(a), (h); 2001-424, s. 22.8(g).)

§ 7A-801. Monitoring and annual report.

The Administrative Office of the Courts shall monitor all State-recognized and funded local drug treatment courts, prepare an annual report on the implementation, operation, and effectiveness of the statewide drug treatment court program, and submit the report to the General Assembly by March 1 of each year. Each local drug treatment court program shall submit evaluation reports to the Administrative Office of the Courts as requested. (1995, c. 507, s. 21.6(a); 1998-23, s. 9; 1998-212, s. 16.15(a), (i); 2007-393, s. 14.)

§ 7A-802. Reserved for future codification purposes.

§ 7A-803. Reserved for future codification purposes.

§ 7A-804. Reserved for future codification purposes.

SUBCHAPTER XV. CONFERENCE OF CLERKS OF SUPERIOR COURT.

Article 63.

Conference of Clerks of Superior Court.

§ 7A-805. Establishment and purpose.

There is created the Conference of Clerks of Superior Court of North Carolina, of which each clerk of superior court is a member. The purpose of the Conference is to assist in improving the administration of justice in North Carolina by coordinating the efforts of the various clerks of superior court, by assisting them in the administration of their offices, and by exercising the powers and performing the duties provided for in this Article. (2005-100, s. 1.)

§ 7A-806. Annual meetings; organization; election of officers.

(a) Annual Meetings. - The Conference shall meet each summer and winter at a time and place selected by the President of the Conference.

(b) Election of Officers. - Officers of the Conference are a President, two Vice Presidents, a Secretary, a Treasurer, and other officers from among its membership that the Conference may designate in its bylaws. Officers are elected for one-year terms at the annual summer conference and take office immediately following their election.

(c) Executive Committee. - The Executive Committee of the Conference consists of the President, the two Vice Presidents, the Secretary, the Treasurer, and seven other members of the Conference. One of these seven members shall be the immediate past president if there is one and that past president continues to be a member.

(d) Organization and Functioning; Bylaws. - The bylaws may provide for the organization and functioning of the Conference, including the powers and duties of its officers and committees. The bylaws shall state the number of members required to constitute a quorum at any meeting of the Conference or the Executive Committee. The bylaws shall set out the procedure for amending the bylaws.

(e) Calling Meetings; Duty to Attend. - The President or the Executive Committee may call a meeting of the Conference upon 10 days' notice to the members, except upon written waiver of notice signed by at least three-fourths of the members. A member should attend each meeting of the Conference and the Executive Committee of which he is given notice. Members are entitled to reimbursement for travel and subsistence expenses at the rate applicable to State employees. (2005-100, s. 1; 2006-66, s. 14.20(a); 2006-221, s. 15.)

§ 7A-807. Powers of Conference.

(a) The Conference may:

(1) Cooperate with citizens and other public and private agencies to promote the effective administration of justice.

(2) Develop advisory manuals to assist in the organization and administration of their offices, case management, calendaring, case tracking, filing, and office procedures.

(3) Work with the cooperation of the Administrative Office of the Courts and the Institute of Government of the School of Government at UNC-Chapel Hill to provide education and training programs for the clerks of superior court and their staff.

(b) The Conference may not adopt rules pursuant to Chapter 150B of the General Statutes. (2005-100, s. 1.)

§ 7A-808. Executive secretary; clerical support.

The Conference may employ an executive secretary and any necessary supporting staff to assist it in carrying out its duties. (2005-100, s. 1.)

§ 7A-809. Reports.

The Conference of Clerks of Superior Court shall, in consultation with the registers of deeds, annually study the status of the individual counties and judicial districts as to whether or not the clerks of superior court or the registers of deeds are implementing G.S. 132-1.10(f1) and report results of the study to the Joint Legislative Commission on Governmental Operations on or before March 1 of each year.  (2009-355, s. 4; 2010-96, s. 1.)

Chapter 7B.

Juvenile Code.

SUBCHAPTER I. ABUSE, NEGLECT, DEPENDENCY.

Article 1.

Purposes; Definitions.

§ 7B-100. Purpose.

This Subchapter shall be interpreted and construed so as to implement the following purposes and policies:

(1)     To provide procedures for the hearing of juvenile cases that assure fairness and equity and that protect the constitutional rights of juveniles and parents;

(2)     To develop a disposition in each juvenile case that reflects consideration of the facts, the needs and limitations of the juvenile, and the strengths and weaknesses of the family.

(3)     To provide for services for the protection of juveniles by means that respect both the right to family autonomy and the juveniles' needs for safety, continuity, and permanence; and

(4)     To provide standards for the removal, when necessary, of juveniles from their homes and for the return of juveniles to their homes consistent with preventing the unnecessary or inappropriate separation of juveniles from their parents.

(5)     To provide standards, consistent with the Adoption and Safe Families Act of 1997, P.L. 105-89, for ensuring that the best interests of the juvenile are of paramount consideration by the court and that when it is not in the juvenile's best interest to be returned home, the juvenile will be placed in a safe, permanent home within a reasonable amount of time. (1979, c. 815, s. 1; 1987 (Reg. Sess., 1988), c. 1090, s. 1; 1998-202, s. 6; 1999-456, s. 60; 2003-140, s. 5.)

§ 7B-101. Definitions.

As used in this Subchapter, unless the context clearly requires otherwise, the following words have the listed meanings:

(1)     Abused juveniles. - Any juvenile less than 18 years of age whose parent, guardian, custodian, or caretaker:

a.     Inflicts or allows to be inflicted upon the juvenile a serious physical injury by other than accidental means;

b.     Creates or allows to be created a substantial risk of serious physical injury to the juvenile by other than accidental means;

c.     Uses or allows to be used upon the juvenile cruel or grossly inappropriate procedures or cruel or grossly inappropriate devices to modify behavior;

d.     Commits, permits, or encourages the commission of a violation of the following laws by, with, or upon the juvenile: first-degree rape, as provided in G.S. 14-27.2; rape of a child by an adult offender, as provided in G.S. 14-27.2A; second degree rape as provided in G.S. 14-27.3; first-degree sexual offense, as provided in G.S. 14-27.4; sexual offense with a child by an adult offender, as provided in G.S. 14-27.4A; second degree sexual offense, as provided in G.S. 14-27.5; sexual act by a custodian, as provided in G.S. 14-27.7; unlawful sale, surrender, or purchase of a minor, as provided in G.S. 14-43.14; crime against nature, as provided in G.S. 14-177; incest, as provided in G.S. 14-178; preparation of obscene photographs, slides, or motion pictures of the juvenile, as provided in G.S. 14-190.5; employing or permitting the juvenile to assist in a violation of the obscenity laws as provided in G.S. 14-190.6; dissemination of obscene material to the juvenile as provided in G.S. 14-190.7 and G.S. 14-190.8; displaying or disseminating material harmful to the juvenile as provided in

G.S. 14-190.14 and G.S. 14-190.15; first and second degree sexual exploitation of the juvenile as provided in G.S. 14-190.16 and G.S. 14-190.17; promoting the prostitution of the juvenile as provided in G.S. 14-205.3(b); and taking indecent liberties with the juvenile, as provided in G.S. 14-202.1;

e. Creates or allows to be created serious emotional damage to the juvenile; serious emotional damage is evidenced by a juvenile's severe anxiety, depression, withdrawal, or aggressive behavior toward himself or others;

f. Encourages, directs, or approves of delinquent acts involving moral turpitude committed by the juvenile; or

g. Commits or allows to be committed an offense under G.S. 14-43.11 (human trafficking), G.S. 14-43.12 (involuntary servitude), or G.S. 14-43.13 (sexual servitude) against the child.

(2) Aggravated circumstances. - Any circumstance attending to the commission of an act of abuse or neglect which increases its enormity or adds to its injurious consequences, including, but not limited to, abandonment, torture, chronic abuse, or sexual abuse.

(3) Caretaker. - Any person other than a parent, guardian, or custodian who has responsibility for the health and welfare of a juvenile in a residential setting. A person responsible for a juvenile's health and welfare means a stepparent, foster parent, an adult member of the juvenile's household, an adult relative entrusted with the juvenile's care, any person such as a house parent or cottage parent who has primary responsibility for supervising a juvenile's health and welfare in a residential child care facility or residential educational facility, or any employee or volunteer of a division, institution, or school operated by the Department of Health and Human Services. "Caretaker" also means any person who has the responsibility for the care of a juvenile in a child care facility as defined in Article 7 of Chapter 110 of the General Statutes and includes any person who has the approval of the care provider to assume responsibility for the juveniles under the care of the care provider. Nothing in this subdivision shall be construed to impose a legal duty of support under Chapter 50 or Chapter 110 of the General Statutes. The duty imposed upon a caretaker as defined in this subdivision shall be for the purpose of this Subchapter only.

(4) Clerk. - Any clerk of superior court, acting clerk, or assistant or deputy clerk.

(5) Repealed by Session Laws 2013-129, s. 1, effective October 1, 2013, and applicable to actions filed or pending on or after that date.

(6) Court. - The district court division of the General Court of Justice.

(7) Court of competent jurisdiction. - A court having the power and authority of law to act at the time of acting over the subject matter of the cause.

(7a) Criminal history. - A local, State, or federal criminal history of conviction or pending indictment of a crime, whether a misdemeanor or a felony, involving violence against a person.

(8) Custodian. - The person or agency that has been awarded legal custody of a juvenile by a court.

(9) Dependent juvenile. - A juvenile in need of assistance or placement because (i) the juvenile has no parent, guardian, or custodian responsible for the juvenile's care or supervision or (ii) the juvenile's parent, guardian, or custodian is unable to provide for the juvenile's care or supervision and lacks an appropriate alternative child care arrangement.

(10) Director. - The director of the county department of social services in the county in which the juvenile resides or is found, or the director's representative as authorized in G.S. 108A-14.

(11) District. - Any district court district as established by G.S. 7A-133.

(11a) Family assessment response. - A response to selected reports of child neglect and dependency as determined by the Director using a family-centered approach that is protection and prevention oriented and that evaluates the strengths and needs of the juvenile's family, as well as the condition of the juvenile.

(11b) Investigative assessment response. - A response to reports of child abuse and selected reports of child neglect and dependency as determined by the Director using a formal information gathering process to determine whether a juvenile is abused, neglected, or dependent.

(12) Judge. - Any district court judge.

(13)    Judicial district. - Any district court district as established by G.S. 7A-133.

(14)    Juvenile. - A person who has not reached the person's eighteenth birthday and is not married, emancipated, or a member of the Armed Forces of the United States.

(15)    Neglected juvenile. - A juvenile who does not receive proper care, supervision, or discipline from the juvenile's parent, guardian, custodian, or caretaker; or who has been abandoned; or who is not provided necessary medical care; or who is not provided necessary remedial care; or who lives in an environment injurious to the juvenile's welfare; or who has been placed for care or adoption in violation of law. In determining whether a juvenile is a neglected juvenile, it is relevant whether that juvenile lives in a home where another juvenile has died as a result of suspected abuse or neglect or lives in a home where another juvenile has been subjected to abuse or neglect by an adult who regularly lives in the home.

(16)    Petitioner. - The individual who initiates court action, whether by the filing of a petition or of a motion for review alleging the matter for adjudication.

(17)    Prosecutor. - The district attorney or assistant district attorney assigned by the district attorney to juvenile proceedings.

(18)    Reasonable efforts. - The diligent use of preventive or reunification services by a department of social services when a juvenile's remaining at home or returning home is consistent with achieving a safe, permanent home for the juvenile within a reasonable period of time. If a court of competent jurisdiction determines that the juvenile is not to be returned home, then reasonable efforts means the diligent and timely use of permanency planning services by a department of social services to develop and implement a permanent plan for the juvenile.

(18a)   Responsible individual. - A parent, guardian, custodian, or caretaker who abuses or seriously neglects a juvenile.

(18b)   Return home or reunification. - Placement of the juvenile in the home of either parent or placement of the juvenile in the home of a guardian or custodian from whose home the child was removed by court order.

(19)     Safe home. - A home in which the juvenile is not at substantial risk of physical or emotional abuse or neglect.

(19a)    Serious neglect. - Conduct, behavior, or inaction of the juvenile's parent, guardian, custodian, or caretaker that evidences a disregard of consequences of such magnitude that the conduct, behavior, or inaction constitutes an unequivocal danger to the juvenile's health, welfare, or safety, but does not constitute abuse.

(20)     Repealed by Session Laws 2013-129, s. 1, effective October 1, 2013, and applicable to actions filed or pending on or after that date.

(21)     Substantial evidence. - Relevant evidence a reasonable mind would accept as adequate to support a conclusion.

(22)     Working day. - Any day other than a Saturday, Sunday, or a legal holiday when the courthouse is closed for transactions.

The singular includes the plural, the masculine singular includes the feminine singular and masculine and feminine plural unless otherwise specified. (1979, c. 815, s. 1; 1981, c. 336; c. 359, s. 2; c. 469, ss. 1-3; c. 716, s. 1; 1985, c. 648; c. 757, s. 156(q); 1985 (Reg. Sess., 1986), c. 852, s. 16; 1987, c. 162; c. 695; 1987 (Reg. Sess., 1988), c. 1037, ss. 36, 37; 1989 (Reg. Sess., 1990), c. 815, s. 1; 1991, c. 258, s. 3; c. 273, s. 11; 1991 (Reg. Sess., 1992), c. 1030, s. 3; 1993, c. 324, s. 1; c. 516, ss. 1-3; 1997-113, s. 1; 1997-390, s. 3; 1997-390, s. 3.2; 1997-443, s. 11A.118(a); 1997-506, s. 30; 1998-202, s. 6; 1998-229, ss. 1, 18; 1999-190, s. 1; 1999-318, s. 1; 1999-456, s. 60; 2005-55, s. 1; 2005-399, s. 1; 2009-38, s. 1; 2010-90, ss. 1, 2; 2011-183, s. 2; 2012-153, s. 2; 2013-129, s. 1; 2013-368, s. 16.)

ARTICLE 2.

Jurisdiction

§ 7B-200. Jurisdiction.

(a)      The court has exclusive, original jurisdiction over any case involving a juvenile who is alleged to be abused, neglected, or dependent. This jurisdiction does not extend to cases involving adult defendants alleged to be guilty of abuse or neglect.

The court also has exclusive original jurisdiction of the following proceedings:

(1) Proceedings under the Interstate Compact on the Placement of Children set forth in Article 38 of this Chapter.

(2) Proceedings involving judicial consent for emergency surgical or medical treatment for a juvenile when the juvenile's parent, guardian, custodian, or other person who has assumed the status and obligation of a parent without being awarded legal custody of the juvenile by a court refuses to consent for treatment to be rendered.

(3) Proceedings to determine whether a juvenile should be emancipated.

(4) Proceedings to terminate parental rights.

(4a) Proceedings for reinstatement of parental rights.

(5) Proceedings to review the placement of a juvenile in foster care pursuant to an agreement between the juvenile's parents or guardian and a county department of social services.

(6) Proceedings in which a person is alleged to have obstructed or interfered with an investigation required by G.S. 7B-302.

(7) Proceedings involving consent for an abortion on an unemancipated minor under Article 1A, Part 2 of Chapter 90 of the General Statutes.

(8) Proceedings by an underage party seeking judicial authorization to marry under Article 1 of Chapter 51 of the General Statutes.

(9) Petitions for judicial review of a director's determination under Article 3A of this Chapter.

(b) The court shall have jurisdiction over the parent, guardian, custodian, or caretaker of a juvenile who has been adjudicated abused, neglected, or dependent, provided the parent, guardian, custodian, or caretaker has (i) been properly served with summons pursuant to G.S. 7B-406, (ii) waived service of process, or (iii) automatically become a party pursuant to G.S. 7B-401.1(c) or (d).

(c) When the court obtains jurisdiction over a juvenile as the result of a petition alleging that the juvenile is abused, neglected, or dependent:

(1) Any other civil action in this State in which the custody of the juvenile is an issue is automatically stayed as to that issue, unless the juvenile proceeding and the civil custody action or claim are consolidated pursuant to subsection (d) of this section or the court in the juvenile proceeding enters an order dissolving the stay.

(2) If an order entered in the juvenile proceeding and an order entered in another civil custody action conflict, the order in the juvenile proceeding controls as long as the court continues to exercise jurisdiction in the juvenile proceeding.

(d) Notwithstanding G.S. 50-13.5(f), the court in a juvenile proceeding may order that any civil action or claim for custody filed in the district be consolidated with the juvenile proceeding. If a civil action or claim for custody of the juvenile is filed in another district, the court in the juvenile proceeding, for good cause and after consulting with the court in the other district, may: (i) order that the civil action or claim for custody be transferred to the county in which the juvenile proceeding is filed; or (ii) order a change of venue in the juvenile proceeding and transfer the juvenile proceeding to the county in which the civil action or claim is filed. The court in the juvenile proceeding may also proceed in the juvenile proceeding while the civil action or claim remains stayed or dissolve the stay of the civil action or claim and stay the juvenile proceeding pending a resolution of the civil action or claim. (1979, c. 815, s. 1; 1983, c. 837, s. 1; 1985, c. 459, s. 2; 1987, c. 409, s. 2; 1995, c. 328, s. 3; c. 462, s. 2; 1996, 2nd Ex. Sess., c. 18, s. 23.2(c); 1998-202, s. 6; 1999-456, s. 60; 2001-62, s. 13; 2005-320, s. 1; 2005-399, s. 4; 2010-90, s. 3; 2011-295, s. 1; 2013-129, s. 2.)

§ 7B-201. Retention and termination of jurisdiction.

(a) When the court obtains jurisdiction over a juvenile, jurisdiction shall continue until terminated by order of the court or until the juvenile reaches the age of 18 years or is otherwise emancipated, whichever occurs first.

(b) When the court's jurisdiction terminates, whether automatically or by court order, the court thereafter shall not modify or enforce any order previously entered in the case, including any juvenile court order relating to the custody, placement, or guardianship of the juvenile. The legal status of the juvenile and the custodial rights of the parties shall revert to the status they were before the juvenile petition was filed, unless applicable law or a valid court order in another civil action provides otherwise. Termination of the court's jurisdiction in an abuse, neglect, or dependency proceeding, however, shall not affect any of the following:

(1)  A civil custody order entered pursuant to G.S. 7B-911.

(2)  An order terminating parental rights.

(3)  A pending action to terminate parental rights, unless the court orders otherwise.

(4)  Any proceeding in which the juvenile is alleged to be or has been adjudicated undisciplined or delinquent.

(5)  The court's jurisdiction in relation to any new abuse, neglect, or dependency petition that is filed. (1979, c. 815, s. 1; 1981, c. 469, s. 4; 1996, 2nd Ex. Sess., c. 18, s. 23.2(d); 1998-202, s. 6; 1999-456, s. 60; 2005-320, s. 2.)

§ 7B-202.  Permanency mediation.

(a)  The Administrative Office of the Courts shall establish a Permanency Mediation Program to provide statewide and uniform services to resolve issues in cases under this Subchapter in which a juvenile is alleged or has been adjudicated to be abused, neglected, or dependent, or in which a petition or motion to terminate a parent's rights has been filed. Participants in the mediation shall include the parties and their attorneys, including the guardian ad litem and attorney advocate for the child; provided, the court may allow mediation to proceed without the participation of a parent whose identity is unknown, a party who was served and has not made an appearance, or a parent, guardian, or custodian who has not been served despite a diligent attempt to serve the person. Upon a finding of good cause, the court may allow mediation to proceed without the participation of a parent who is unable to participate due to incarceration, illness, or some other cause. Others may participate by agreement of the parties, their attorneys, and the mediator, or by order of the court.

(b)  The Administrative Office of the Courts shall establish in phases a statewide Permanency Mediation Program consisting of local district programs to be established in all judicial districts of the State. The Director of the Administrative Office of the Courts is authorized to approve contractual agreements for such services as executed by order of the Chief District Court Judge of a district court district, such contracts to be exempt from competitive bidding procedures under Chapter 143 of the General Statutes. The Administrative Office of the Courts shall promulgate policies and regulations necessary and appropriate for the administration of the program. Any funds appropriated by the General Assembly for the establishment and maintenance of permanency mediation programs under this Article shall be administered by the Administrative Office of the Courts.

(c)     Mediation proceedings shall be held in private and shall be confidential. Except as provided otherwise in this section, all verbal or written communications from participants in the mediation to the mediator or between or among the participants in the presence of the mediator are absolutely privileged and inadmissible in court.

(d)     Neither the mediator nor any party or other person involved in mediation sessions under this section shall be competent to testify to communications made during or in furtherance of such mediation sessions; provided, there is no confidentiality or privilege as to communications made in furtherance of a crime or fraud. Nothing in this subsection shall be construed as permitting an individual to obtain immunity from prosecution for criminal conduct or as excusing an individual from the reporting requirements of Article 3 of Chapter 7B of the General Statutes or G.S. 108A-102.

(e)     Any agreement reached by the parties as a result of the mediation, whether referred to as a "placement agreement," "case plan," or some similar name, shall be reduced to writing, signed by each party, and submitted to the court as soon as practicable. Unless the court finds good reason not to, the court shall incorporate the agreement in a court order, and the agreement shall become enforceable as a court order. If some or all of the issues referred to mediation are not resolved by mediation, the mediator shall report that fact to the court. (2006-187, s. 4(a).)

§§ 7B-203 through 7B-299.  Reserved for future codification purposes.

Article 3.

Screening of Abuse and Neglect Complaints.

§ 7B-300. Protective services.

The director of the department of social services in each county of the State shall establish protective services for juveniles alleged to be abused, neglected, or dependent.

Protective services shall include the screening of reports, the performance of an assessment using either a family assessment response or an investigative assessment response, casework, or other counseling services to parents, guardians, or other caretakers as provided by the director to help the parents, guardians, or other caretakers and the court to prevent abuse or neglect, to improve the quality of child care, to be more adequate parents, guardians, or caretakers, and to preserve and stabilize family life.

The provisions of this Article shall also apply to child care facilities as defined in G.S. 110-86. (1979, c. 815, s. 1; 1981, c. 359, s. 1; 1991 (Reg. Sess., 1992), c. 923, s. 1; 1997-506, s. 31; 1998-202, s. 6; 1999-456, s. 60; 2005-55, s. 2.)

§ 7B-301. Duty to report abuse, neglect, dependency, or death due to maltreatment.

(a)     Any person or institution who has cause to suspect that any juvenile is abused, neglected, or dependent, as defined by G.S. 7B-101, or has died as the result of maltreatment, shall report the case of that juvenile to the director of the department of social services in the county where the juvenile resides or is found. The report may be made orally, by telephone, or in writing. The report shall include information as is known to the person making it including the name and address of the juvenile; the name and address of the juvenile's parent, guardian, or caretaker; the age of the juvenile; the names and ages of other juveniles in the home; the present whereabouts of the juvenile if not at the home address; the nature and extent of any injury or condition resulting from abuse, neglect, or dependency; and any other information which the person making the report believes might be helpful in establishing the need for protective services or court intervention. If the report is made orally or by telephone, the person making the report shall give the person's name, address, and telephone number. Refusal of the person making the report to give a name shall not preclude the department's assessment of the alleged abuse, neglect, dependency, or death as a result of maltreatment.

Upon receipt of any report of sexual abuse of the juvenile in a child care facility, the director shall notify the State Bureau of Investigation within 24 hours or on the next workday. If sexual abuse in a child care facility is not alleged in the initial report, but during the course of the assessment there is reason to suspect that sexual abuse has occurred, the director shall immediately notify the State Bureau of Investigation. Upon notification that sexual abuse may have occurred in a child care facility, the State Bureau of Investigation may form a task force to investigate the report.

(b)     Any person or institution who knowingly or wantonly fails to report the case of a juvenile as required by subsection (a) of this section, or who knowingly or wantonly prevents another person from making a report as required by subsection (a) of this section, is guilty of a Class 1 misdemeanor.

(c)     A director of social services who receives a report of sexual abuse of a juvenile in a child care facility and who knowingly fails to notify the State Bureau of Investigation of the report pursuant to subsection (a) of this section is guilty of a Class 1 misdemeanor. (1979, c. 815, s. 1; 1991 (Reg. Sess., 1992), c. 923, s. 2; 1993, c. 516, s. 4; 1997-506, s. 32; 1998-202, s. 6; 1999-456, s. 60; 2005-55, s. 3; 2013-52, s. 7.)


§ 7B-302. Assessment by director; access to confidential information; notification of person making the report.

(a)     When a report of abuse, neglect, or dependency is received, the director of the department of social services shall make a prompt and thorough assessment, using either a family assessment response or an investigative assessment response, in order to ascertain the facts of the case, the extent of the abuse or neglect, and the risk of harm to the juvenile, in order to determine whether protective services should be provided or the complaint filed as a petition. When the report alleges abuse, the director shall immediately, but no later than 24 hours after receipt of the report, initiate the assessment. When the report alleges neglect or dependency, the director shall initiate the assessment within 72 hours following receipt of the report. When the report alleges abandonment, the director shall immediately initiate an assessment, take appropriate steps to assume temporary custody of the juvenile, and take appropriate steps to secure an order for nonsecure custody of the juvenile. The assessment and evaluation shall include a visit to the place where the juvenile resides, except when the report alleges abuse or neglect in a child care facility as defined in Article 7 of Chapter 110 of the General Statutes. When a report alleges abuse or neglect in a child care facility as defined in Article 7 of Chapter 110 of the General Statutes, a visit to the place where the juvenile resides is not required. When the report alleges abandonment, the assessment shall include a request from the director to law enforcement officials to investigate through the North Carolina Center for Missing Persons and other national and State resources whether the juvenile is a missing child.

(a1) All information received by the department of social services, including the identity of the reporter, shall be held in strictest confidence by the department, except under the following circumstances:

(1) The department shall disclose confidential information to any federal, State, or local government entity or its agent in order to protect a juvenile from abuse or neglect. Any confidential information disclosed to any federal, State, or local government entity or its agent under this subsection shall remain confidential with the other government entity or its agent and shall only be redisclosed for purposes directly connected with carrying out that entity's mandated responsibilities.

(1a) The department shall disclose confidential information regarding the identity of the reporter to any federal, State, or local government entity or its agent with a court order. The department may only disclose confidential information regarding the identity of the reporter to a federal, State, or local government entity or its agent without a court order when the entity demonstrates a need for the reporter's name to carry out the entity's mandated responsibilities.

(2) The information may be examined upon request by the juvenile's guardian ad litem or the juvenile, including a juvenile who has reached age 18 or been emancipated.

(3) A district or superior court judge of this State presiding over a civil matter in which the department of social services is not a party may order the department to release confidential information, after providing the department with reasonable notice and an opportunity to be heard and then determining that the information is relevant and necessary to the trial of the matter before the court and unavailable from any other source. This subdivision shall not be construed to relieve any court of its duty to conduct hearings and make findings

required under relevant federal law, before ordering the release of any private medical or mental health information or records related to substance abuse or HIV status or treatment. The department of social services may surrender the requested records to the court, for in camera review, if the surrender is necessary to make the required determinations.

(4)     A district or superior court judge of this State presiding over a criminal or delinquency matter shall conduct an in camera review prior to releasing to the defendant or juvenile any confidential records maintained by the department of social services, except those records the defendant or juvenile is entitled to pursuant to subdivision (2) of this subsection.

(5)     The department may disclose confidential information to a parent, guardian, custodian, or caretaker in accordance with G.S. 7B-700 of this Subchapter.

(a2)    If the director, at any time after receiving a report that a juvenile may be abused, neglected, or dependent, determines that the juvenile's legal residence is in another county, the director shall promptly notify the director in the county of the juvenile's residence, and the two directors shall coordinate efforts to ensure that appropriate actions are taken.

(b)     When a report of a juvenile's death as a result of suspected maltreatment or a report of suspected abuse, neglect, or dependency of a juvenile in a noninstitutional setting is received, the director of the department of social services shall immediately ascertain if other juveniles live in the home, and, if so, initiate an assessment in order to determine whether they require protective services or whether immediate removal of the juveniles from the home is necessary for their protection. When a report of a juvenile's death as a result of maltreatment or a report of suspected abuse, neglect, or dependency of a juvenile in an institutional setting such as a residential child care facility or residential educational facility is received, the director of the department of social services shall immediately ascertain if other juveniles remain in the facility subject to the alleged perpetrator's care or supervision, and, if so, assess the circumstances of those juveniles in order to determine whether they require protective services or whether immediate removal of those juveniles from the facility is necessary for their protection.

(c)     If the assessment indicates that abuse, neglect, or dependency has occurred, the director shall decide whether immediate removal of the juvenile or any other juveniles in the home is necessary for their protection. If immediate removal does not seem necessary, the director shall immediately provide or arrange for protective services. If the parent, guardian, custodian, or caretaker refuses to accept the protective services provided or arranged by the director, the director shall sign a petition seeking to invoke the jurisdiction of the court for the protection of the juvenile or juveniles.

(d)     If immediate removal seems necessary for the protection of the juvenile or other juveniles in the home, the director shall sign a petition that alleges the applicable facts to invoke the jurisdiction of the court. Where the assessment shows that it is warranted, a protective services worker may assume temporary custody of the juvenile for the juvenile's protection pursuant to Article 5 of this Chapter.

(d1)    Whenever a juvenile is removed from the home of a parent, guardian, custodian, stepparent, or adult relative entrusted with the juvenile's care due to physical abuse, the director shall conduct a thorough review of the background of the alleged abuser or abusers. This review shall include a criminal history check and a review of any available mental health records. If the review reveals that the alleged abuser or abusers have a history of violent behavior against people, the director shall petition the court to order the alleged abuser or abusers to submit to a complete mental health evaluation by a licensed psychologist or psychiatrist.

(e)     In performing any duties related to the assessment of the report or the provision or arrangement for protective services, the director may consult with any public or private agencies or individuals, including the available State or local law enforcement officers who shall assist in the assessment and evaluation of the seriousness of any report of abuse, neglect, or dependency when requested by the director. The director or the director's representative may make a written demand for any information or reports, whether or not confidential, that may in the director's opinion be relevant to the assessment or provision of protective services. Upon the director's or the director's representative's request and unless protected by the attorney-client privilege, any public or private agency or individual shall provide access to and copies of this confidential information and these records to the extent permitted by federal law and regulations. If a custodian of criminal investigative information or records believes that release of the information will jeopardize the right of the State to prosecute a defendant or the right of a defendant to receive a fair trial or will undermine an ongoing or future investigation, it may seek an order from a court of competent jurisdiction to prevent disclosure of the information. In such an action, the custodian of the records shall have the burden of showing by a preponderance of the evidence that disclosure of the information in question will jeopardize the right of the State to prosecute a defendant or the right of a defendant to receive a fair trial or will undermine an ongoing or future investigation. Actions brought pursuant to this paragraph shall be set down for immediate hearing, and subsequent proceedings in the actions shall be accorded priority by the trial and appellate courts.

(f)     Within five working days after receipt of the report of abuse, neglect, or dependency, the director shall give written notice to the person making the report, unless requested by that person not to give notice, as to whether the report was accepted for assessment and whether the report was referred to the appropriate State or local law enforcement agency.

(g)     Within five working days after completion of the protective services assessment, the director shall give subsequent written notice to the person making the report, unless requested by that person not to give notice, as to whether there is a finding of abuse, neglect, or dependency, whether the county department of social services is taking action to protect the juvenile, and what action it is taking, including whether or not a petition was filed. The person making the report shall be informed of procedures necessary to request a review by the prosecutor of the director's decision not to file a petition. A request for review by the prosecutor shall be made within five working days of receipt of the second notification. The second notification shall include notice that, if the person making the report is not satisfied with the director's decision, the person may request review of the decision by the prosecutor within five working days of receipt. The person making the report may waive the person's right to this notification, and no notification is required if the person making the report does not identify himself to the director.

(h)     The director or the director's representative may not enter a private residence for assessment purposes without at least one of the following:

(1)     The reasonable belief that a juvenile is in imminent danger of death or serious physical injury.

(2)     The permission of the parent or person responsible for the juvenile's care.

(3)     The accompaniment of a law enforcement officer who has legal authority to enter the residence.

(4) An order from a court of competent jurisdiction. (1979, c. 815, s. 1; 1985, c. 205; 1991, c. 593, s. 1; 1991 (Reg. Sess., 1992), c. 923, s. 3; 1993, c. 516, s. 5; 1995, c. 411, s. 1; 1997-390, s. 3.1; 1998-202, s. 6; 1998-229, ss. 2, 19; 1999-190, s. 2; 1999-318, s. 2; 1999-456, s. 60; 2001-291, s. 1; 2003-304, s. 4.1; 2005-55, s. 4; 2006-205, s. 1; 2009-311, s. 1; 2012-153, s. 6.)

§ 7B-303. Interference with assessment.

(a) If any person obstructs or interferes with an assessment required by G.S. 7B-302, the director may file a petition naming that person as respondent and requesting an order directing the respondent to cease the obstruction or interference. The petition shall contain the name and date of birth and address of the juvenile who is the subject of the assessment; shall include a concise statement of the basis for initiating the assessment, shall specifically describe the conduct alleged to constitute obstruction of or interference with the assessment; and shall be verified.

(b) For purposes of this section, obstruction of or interference with an assessment means refusing to disclose the whereabouts of the juvenile, refusing to allow the director to have personal access to the juvenile, refusing to allow the director to observe or interview the juvenile in private, refusing to allow the director access to confidential information and records upon request pursuant to G.S. 7B-302, refusing to allow the director to arrange for an evaluation of the juvenile by a physician or other expert, or other conduct that makes it impossible for the director to carry out the duty to assess the juvenile's condition.

(c) Upon filing of the petition, the court shall schedule a hearing to be held not less than five days after service of the petition and summons on the respondent. Service of the petition and summons and notice of hearing shall be made as provided by the Rules of Civil Procedure on the respondent; the juvenile's parent, guardian, custodian, or caretaker; and any other person determined by the court to be a necessary party. If at the hearing on the petition the court finds by clear, cogent, and convincing evidence that the respondent, without lawful excuse, has obstructed or interfered with an assessment required by G.S. 7B-302, the court may order the respondent to cease such obstruction or interference. The burden of proof shall be on the petitioner.

(d) If the director has reason to believe that the juvenile is in need of immediate protection or assistance, the director shall so allege in the petition and may seek an ex parte order from the court. If the court, from the verified petition and any inquiry the court makes of the director, finds probable cause to believe both that the juvenile is at risk of immediate harm and that the respondent is obstructing or interfering with the director's ability to assess the juvenile's condition, the court may enter an ex parte order directing the respondent to cease the obstruction or interference. The order shall be limited to provisions necessary to enable the director to conduct an assessment sufficient to determine whether the juvenile is in need of immediate protection or assistance. Within 10 days after the entry of an ex parte order under this subsection, a hearing shall be held to determine whether there is good cause for the continuation of the order or the entry of a different order. An order entered under this subsection shall be served on the respondent along with a copy of the petition, summons, and notice of hearing.

(e) The director may be required at a hearing under this section to reveal the identity of any person who made a report of suspected abuse, neglect, or dependency as required by G.S. 7B-301.

(f) An order entered pursuant to this section is enforceable by civil or criminal contempt as provided in Chapter 5A of the General Statutes. (1987, c. 409, s. 1; 1993, c. 516, s. 6; 1998-202, s. 6; 1999-456, s. 60; 2005-55, s. 5.)

§ 7B-304: Repealed by Session Laws 2003, c. 140, s. 1, effective June 4, 2003.

§ 7B-305. Request for review by prosecutor.

The person making the report shall have five working days, from receipt of the decision of the director of the department of social services not to petition the court, to notify the prosecutor that the person is requesting a review. The prosecutor shall notify the person making the report and the director of the time and place for the review, and the director shall immediately transmit to the prosecutor a copy of a summary of the assessment. (1979, c. 815, s. 1; 1998-202, s. 6; 1999-456, s. 60; 2005-55, s. 6.)

§ 7B-306. Review by prosecutor.

The prosecutor shall review the director's determination that a petition should not be filed within 20 days after the person making the report is notified. The review shall include conferences with the person making the report, the protective services worker, the juvenile, if practicable, and other persons known to have pertinent information about the juvenile or the juvenile's family. At the conclusion of the conferences, the prosecutor may affirm the decision made by the director, may request the appropriate local law enforcement agency to investigate the allegations, or may direct the director to file a petition. (1979, c. 815, s. 1; 1981, c. 469, s. 7; 1993, c. 516, s. 7; 1998-202, s. 6; 1999-456, s. 60.)

§ 7B-307. Duty of director to report evidence of abuse, neglect; investigation by local law enforcement; notification of Department of Health and Human Services and State Bureau of Investigation.

(a) If the director finds evidence that a juvenile may have been abused as defined by G.S. 7B-101, the director shall make an immediate oral and subsequent written report of the findings to the district attorney or the district attorney's designee and the appropriate local law enforcement agency within 48 hours after receipt of the report. The local law enforcement agency shall immediately, but no later than 48 hours after receipt of the information, initiate and coordinate a criminal investigation with the protective services assessment being conducted by the county department of social services. Upon completion of the investigation, the district attorney shall determine whether criminal prosecution is appropriate and may request the director or the director's designee to appear before a magistrate.

If the director receives information that a juvenile may have been physically harmed in violation of any criminal statute by any person other than the juvenile's parent, guardian, custodian, or caretaker, the director shall make an immediate oral and subsequent written report of that information to the district attorney or the district attorney's designee and to the appropriate local law enforcement agency within 48 hours after receipt of the information. The local law enforcement agency shall immediately, but no later than 48 hours after receipt of the information, initiate a criminal investigation. Upon completion of the investigation, the district attorney shall determine whether criminal prosecution is appropriate.

If the report received pursuant to G.S. 7B-301 involves abuse or neglect of a juvenile in child care, the director shall notify the Department of Health and Human Services within 24 hours or on the next working day of receipt of the report.

(b) If the director finds evidence that a juvenile has been abused or neglected as defined by G.S. 7B-101 in a child care facility, the director shall immediately so notify the Department of Health and Human Services and, in the case of sexual abuse, the State Bureau of Investigation, in such a way as does not violate the law guaranteeing the confidentiality of the records of the department of social services.

(c) Upon completion of the assessment, the director shall give the Department written notification of the results of the assessment required by G.S. 7B-302. Upon completion of an assessment of sexual abuse in a child care facility, the director shall also make written notification of the results of the assessment to the State Bureau of Investigation.

The director of the department of social services shall submit a report of alleged abuse, neglect, or dependency cases or child fatalities that are the result of alleged maltreatment to the central registry under the policies adopted by the Social Services Commission. (1979, c. 815, s. 1; 1983, c. 199; 1985, c. 757, s. 156(s)-(u); 1991, c. 593, s. 2; 1991 (Reg. Sess., 1992), c. 923, s. 4; 1993, c. 516, s. 8; 1997-443, s. 11A.118(a); 1997-506, s. 33; 1998-202, s. 6; 1999-456, s. 60; 2005-55, s. 7.)

§ 7B-308. Authority of medical professionals in abuse cases.

(a) Any physician or administrator of a hospital, clinic, or other medical facility to which a suspected abused juvenile is brought for medical diagnosis or treatment shall have the right, when authorized by the chief district court judge of the district or the judge's designee, to retain physical custody of the juvenile in the facility when the physician who examines the juvenile certifies in writing that the juvenile who is suspected of being abused should remain for medical treatment or that, according to the juvenile's medical evaluation, it is unsafe for the juvenile to return to the juvenile's parent, guardian, custodian, or caretaker. This written certification must be signed by the certifying physician and must include the time and date that the judicial authority to retain custody is given. Copies of the written certification must be appended to the juvenile's medical and judicial records and another copy must be given to the juvenile's parent, guardian, custodian, or caretaker. The right to retain custody in the facility shall exist for up to 12 hours from the time and date contained in the written certification.

(b) Immediately upon receipt of judicial authority to retain custody, the physician, the administrator, or that person's designee shall so notify the director of social services for the county in which the facility is located. The director shall treat this notification as a report of suspected abuse and shall immediately begin an assessment of the case.

(1) If the assessment reveals (i) that it is the opinion of the certifying physician that the juvenile is in need of medical treatment to cure or alleviate physical distress or to prevent the juvenile from suffering serious physical injury, and (ii) that it is the opinion of the physician that the juvenile should for these reasons remain in the custody of the facility for 12 hours, but (iii) that the juvenile's parent, guardian, custodian, or caretaker cannot be reached or, upon request, will not consent to the treatment within the facility, the director shall within the initial 12-hour period file a juvenile petition alleging abuse and setting forth supporting allegations and shall seek a nonsecure custody order. A petition filed and a nonsecure custody order obtained in accordance with this subdivision shall come on for hearing under the regular provisions of this Subchapter unless the director and the certifying physician together voluntarily dismiss the petition.

(2) In all cases except those described in subdivision (1) above, the director shall conduct the assessment and may initiate juvenile proceedings and take all other steps authorized by the regular provisions of this Subchapter. If the director decides not to file a petition, the physician, the administrator, or that person's designee may ask the prosecutor to review this decision according to the provisions of G.S. 7B-305 and G.S. 7B-306.

(c) If, upon hearing, the court determines that the juvenile is found in a county other than the county of legal residence, in accord with G.S. 153A-257, the juvenile may be transferred, in accord with G.S. 7B-903(2), to the custody of the department of social services in the county of residence.

(d) If the court, upon inquiry, determines that the medical treatment rendered was necessary and appropriate, the cost of that treatment may be charged to the parents, guardian, custodian, or caretaker, or, if the parents are unable to pay, to the county of residence in accordance with G.S. 7B-903 and G.S. 7B-904.

(e) Except as otherwise provided, a petition begun under this section shall proceed in like manner with petitions begun under G.S. 7B-302.

(f) The procedures in this section are in addition to, and not in derogation of, the abuse and neglect reporting provisions of G.S. 7B-301 and the temporary custody provisions of G.S. 7B-500. Nothing in this section shall preclude a physician or administrator and a director of social services from following the procedures of G.S. 7B-301 and G.S. 7B-500 whenever these procedures are more appropriate to the juvenile's circumstances. (1979, c. 815, s. 1; 1981, c. 716, s. 2; 1995, c. 255, s. 1; 1998-202, s. 6; 1999-456, s. 60; 2005-55, s. 8.)

§ 7B-309. Immunity of persons reporting and cooperating in an assessment.

Anyone who makes a report pursuant to this Article, cooperates with the county department of social services in a protective services assessment, testifies in any judicial proceeding resulting from a protective services report or assessment, or otherwise participates in the program authorized by this Article, is immune from any civil or criminal liability that might otherwise be incurred or imposed for that action provided that the person was acting in good faith. In any proceeding involving liability, good faith is presumed. (1979, c. 815, s. 1; 1981, s. 469, s. 8; 1993, c. 516, s. 9; 1998-202, s. 6; 1999-456, s. 60; 2005-55, s. 9.)

§ 7B-310. Privileges not grounds for failing to report or for excluding evidence.

No privilege shall be grounds for any person or institution failing to report that a juvenile may have been abused, neglected, or dependent, even if the knowledge or suspicion is acquired in an official professional capacity, except when the knowledge or suspicion is gained by an attorney from that attorney's client during representation only in the abuse, neglect, or dependency case. No privilege, except the attorney-client privilege, shall be grounds for excluding evidence of abuse, neglect, or dependency in any judicial proceeding (civil, criminal, or juvenile) in which a juvenile's abuse, neglect, or dependency is in issue nor in any judicial proceeding resulting from a report submitted under this Article, both as this privilege relates to the competency of the witness and to the exclusion of confidential communications. (1979, c. 815, s. 1; 1987, c. 323, s. 1; 1993, c. 514, s. 3; c. 516, s. 10; 1995, c. 509, s. 133; 1998-202, s. 6; 1999-456, s. 60.)

§ 7B-311. Central registry; responsible individuals list.

(a) The Department of Health and Human Services shall maintain a central registry of abuse, neglect, and dependency cases and child fatalities that are the result of alleged maltreatment that are reported under this Article in order to compile data for appropriate study of the extent of abuse and neglect within the State and to identify repeated abuses of the same juvenile or of other juveniles in the same family. This data shall be furnished by county directors of social services to the Department of Health and Human Services and shall be confidential, subject to rules adopted by the Social Services Commission providing for its use for study and research and for other appropriate disclosure. Data shall not be used at any hearing or court proceeding unless based upon a final judgment of a court of law.

(b) The Department shall also maintain a list of responsible individuals. The Department may provide information from this list to child caring institutions, child placing agencies, group home facilities, and other providers of foster care, child care, or adoption services that need to determine the fitness of individuals to care for or adopt children. The name of an individual who has been identified as a responsible individual shall be placed on the responsible individuals list only after one of the following:

(1) The individual is properly notified pursuant to G.S. 7B-320 and fails to file a petition for judicial review in a timely manner.

(2) The court determines that the individual is a responsible individual as a result of a hearing on the individual's petition for judicial review.

(3) The individual is criminally convicted as a result of the same incident involved in an investigative assessment response.

(c) It is unlawful for any public official or public employee to knowingly and willfully release information from either the central registry or the responsible individuals list to a person who is not authorized to receive the information. It is unlawful for any person who is authorized to receive information from the central registry or the responsible individuals list to release that information to an unauthorized person. It is unlawful for any person who is not authorized to receive information from the central registry or the responsible individuals list to access or attempt to access that information. A person who commits an offense described in this subsection is guilty of a Class 3 misdemeanor.

(d) The Social Services Commission shall adopt rules regarding the operation of the central registry and responsible individuals list, including procedures for each of the following:

(1) Filing data.

(2) Notifying an individual that the individual has been determined by the director to be a responsible individual.

(3) Correcting and expunging information.

(4) Determining persons who are authorized to receive information from the responsible individuals list.

(5) Releasing information from the responsible individuals list to authorized requestors.

(6) Gathering statistical information.

(7) Keeping and maintaining information placed in the registry and on the responsible individuals list.

(8) Repealed by Session Laws 2010-90, s. 4, effective July 11, 2010. (1979, c. 815, s. 1; 1993, c. 516, s. 11; 1997-443, s. 11A.118(a); 1998-202, s. 6; 1999-456, s. 60; 2005-399, s. 2; 2010-90, s. 4; 2013-129, s. 3.)

§§ 7B-312 through 7B-319: Reserved for future codification purposes.

ARTICLE 3A.

Judicial Review; Responsible Individuals List.

§ 7B-320. Notification to individual determined to be a responsible individual.

(a) Within five working days after the completion of an investigative assessment response that results in a determination of abuse or serious neglect and the identification of a responsible individual, the director shall personally deliver written notice of the determination to the identified individual.

(b) If personal written notice is not made within 15 days of the determination and the director has made diligent efforts to locate the identified individual, the director shall send the notice to the individual by registered or certified mail, return receipt requested, and addressed to the individual at the individual's last known address.

(c) The notice shall include all of the following:

(1) A statement informing the individual of the nature of the investigative assessment response and whether the director determined abuse or serious neglect or both.

(1a) A statement that the individual has been identified as a responsible individual.

(2) A statement summarizing the substantial evidence supporting the director's determination without identifying the reporter or collateral contacts.

(3) A statement informing the individual that unless the individual petitions for judicial review, the individual's name will be placed on the responsible individuals list as provided in G.S. 7B-311, and that the Department of Health and Human Services may provide information from this list to child caring institutions, child placing agencies, group home facilities, and other providers of foster care, child care, or adoption services that need to determine the fitness of individuals to care for or adopt children.

(4) A clear description of the actions the individual must take to seek judicial review of the director's determination.

(d) In addition to the notice, the director shall provide the individual with a copy of a petition for judicial review form. (2005-399, s. 3; 2010-90, s. 5; 2013-129, s. 4.)


§ 7B-321: Repealed by Session Laws 2010-90, s. 6, effective July 11, 2010.

§ 7B-322: Repealed by Session Laws 2010-90, s. 6, effective July 11, 2010.

§ 7B-323. Petition for judicial review; district court.

(a) Within 15 days of the receipt of notice of the director's determination under G.S. 7B-320(a) or (b), an individual may file a petition for judicial review with the district court of the county in which the abuse or serious neglect report arose. The request shall be by a petition for judicial review filed with the appropriate clerk of court's office with a copy delivered in person or by certified mail, return receipt requested, to the director who determined the abuse or serious neglect and identified the individual as a responsible individual. The petition for judicial review shall contain the name, date of birth, and address of the individual seeking judicial review, the name of the juvenile who was the subject of the determination of abuse or serious neglect, and facts that invoke the jurisdiction of the court. Failure to timely file a petition for judicial review constitutes a waiver of the individual's right to a district court hearing and to contest the placement of the individual's name on the responsible individuals list.

(a1) If the director cannot show that the individual has received actual notice, the director shall not place the individual on the responsible individuals list until an ex parte hearing is held at which a district court judge determines that the director made diligent efforts to find the individual. A finding that the individual is evading service is relevant to the determination that the director made diligent efforts.

(b) The clerk of court shall maintain a separate docket for judicial review actions. Upon the filing of a petition for judicial review, the clerk shall calendar the matter for hearing within 45 days from the date the petition is filed at a session of district court hearing juvenile matters or, if there is no such session, at the next session of juvenile court. The clerk shall send notice of the hearing to the petitioner and to the director who determined the abuse or serious neglect and identified the individual as a responsible individual. Upon the request of a party, the court shall close the hearing to all persons, except officers of the court, the parties, and their witnesses. At the hearing, the director shall have the burden of proving by a preponderance of the evidence the abuse or serious neglect and the identification of the individual seeking judicial review as a responsible individual. The hearing shall be before a judge without a jury. The rules of evidence applicable in civil cases shall apply. However, the court, in its discretion, may permit the admission of any reliable and relevant evidence if the general purposes of the rules of evidence and the interests of justice will best be served by its admission.

(b1) Upon receipt of a notice of hearing for judicial review, the director who identified the individual as a responsible individual shall review all records, reports, and other information gathered during the investigative assessment response. If after a review, the director determines that there is not sufficient evidence to support a determination that the individual abused or seriously neglected the juvenile and is a responsible individual, the director shall prepare a written statement of the director's determination and either deliver the statement personally to the individual seeking judicial review or send the statement by first-class mail. The director shall also give written notice of the director's determination to the clerk to be placed in the court file, and the judicial review hearing shall be cancelled with notice of the cancellation given by the clerk to the petitioner.

(c)     At the hearing, the following rights of the parties shall be preserved:

(1)     The right to present sworn evidence, law, or rules that bear upon the case.

(2)     The right to represent themselves or obtain the services of an attorney at their own expense.

(3)     The right to subpoena witnesses, cross-examine witnesses of the other party, and make a closing argument summarizing the party's view of the case and the law.

(d)     Within 30 days after completion of the hearing, the court shall enter an order containing findings of fact and conclusions of law. The clerk shall serve a copy of the order on each party or the party's attorney of record. If the court concludes that the director has not established by a preponderance of the evidence abuse or serious neglect or the identification of the responsible individual, the court shall reverse the director's determination and order the director not to place the individual's name on the responsible individuals list. If the court concludes that the director has established by a preponderance of the evidence abuse or serious neglect and the identification of the individual seeking judicial review as a responsible individual, the court shall order the director to place the individual's name on the responsible individuals list, consistent with the court's order.

(e)     Notwithstanding any time limitations contained in this section or the provisions of G.S. 7B-324(a)(4), upon the filing of a petition for judicial review by an individual identified by a director as a responsible individual, the district court of the county in which the abuse or neglect report arose may review a director's determination of abuse or serious neglect at any time if the review serves the interests of justice or for extraordinary circumstances. If the district court undertakes such a review, a hearing shall be held pursuant to this section at which the director shall have the burden of establishing by a preponderance of the evidence abuse or serious neglect and the identification of the individual seeking judicial review as a responsible individual. If the court concludes that the director has not established by a preponderance of the evidence abuse or serious neglect or the identification of the responsible individual, the court shall reverse the director's determination and order the director to expunge the individual's name from the responsible individuals list.

(f)     A party may appeal the district court's decision under G.S. 7A-27(c). (2005-399, s. 3; 2010-90, s. 7; 2013-129, s. 5.)


§ 7B-324. Persons ineligible to petition for judicial review.

(a)     An individual who has been identified by a director as a responsible individual may not petition for judicial review if any of the following apply:

(1)     The individual is criminally convicted as a result of the same incident. The district attorney shall inform the director of the result of the criminal proceeding.

(2)     Repealed by Session Laws 2013-129, s. 6, effective October 1, 2013, and applicable to actions filed or pending on or after that date.

(3)     Repealed by Session Laws 2010-90, s. 8, effective July 11, 2010.

(4)     After proper notice, the individual fails to file a petition for judicial review with the district court in a timely manner.

(5)     Repealed by Session Laws 2010-90, s. 8, effective July 11, 2010.

(b)     If an individual seeking judicial review is named as a respondent in a juvenile court case or a defendant in a criminal court case resulting from the same incident, the district court judge may stay the judicial review proceeding. (2005-399, s. 3; 2010-90, s. 8; 2013-129, s. 6.)


§§ 7B-325 through 7B-329: Reserved for future codification purposes.

Article 4.

Venue; Petitions.

§ 7B-400. Venue.

(a) A proceeding in which a juvenile is alleged to be abused, neglected, or dependent may be commenced in the district in which the juvenile resides or is present. Notwithstanding G.S. 153A-257, the absence of a juvenile from the juvenile's home pursuant to a protection plan during an assessment or the provision of case management services by a department of social services shall not change the original venue if it subsequently becomes necessary to file a juvenile petition.

(b) When the director in one county conducts an assessment pursuant to G.S. 7B-302 in another county because a conflict of interest exists, the director in the county conducting the assessment may file a resulting petition in either county.

(c) For good cause, the court may grant motion for change of venue before adjudication. A pre-adjudication change of venue shall not affect the identity of the petitioner.

(d) Any change of venue after adjudication shall be pursuant to G.S. 7B-900.1. (1979, c. 815, s. 1; 1998-202, s. 6; 1999-456, s. 60; 2009-311, s. 2; 2013-129, s. 7.)

§ 7B-401. Pleading and process.

(a) The pleading in an abuse, neglect, or dependency action is the petition. The process in an abuse, neglect, or dependency action is the summons.

(b) If the court has retained jurisdiction over a juvenile whose custody was granted to a parent and there are no periodic judicial reviews of the placement, the provisions of Article 8 of this subchapter shall apply to any subsequent report of abuse, neglect, or dependency determined by the director of social services to require court action pursuant to G.S. 7B-302. (1979, c. 815, s. 1; 1998-202, s. 6; 1999-456, s. 60; 2013-129, s. 8.)

§ 7B-401.1.  Parties.

(a)  Petitioner. - Only a county director of social services or the director's authorized representative may file a petition alleging that a juvenile is abused, neglected, or dependent. The petitioner shall remain a party until the court terminates its jurisdiction in the case.

(b)  Parents. - The juvenile's parent shall be a party unless one of the following applies:

(1)  The parent's rights have been terminated.

(2)  The parent has relinquished the juvenile for adoption, unless the court orders that the parent be made a party.

(3)  The parent has been convicted under G.S. 14-27.2 or G.S. 14-27.3 for an offense that resulted in the conception of the juvenile.

(c)  Guardian. - A person who is the child's court-appointed guardian of the person or general guardian when the petition is filed shall be a party. A person appointed as the child's guardian pursuant to G.S. 7B-600 shall automatically become a party but only if the court has found that the guardianship is the permanent plan for the juvenile.

(d)  Custodian. - A person who is the juvenile's custodian, as defined in G.S. 7B-101(8), when the petition is filed shall be a party. A person to whom custody of the juvenile is awarded in the juvenile proceeding shall automatically become a party but only if the court has found that the custody arrangement is the permanent plan for the juvenile.

(e)  Caretaker. - A caretaker shall be a party only if (i) the petition includes allegations relating to the caretaker, (ii) the caretaker has assumed the status and obligation of a parent, or (iii) the court orders that the caretaker be made a party.

(f)  The Juvenile. - The juvenile shall be a party.

(g)  Removal of a Party. - If a guardian, custodian, or caretaker is a party, the court may discharge that person from the proceeding, making the person no longer a party, if the court finds that the person does not have legal rights that may be affected by the action and that the person's continuation as a party is not necessary to meet the juvenile's needs.

(h) Intervention. - Except as provided in G.S. 7B-1103(b), the court shall not allow intervention by a person who is not the juvenile's parent, guardian, custodian, or caretaker but may allow intervention by another county department of social services that has an interest in the proceeding. This section shall not prohibit the court from consolidating a juvenile proceeding with a civil action or claim for custody pursuant to G.S. 7B-200. (2013-129, s. 9.)

§ 7B-402. Petition.

(a) The petition shall contain the name, date of birth, address of the juvenile, the name and last known address of each party as determined by G.S. 7B-401.1, and allegations of facts sufficient to invoke jurisdiction over the juvenile. The petition may contain information on more than one juvenile when the juveniles are from the same home and are before the court for the same reason.

(b) The petition, or an affidavit attached to the petition, shall contain the information required by G.S. 50A-209.

(c) Sufficient copies of the petition shall be prepared so that copies will be available for each party named in the petition, except the juvenile, and for the juvenile's guardian ad litem, the social worker, and any person determined by the court to be a necessary party.

(d) If the petition is filed in a county other than the county of the juvenile's residence, the petitioner shall provide a copy of the petition and any notices of hearing to the director of the department of social services in the county of the juvenile's residence. (1979, c. 815, s. 1; 1981, c. 469, s. 9; 1998-202, s. 6; 1999-456, s. 60; 2004-128, s. 11; 2005-320, s. 3; 2009-311, s. 3; 2010-90, s. 9; 2013-129, s. 10.)

§ 7B-403. Receipt of reports; filing of petition.

(a) All reports concerning a juvenile alleged to be abused, neglected, or dependent shall be referred to the director of the department of social services for screening. Thereafter, if it is determined by the director that a report should be filed as a petition, the petition shall be drawn by the director, verified before an official authorized to administer oaths, and filed by the clerk, recording the date of filing.

(b)     A decision of the director of social services not to file a report as a petition shall be reviewed by the prosecutor if review is requested pursuant to G.S. 7B-305. (1979, c. 815, s. 1; 1981, c. 469, ss. 10, 11; 1998-202, s. 6; 1999-456, s. 60.)


§ 7B-404.  Immediate need for petition when clerk's office is closed.

(a)     When the office of the clerk is closed, a magistrate may be authorized by the chief district court judge to draw, verify, and issue petitions as follows:

(1)     When the director of the department of social services requests a petition alleging a juvenile to be abused, neglected, or dependent, or

(2)     When the director of the department of social services requests a petition alleging the obstruction of or interference with an assessment required by G.S. 7B-302.

(b)     The authority of the magistrate under this section is limited to emergency situations when a petition is required in order to obtain a nonsecure custody order or an order under G.S. 7B-303. Any petition issued under this section shall be delivered to the clerk's office for processing as soon as that office is open for business. (1979, c. 815, s. 1; 1987, c. 409, s. 3; 1998-202, s. 6; 1999-456, s. 60; 2005-55, s. 10.)


§ 7B-405.  Commencement of action.

An action is commenced by the filing of a petition in the clerk's office when that office is open or by the issuance of a juvenile petition by a magistrate when the clerk's office is closed, which issuance shall constitute filing. (1979, c. 815, s. 1; 1998-202, s. 6; 1999-456, s. 60.)


§ 7B-406.  Issuance of summons.

(a) Immediately after a petition has been filed alleging that a juvenile is abused, neglected, or dependent, the clerk shall issue a summons to each party named in the petition, except the juvenile, requiring them to appear for a hearing at the time and place stated in the summons. A copy of the petition shall be attached to each summons. Service of the summons shall be completed as provided in G.S. 7B-407, but the parent of the juvenile shall not be deemed to be under a disability even though the parent is a minor.

(b) A summons shall be on a printed form supplied by the Administrative Office of the Courts and shall include each of the following:

(1) Notice of the nature of the proceeding.

(2) Notice of any right to counsel and information about how a parent may seek the appointment of counsel prior to a hearing if provisional counsel is not identified.

(2a) Repealed by Session Laws 2013-129, s. 11, effective October 1, 2013, and applicable to actions filed or pending on or after that date.

(3) Notice that, if the court determines at the hearing that the allegations of the petition are true, the court will conduct a dispositional hearing to consider the needs of the juvenile and enter an order designed to meet those needs and the objectives of the State.

(4) Notice that the dispositional order or a subsequent order:

a. May remove the juvenile from the custody of the parent, guardian, or custodian.

b. May require that the juvenile receive medical, psychiatric, psychological, or other treatment and that the parent participate in the treatment.

c. May require the parent to undergo psychiatric, psychological, or other treatment or counseling for the purpose of remedying the behaviors or conditions that are alleged in the petition or that contributed to the removal of the juvenile from the custody of that person.

d. May order the parent to pay for treatment that is ordered for the juvenile or the parent.

e. May, upon proper notice and hearing and a finding based on the criteria set out in G.S. 7B-1111, terminate the parental rights of the respondent parent.

(c) The summons shall advise the parent that upon service, jurisdiction over that person is obtained and that failure to comply with any order of the court pursuant to G.S. 7B-904 may cause the court to issue a show cause order for contempt.

(d) A summons shall be directed to the person summoned to appear and shall be delivered to any person authorized to serve process. (1979, c. 815, s. 1; 1987 (Reg. Sess., 1988), c. 1090, s. 2; 1995, c. 328, s. 1; 1998-202, s. 6; 1999-456, s. 60; 2000-183, s. 1; 2001-208, s. 1; 2001-487, s. 101; 2004-128, s. 12; 2010-90, s. 10; 2013-129, s. 11.)

§ 7B-407. Service of summons.

The summons shall be served under G.S. 1A-1, Rule 4(j) upon the parent, guardian, custodian, or caretaker, not less than five days prior to the date of the scheduled hearing. The time for service may be waived in the discretion of the court.

If service by publication under G.S. 1A-1, Rule 4(j1) is required, the cost of the service by publication shall be advanced by the petitioner and may be charged as court costs as the court may direct. (1979, c. 815, s. 1; 1998-202, s. 6; 1999-456, s. 60; 2003-304, s. 1; 2013-129, s. 12.)

§ 7B-408. Copy of petition and notices to guardian ad litem.

Immediately after a petition has been filed alleging that a juvenile is abused or neglected, the clerk shall provide a copy of the petition and any notices of hearings to the local guardian ad litem office. (2003-140, s. 6)

§§ 7B-409 through 7B-413: Reserved for future codification purposes.

Article 5.

Temporary Custody; Nonsecure Custody; Custody Hearings.

§ 7B-500. Taking a juvenile into temporary custody; civil and criminal immunity.

(a) Temporary custody means the taking of physical custody and providing personal care and supervision until a court order for nonsecure custody can be obtained. A juvenile may be taken into temporary custody without a court order by a law enforcement officer or a department of social services worker if there are reasonable grounds to believe that the juvenile is abused, neglected, or dependent and that the juvenile would be injured or could not be taken into custody if it were first necessary to obtain a court order. If a department of social services worker takes a juvenile into temporary custody under this section, the worker may arrange for the placement, care, supervision, and transportation of the juvenile.

(b) The following individuals shall, without a court order, take into temporary custody an infant under seven days of age that is voluntarily delivered to the individual by the infant's parent who does not express an intent to return for the infant:

(1) A health care provider, as defined under G.S. 90-21.11, who is on duty or at a hospital or at a local or district health department or at a nonprofit community health center.

(2) A law enforcement officer who is on duty or at a police station or sheriff's department.

(3) A social services worker who is on duty or at a local department of social services.

(4) A certified emergency medical service worker who is on duty or at a fire or emergency medical services station.

(c) An individual who takes an infant into temporary custody under subsection (b) of this section shall perform any act necessary to protect the physical health and well-being of the infant and shall immediately notify the department of social services or a local law enforcement agency. Any individual who takes an infant into temporary custody under subsection (b) of this section may inquire as to the parents' identities and as to any relevant medical history, but the parent is not required to provide the information. The individual shall notify the parent that the parent is not required to provide the information.

(d)     Any adult may, without a court order, take into temporary custody an infant under seven days of age that is voluntarily delivered to the individual by the infant's parent who does not express an intent to return for the infant. Any individual who takes an infant into temporary custody under this section shall perform any act necessary to protect the physical health and well-being of the infant and shall immediately notify the department of social services or a local law enforcement agency. An individual who takes an infant into temporary custody under this subsection may inquire as to the parents' identities and as to any relevant medical history, but the parent is not required to provide the information. The individual shall notify the parent that the parent is not required to provide the information.

(e)     An individual described in subsection (b) or (d) of this section is immune from any civil or criminal liability that might otherwise be incurred or imposed as a result of any omission or action taken pursuant to the requirements of subsection (c) or (d) of this section as long as that individual was acting in good faith. The immunity established by this subsection does not extend to gross negligence, wanton conduct, or intentional wrongdoing that would otherwise be actionable. (1979, c. 815, s. 1; 1985, c. 408, s. 1; 1985 (Reg. Sess., 1986), c. 863, s. 1; 1994, Ex. Sess., c. 27, s. 2; 1995, c. 391, s. 1; 1997-443, s. 11A.118(a); 1998-202, s. 6; 1999-456, s. 60; 2001-291, s. 2.)

§ 7B-501.  Duties of person taking juvenile into temporary custody.

(a)     A person who takes a juvenile into custody without a court order under G.S. 7B-500 shall proceed as follows:

(1)     Notify the juvenile's parent, guardian, custodian, or caretaker that the juvenile has been taken into temporary custody and advise the parent, guardian, custodian, or caretaker of the right to be present with the juvenile until a determination is made as to the need for nonsecure custody. Failure to notify the parent that the juvenile is in custody shall not be grounds for release of the juvenile.

(2)     Release the juvenile to the juvenile's parent, guardian, custodian, or caretaker if the person having the juvenile in temporary custody decides that continued custody is unnecessary.

(3) The person having temporary custody shall communicate with the director of the department of social services who shall consider prehearing diversion. If the decision is made to file a petition, the director shall contact the judge or person delegated authority pursuant to G.S. 7B-502 for a determination of the need for continued custody.

(b) A juvenile taken into temporary custody under this Article shall not be held for more than 12 hours, or for more than 24 hours if any of the 12 hours falls on a Saturday, Sunday, or legal holiday, unless:

(1) A petition or motion for review has been filed by the director of the department of social services, and

(2) An order for nonsecure custody has been entered by the court. (1979, c. 815, s. 1; 1981, c. 335, ss. 1, 2; 1994, Ex. Sess., c. 17, s. 1; c. 27, s. 3; 1995, c. 391, s. 2; 1998-202, s. 6; 1999-456, s. 60.)

§ 7B-502. Authority to issue custody orders; delegation.

In the case of any juvenile alleged to be within the jurisdiction of the court, the court may order that the juvenile be placed in nonsecure custody pursuant to criteria set out in G.S. 7B-503 when custody of the juvenile is necessary.

Any district court judge shall have the authority to issue nonsecure custody orders pursuant to G.S. 7B-503. The chief district court judge may delegate the court's authority to persons other than district court judges by administrative order which shall be filed in the office of the clerk of superior court. The administrative order shall specify which persons shall be contacted for approval of a nonsecure custody order pursuant to G.S. 7B-503. (1979, c. 815, s. 1; 1981, c. 425; 1983, c. 590, s. 1; 1998-202, s. 6; 1999-456, s. 60.)

§ 7B-503. Criteria for nonsecure custody.

(a) When a request is made for nonsecure custody, the court shall first consider release of the juvenile to the juvenile's parent, relative, guardian, custodian, or other responsible adult. An order for nonsecure custody shall be made only when there is a reasonable factual basis to believe the matters alleged in the petition are true, and any of the following apply:

(1)     The juvenile has been abandoned.

(2)     The juvenile has suffered physical injury or sexual abuse.

(3)     The juvenile is exposed to a substantial risk of physical injury or sexual abuse because the parent, guardian, custodian, or caretaker has created the conditions likely to cause injury or abuse or has failed to provide, or is unable to provide, adequate supervision or protection.

(4)     The juvenile is in need of medical treatment to cure, alleviate, or prevent suffering serious physical harm which may result in death, disfigurement, or substantial impairment of bodily functions, and the juvenile's parent, guardian, custodian, or caretaker is unwilling or unable to provide or consent to the medical treatment.

(5)     The parent, guardian, custodian, or caretaker consents to the nonsecure custody order.

(6)     The juvenile is a runaway and consents to nonsecure custody.

A juvenile alleged to be abused, neglected, or dependent shall be placed in nonsecure custody only when there is a reasonable factual basis to believe that there are no other reasonable means available to protect the juvenile. In no case shall a juvenile alleged to be abused, neglected, or dependent be placed in secure custody.

(b)     Whenever a petition is filed under G.S. 7B-302(d1), the court shall rule on the petition prior to returning the child to a home where the alleged abuser or abusers are or have been present. If the court finds that the alleged abuser or abusers have a history of violent behavior against people, the court shall order the alleged abuser or abusers to submit to a complete mental health evaluation by a licensed psychologist or psychiatrist. The court may order the alleged abuser or abusers to pay the cost of any mental health evaluation required under this section. (1979, c. 815, s. 1; 1981, c. 426, ss. 1-4; c. 526; 1983, c. 590, ss. 2-6; 1987, c. 101; 1987 (Reg. Sess., 1988), c. 1090, s. 3; 1989, c. 550; 1998-202, s. 6; 1999-318, s. 4; 1999-456, s. 60; 2011-295, s. 2.)

§ 7B-504.  Order for nonsecure custody.

The custody order shall be in writing and shall direct a law enforcement officer or other authorized person to assume custody of the juvenile and to make due return on the order. A copy of the order shall be given to the juvenile's parent, guardian, custodian, or caretaker by the official executing the order.

An officer receiving an order for custody which is complete and regular on its face may execute it in accordance with its terms. The officer is not required to inquire into the regularity or continued validity of the order and shall not incur criminal or civil liability for its due service. (1979, c. 815, s. 1; 1989, c. 124; 1998-202, s. 6; 1999-456, s. 60.)

§ 7B-505. Placement while in nonsecure custody.

(a) A juvenile meeting the criteria set out in G.S. 7B-503 may be placed in nonsecure custody with the department of social services or a person designated in the order for temporary residential placement in:

(1) A licensed foster home or a home otherwise authorized by law to provide such care; or

(2) A facility operated by the department of social services; or

(3) Any other home or facility, including a relative's home approved by the court and designated in the order.

(b) In placing a juvenile in nonsecure custody under this section, the court shall first consider whether a relative of the juvenile is willing and able to provide proper care and supervision of the juvenile in a safe home. If the court finds that the relative is willing and able to provide proper care and supervision in a safe home, then the court shall order placement of the juvenile with the relative unless the court finds that placement with the relative would be contrary to the best interests of the juvenile.

(c) If the court does not place the juvenile with a relative, the court may consider whether nonrelative kin is willing and able to provide proper care and supervision of the juvenile in a safe home. Nonrelative kin is an individual having a substantial relationship with the juvenile. In the case of a juvenile member of a State-recognized tribe as set forth in G.S. 143B-407(a), nonrelative kin also includes any member of a State-recognized tribe or a member of a federally recognized tribe, whether or not there is a substantial relationship with the juvenile. The court may order the Department to notify the juvenile's State-recognized tribe of the need for nonsecure custody for the purpose of locating relatives or nonrelative kin for placement. The court may order placement of the juvenile with nonrelative kin if the court finds the placement is in the juvenile's best interests.

(d)     In placing a juvenile in nonsecure custody under this section, the court shall also consider whether it is in the juvenile's best interest to remain in the juvenile's community of residence. In placing a juvenile in nonsecure custody under this section, the court shall consider the Indian Child Welfare Act, Pub. L. No. 95-608, 25 U.S.C. §§ 1901, et seq., as amended, and the Howard M. Metzenbaum Multiethnic Placement Act of 1994, Pub. L. No. 103-382, 108 Stat. 4056, as amended, as they may apply. Placement of a juvenile with a relative outside of this State must be in accordance with the Interstate Compact on the Placement of Children, Article 38 of this Chapter. (1979, c. 815, s. 1; 1983, c. 639, ss. 1, 2; 1997-390, s. 4; 1997-443, s. 11A.118(a); 1998-202, s. 6; 1998-229, ss. 3, 20; 1999-456, s. 60; 2002-164, s. 4.7; 2013-129, s. 13.)

§ 7B-506. Hearing to determine need for continued nonsecure custody.

(a)     No juvenile shall be held under a nonsecure custody order for more than seven calendar days without a hearing on the merits or a hearing to determine the need for continued custody. A hearing on nonsecure custody conducted under this subsection may be continued for up to 10 business days with the consent of the juvenile's parent, guardian, custodian, or caretaker and, if appointed, the juvenile's guardian ad litem. In addition, the court may require the consent of additional parties or may schedule the hearing on custody despite a party's consent to a continuance. In every case in which an order has been entered by an official exercising authority delegated pursuant to G.S. 7B-502, a hearing to determine the need for continued custody shall be conducted on the day of the next regularly scheduled session of district court in the city or county where the order was entered if such session precedes the expiration of the applicable time period set forth in this subsection: Provided, that if such session does not precede the expiration of the time period, the hearing may be conducted at another regularly scheduled session of district court in the district where the order was entered.

(b)     At a hearing to determine the need for continued custody, the court shall receive testimony and shall allow the guardian ad litem, or juvenile, and the juvenile's parent, guardian, custodian, or caretaker the right to introduce evidence, to be heard in the person's own behalf, and to examine witnesses. The petitioner shall bear the burden at every stage of the proceedings to provide clear and convincing evidence that the juvenile's placement in custody is necessary. The court shall not be bound by the usual rules of evidence at such hearings.

(c) The court shall be bound by criteria set forth in G.S. 7B-503 in determining whether continued custody is warranted.

(c1) In determining whether continued custody is warranted, the court shall consider the opinion of the mental health professional who performed an evaluation under G.S. 7B-503(b) before returning the juvenile to the custody of that individual.

(d) If the court determines that the juvenile meets the criteria in G.S. 7B-503 and should continue in custody, the court shall issue an order to that effect. The order shall be in writing with appropriate findings of fact and signed and entered within 30 days of the completion of the hearing. The findings of fact shall include the evidence relied upon in reaching the decision and purposes which continued custody is to achieve.

(e) If the court orders at the hearing required in subsection (a) of this section that the juvenile remain in custody, a subsequent hearing on continued custody shall be held within seven business days of that hearing, excluding Saturdays, Sundays, and legal holidays when the courthouse is closed for transactions, and pending a hearing on the merits, hearings thereafter shall be held at intervals of no more than 30 calendar days.

(f) Hearings conducted under subsection (e) of this section may be waived only with the consent of the juvenile's parent, guardian, custodian, or caretaker, and, if appointed, the juvenile's guardian ad litem.

The court may require the consent of additional parties or schedule a hearing despite a party's consent to waiver.

(g) In addition to the hearings required under this section, any party may schedule a hearing on the issue of placement.

(h) At each hearing to determine the need for continued custody, the court shall determine the following:

(1) Inquire as to the identity and location of any missing parent and whether paternity is at issue. The court shall include findings as to the efforts undertaken to locate the missing parent and to serve that parent, as well as efforts undertaken to establish paternity when paternity is an issue. The order may provide for specific efforts aimed at determining the identity and location of any missing parent, as well as specific efforts aimed at establishing paternity.

(2) Inquire about efforts made to identify and notify relatives as potential resources for placement or support and as to whether a relative of the juvenile is willing and able to provide proper care and supervision of the juvenile in a safe home. If the court finds that the relative is willing and able to provide proper care and supervision in a safe home, then the court shall order temporary placement of the juvenile with the relative unless the court finds that placement with the relative would be contrary to the best interests of the juvenile. In placing a juvenile in nonsecure custody under this section, the court shall consider the Indian Child Welfare Act, Pub. L. No. 95-608, 25 U.S.C. §§ 1901, et seq., as amended, and the Howard M. Metzenbaum Multiethnic Placement Act of 1994, Pub. L. No. 103-382, 108 Stat. 4056, as amended, as they may apply. Placement of a juvenile with a relative outside of this State must be in accordance with the Interstate Compact on the Placement of Children set forth in Article 38 of this Chapter.

(2a) If the court does not place the juvenile with a relative, the court may consider whether nonrelative kin is willing and able to provide proper care and supervision of the juvenile in a safe home. Nonrelative kin is an individual having a substantial relationship with the juvenile. In the case of a juvenile member of a State-recognized tribe as set forth in G.S. 143B-407(a), nonrelative kin also includes any member of a State-recognized tribe or a member of a federally recognized tribe, whether or not there is a substantial relationship with the juvenile. The court may order the Department to notify the juvenile's State-recognized tribe of the need for nonsecure custody for the purpose of locating relatives or nonrelative kin for placement. The court may order placement of the juvenile with nonrelative kin if the court finds the placement is in the juvenile's best interests.

(3) Inquire as to whether there are other juveniles remaining in the home from which the juvenile was removed and, if there are, inquire as to the specific findings of the assessment conducted under G.S. 7B-302 and any actions taken or services provided by the director for the protection of the other juveniles. (1979, c. 815, s. 1; 1981, c. 469, s. 13; 1987 (Reg. Sess., 1988), c. 1090, s. 4; 1994, Ex. Sess., c. 27, s. 1; 1997-390, ss. 5, 6; 1998-229, s. 4; 1998-202, s. 6;

1998-229, ss. 4.1, 21; 1999-318, s. 5; 1999-456, s. 60; 2001-208, ss. 16, 24; 2001-487, s. 101; 2003-337, s. 9; 2005-55, s. 11; 2007-276, s. 1; 2013-129, s. 14.)

§ 7B-507. Reasonable efforts.

(a)     An order placing or continuing the placement of a juvenile in the custody or placement responsibility of a county department of social services, whether an order for continued nonsecure custody, a dispositional order, or a review order:

(1)     Shall contain a finding that the juvenile's continuation in or return to the juvenile's own home would be contrary to the juvenile's best interest;

(2)     Shall contain specific findings as to whether a county department of social services has made reasonable efforts to either prevent the need for placement or eliminate the need for placement of the juvenile, unless the court has previously determined under subsection (b) of this section that such efforts are not required or shall cease;

(3)     Shall contain findings as to whether a county department of social services should continue to make reasonable efforts to prevent or eliminate the need for placement of the juvenile, unless the court has previously determined or determines under subsection (b) of this section that such efforts are not required or shall cease;

(4)     Shall specify that the juvenile's placement and care are the responsibility of the county department of social services and that the department is to provide or arrange for the foster care or other placement of the juvenile. After considering the department's recommendations, the court may order a specific placement the court finds to be in the juvenile's best interest; and

(5)     May provide for services or other efforts aimed at returning the juvenile to a safe home or at achieving another permanent plan for the juvenile.

A finding that reasonable efforts have not been made by a county department of social services shall not preclude the entry of an order authorizing the juvenile's placement when the court finds that placement is necessary for the protection of the juvenile. Where efforts to prevent the need for the juvenile's placement were precluded by an immediate threat of harm to the juvenile, the court may find that the placement of the juvenile in the absence of such efforts was reasonable.

(b)     In any order placing a juvenile in the custody or placement responsibility of a county department of social services, whether an order for continued nonsecure custody, a dispositional order, or a review order, the court may direct that reasonable efforts to eliminate the need for placement of the juvenile shall not be required or shall cease if the court makes written findings of fact that:

(1)     Such efforts clearly would be futile or would be inconsistent with the juvenile's health, safety, and need for a safe, permanent home within a reasonable period of time;

(2)     A court of competent jurisdiction has determined that the parent has subjected the child to aggravated circumstances as defined in G.S. 7B-101;

(3)     A court of competent jurisdiction has terminated involuntarily the parental rights of the parent to another child of the parent; or

(4)     A court of competent jurisdiction has determined that: the parent has committed murder or voluntary manslaughter of another child of the parent; has aided, abetted, attempted, conspired, or solicited to commit murder or voluntary manslaughter of the child or another child of the parent; has committed a felony assault resulting in serious bodily injury to the child or another child of the parent; has committed sexual abuse against the child or another child of the parent; or has been required to register as a sex offender on any government-administered registry.

(c)     When the court determines that reunification efforts are not required or shall cease, the court shall order a plan for permanence as soon as possible, after providing each party with a reasonable opportunity to prepare and present evidence. If the court's determination to cease reunification efforts is made in a hearing that was duly and timely noticed as a permanency planning hearing, then the court may immediately proceed to consider all of the criteria contained in G.S. 7B-906.1(e), make findings of fact, and set forth the best plan of care to achieve a safe, permanent home within a reasonable period of time. If the court's decision to cease reunification efforts arises in any other hearing, the court shall schedule a subsequent hearing within 30 days to address the permanent plan in accordance with G.S. 7B-906.1. At any hearing at which the court orders that reunification efforts shall cease, the affected parent, guardian, or custodian may give notice to preserve the right to appeal that order in accordance with G.S. 7B-1001. The party giving notice shall be permitted to make a detailed offer of proof as to any evidence that party sought to offer in opposition to cessation of reunification that the court refused to admit.

(d) In determining reasonable efforts to be made with respect to a juvenile and in making such reasonable efforts, the juvenile's health and safety shall be the paramount concern. Reasonable efforts to preserve or reunify families may be made concurrently with efforts to plan for the juvenile's adoption, to place the juvenile with a legal guardian, or to place the juvenile in another permanent arrangement. (1998-229, ss. 4.1, 21.1; 1999-456, s. 60; 2001-487, s. 2; 2005-398, s. 1; 2011-295, s. 3; 2013-129, s. 15; 2013-378, s. 1.)

§ 7B-508. Telephonic communication authorized.

All communications, notices, orders, authorizations, and requests authorized or required by G.S. 7B-501, 7B-503, and 7B-504 may be made by telephone when other means of communication are impractical. All written orders pursuant to telephonic communication shall bear the name and the title of the person communicating by telephone, the signature and the title of the official entering the order, and the hour and the date of the authorization. (1979, c. 815, s. 1; 1981, c. 469, s. 13; 1987 (Reg. Sess., 1988), c. 1090, s. 4; 1994, Ex. Sess., c. 27, s. 1; 1997-390, ss. 5, 6; 1998-202, s. 6; 1998-229, s. 4; 1999-456, s. 60.)

Article 6.

Basic Rights.

§ 7B-600. Appointment of guardian.

(a) In any case when no parent appears in a hearing with the juvenile or when the court finds it would be in the best interests of the juvenile, the court may appoint a guardian of the person for the juvenile. The guardian shall operate under the supervision of the court with or without bond and shall file only such reports as the court shall require. The guardian shall have the care, custody, and control of the juvenile or may arrange a suitable placement for the juvenile and may represent the juvenile in legal actions before any court. The guardian may consent to certain actions on the part of the juvenile in place of the parent including (i) marriage, (ii) enlisting in the Armed Forces of the United States, and (iii) enrollment in school. The guardian may also consent to any necessary remedial, psychological, medical, or surgical treatment for the juvenile. The authority of the guardian shall continue until the guardianship is terminated by court order, until the juvenile is emancipated pursuant to Article 35 of Subchapter IV of this Chapter, or until the juvenile reaches the age of majority.

(b) In any case where the court has determined that the appointment of a relative or other suitable person as guardian of the person for a juvenile is the permanent plan for the juvenile and appoints a guardian under this section, the guardian becomes a party to the proceeding. The court may terminate the guardianship only if (i) the court finds that the relationship between the guardian and the juvenile is no longer in the juvenile's best interest, (ii) the guardian is unfit, (iii) the guardian has neglected a guardian's duties, or (iv) the guardian is unwilling or unable to continue assuming a guardian's duties.

(b1) If a party files a motion under G.S. 7B-906.1 or G.S. 7B-1000, the court may, prior to conducting a review hearing, do one or more of the following:

(1) Order the county department of social services to conduct an investigation and file a written report of the investigation regarding the performance of the guardian of the person of the juvenile and give testimony concerning its investigation.

(2) Utilize the community resources in behavioral sciences and other professions in the investigation and study of the guardian.

(3) Ensure that a guardian ad litem has been appointed for the juvenile in accordance with G.S. 7B-601 and has been notified of the pending motion or petition.

(4) Take any other action necessary in order to make a determination in a particular case.

(c) If the court appoints an individual guardian of the person pursuant to this section, the court shall verify that the person being appointed as guardian of the juvenile understands the legal significance of the appointment and will have adequate resources to care appropriately for the juvenile. (1979, c. 815, s. 1; 1997-390, s. 7; 1998-202, s. 6; 1999-456, s. 60; 2000-124, s. 1; 2003-140, s. 9(a); 2011-183, s. 3; 2011-295, s. 4; 2013-129, s. 16.)

§ 7B-601. Appointment and duties of guardian ad litem.

(a) When in a petition a juvenile is alleged to be abused or neglected, the court shall appoint a guardian ad litem to represent the juvenile. When a juvenile is alleged to be dependent, the court may appoint a guardian ad litem to represent the juvenile. The juvenile is a party in all actions under this Subchapter. The guardian ad litem and attorney advocate have standing to represent the juvenile in all actions under this Subchapter where they have been appointed. The appointment shall be made pursuant to the program established by Article 12 of this Chapter unless representation is otherwise provided pursuant to G.S. 7B-1202 or G.S. 7B-1203. The appointment shall terminate when the permanent plan has been achieved for the juvenile and approved by the court. The court may reappoint the guardian ad litem pursuant to a showing of good cause upon motion of any party, including the guardian ad litem, or of the court. In every case where a nonattorney is appointed as a guardian ad litem, an attorney shall be appointed in the case in order to assure protection of the juvenile's legal rights throughout the proceeding. The duties of the guardian ad litem program shall be to make an investigation to determine the facts, the needs of the juvenile, and the available resources within the family and community to meet those needs; to facilitate, when appropriate, the settlement of disputed issues; to offer evidence and examine witnesses at adjudication; to explore options with the court at the dispositional hearing; to conduct follow-up investigations to insure that the orders of the court are being properly executed; to report to the court when the needs of the juvenile are not being met; and to protect and promote the best interests of the juvenile until formally relieved of the responsibility by the court.

(b) The court may authorize the guardian ad litem to accompany the juvenile to court in any criminal action wherein the juvenile may be called on to testify in a matter relating to abuse.

(c) The guardian ad litem has the authority to obtain any information or reports, whether or not confidential, that may in the guardian ad litem's opinion be relevant to the case. No privilege other than the attorney-client privilege may be invoked to prevent the guardian ad litem and the court from obtaining such information. The confidentiality of the information or reports shall be respected by the guardian ad litem, and no disclosure of any information or reports shall be made to anyone except by order of the court or unless otherwise provided by law. (1979, c. 815, s. 1; 1981, c. 528; 1983, c. 761, s. 159; 1987 (Reg. Sess., 1988), c. 1090, s. 5; 1993, c. 537, s. 1; 1995, c. 324, s. 21.13; 1998-202, s. 6; 1999-432, s. 1; 1999-456, s. 60.)

§ 7B-602. Parent's right to counsel; guardian ad litem.

(a) In cases where the juvenile petition alleges that a juvenile is abused, neglected, or dependent, the parent has the right to counsel and to appointed counsel in cases of indigency unless that person waives the right. When a petition is filed alleging that a juvenile is abused, neglected, or dependent, the clerk shall appoint provisional counsel for each parent named in the petition in accordance with rules adopted by the Office of Indigent Defense Services and shall indicate the appointment on the juvenile summons or attached notice. At the first hearing, the court shall dismiss the provisional counsel if the respondent parent:

(1) Does not appear at the hearing;

(2) Does not qualify for court-appointed counsel;

(3) Has retained counsel; or

(4) Waives the right to counsel.

The court shall confirm the appointment of counsel if subdivisions (1) through (4) of this subsection are not applicable to the respondent parent.

The court may reconsider a parent's eligibility and desire for appointed counsel at any stage of the proceeding.

(a1) A parent qualifying for appointed counsel may be permitted to proceed without the assistance of counsel only after the court examines the parent and makes findings of fact sufficient to show that the waiver is knowing and voluntary. The court's examination shall be reported as provided in G.S. 7B-806.

(b) In addition to the right to appointed counsel set forth above, a guardian ad litem shall be appointed in accordance with the provisions of G.S. 1A-1, Rule 17, to represent a parent who is under the age of 18 years and who is not married or otherwise emancipated. The appointment of a guardian ad litem under this subsection shall not affect the minor parent's entitlement to a guardian ad litem pursuant to G.S. 7B-601 in the event that the minor parent is the subject of a separate juvenile petition.

(c) On motion of any party or on the court's own motion, the court may appoint a guardian ad litem for a parent who is incompetent in accordance with G.S. 1A-1, Rule 17.

(d) The parent's counsel shall not be appointed to serve as the guardian ad litem and the guardian ad litem shall not act as the parent's attorney. Communications between the guardian ad litem appointed under this section and the parent and between the guardian ad litem and the parent's counsel shall be privileged and confidential to the same extent that communications between the parent and the parent's counsel are privileged and confidential.

(e) Repealed by Session Laws 2013-129, s. 17, effective October 1, 2013, and applicable to actions filed or pending on or after that date. (1979, c. 815, s. 1; 1981, c. 469, s. 14; 1998-202, s. 6; 1999-456, s. 60; 2000-144, s. 16; 2001-208, s. 2; 2001-487, s. 101; 2005-398, s. 2; 2011-326, s. 12(a); 2013-129, s. 17.)


§ 7B-603. Payment of court-appointed attorney or guardian ad litem.

(a) An attorney or guardian ad litem appointed pursuant to G.S. 7B-601 shall be paid a reasonable fee fixed by the court or by direct engagement for specialized guardian ad litem services through the Administrative Office of the Courts.

(a1) The court may require payment of the fee for an attorney or guardian ad litem appointed pursuant to G.S. 7B-601 from a person other than the juvenile as provided in G.S. 7A-450.1, 7A-450.2, and 7A-450.3. In no event shall the parent or guardian be required to pay the fees for a court-appointed attorney or guardian ad litem in an abuse, neglect, or dependency proceeding unless the juvenile has been adjudicated to be abused, neglected, or dependent or, in a proceeding to terminate parental rights, unless the parent's rights have been terminated. If the party is ordered to reimburse the State for attorney or guardian ad litem fees and fails to comply with the order at the time of disposition, the court shall file a judgment against the party for the amount due the State.

(b) An attorney appointed pursuant to G.S. 7B-602 or pursuant to any other provision of the Juvenile Code for which the Office of Indigent Defense Services is responsible for providing counsel shall be paid a reasonable fee in accordance with rules adopted by the Office of Indigent Defense Services.

(b1)    The court may require payment of the fee for an attorney appointed pursuant to G.S. 7B-602 or G.S. 7B-1101 from the respondent. In no event shall the respondent be required to pay the fees for a court-appointed attorney in an abuse, neglect, or dependency proceeding unless the juvenile has been adjudicated to be abused, neglected, or dependent or, in a proceeding to terminate parental rights, unless the respondent's rights have been terminated. At the dispositional hearing or other appropriate hearing, the court shall make a determination whether the respondent should be held responsible for reimbursing the State for the respondent's attorneys' fees. This determination shall include the respondent's financial ability to pay.

If the court determines that the respondent is responsible for reimbursing the State for the respondent's attorneys' fees, the court shall so order. If the respondent does not comply with the order at the time of disposition, the court shall file a judgment against the respondent for the amount due the State.

(c)    Repealed by Session Laws 2005-254, s. 2, effective October 1, 2005, and applicable to the appointment of counsel on or after that date. (1979, c. 815, s. 1; 1983, c. 726, ss. 2, 3; 1987 (Reg. Sess., 1988), c. 1090, s. 6; 1991, c. 575, s. 1; 1998-202, s. 6; 1999-456, s. 60; 2000-144, s. 17; 2005-254, s. 2.)

Article 7.

Discovery.

§ 7B-700.  Sharing of information; discovery.

(a)    Sharing of Information. - A department of social services is authorized to share with any other party information relevant to the subject matter of an action pending under this Subchapter. However, this subsection does not authorize the disclosure of the identity of the reporter or any uniquely identifying information that would lead to the discovery of the reporter's identity in accordance with G.S. 7B-302 or the identity of any other person where the agency making the information available determines that the disclosure would be likely to endanger the life or safety of the person.

(b)    Local Rules. - The chief district court judge may adopt local rules or enter an administrative order addressing the sharing of information among parties and the use of discovery.

(c) Discovery. - Any party may file a motion for discovery. The motion shall contain a specific description of the information sought and a statement that the requesting party has made a reasonable effort to obtain the information pursuant to subsections (a) and (b) of this section or that the information cannot be obtained pursuant to subsections (a) and (b) of this section. The motion shall be served upon all parties pursuant to G.S. 1A-1, Rule 5. The motion shall be heard and ruled upon within 10 business days of the filing of the motion. The court may grant, restrict, defer, or deny the relief requested. Any order shall avoid unnecessary delay of the hearing, establish expedited deadlines for completion, and conform to G.S. 7B-803.

(d) Protective Order. - Any party served with a motion for discovery may request that the discovery be denied, restricted, or deferred and shall submit, for in camera inspection, the document, information, or materials the party seeks to protect. If the court enters any order granting relief, copies of the documents, information, or materials submitted in camera shall be preserved for appellate review in the event of an appeal.

(e) Redisclosure. - Information obtained through discovery or sharing of information under this section may not be redisclosed if the redisclosure is prohibited by State or federal law.

(f) Guardian Ad Litem. - Unless provided otherwise by local rules, information or reports obtained by the guardian ad litem pursuant to G.S. 7B-601 are not subject to disclosure pursuant to this subsection, except that reports and records shall be shared with all parties before submission to the court. (1979, c. 815, s. 1; 1998-202, s. 6; 1999-456, s. 60; 2009-311, s. 4.)

Article 8.

Hearing Procedures.

§ 7B-800. Amendment of petition.

The court, in its discretion, may permit a petition to be amended. The court shall direct the manner in which an amended petition shall be served and the time allowed for a party to prepare after the petition has been amended. (1979, c. 815, s. 1; 1998-202, s. 6; 1999-456, s. 60; 2010-90, s. 11.)

§ 7B-800.1. Pre-adjudication hearing.

(a) Prior to the adjudicatory hearing, the court shall consider the following:

(1) Retention or release of provisional counsel.

(2) Identification of the parties to the proceeding.

(3) Whether paternity has been established or efforts made to establish paternity, including the identity and location of any missing parent.

(4) Whether relatives have been identified and notified as potential resources for placement or support.

(5) Whether all summons, service of process, and notice requirements have been met.

(6) Any pretrial motions, including (i) appointment of a guardian ad litem in accordance with G.S. 7B-602, (ii) discovery motions in accordance with G.S. 7B-700, (iii) amendment of the petition in accordance with G.S. 7B-800, or (iv) any motion for a continuance of the adjudicatory hearing in accordance with G.S. 7B-803.

(7) Any other issue that can be properly addressed as a preliminary matter.

(b) The pre-adjudication hearing may be combined with a hearing on the need for nonsecure custody or any pretrial hearing or conducted in accordance with local rules.

(c) The parties may enter stipulations in accordance with G.S. 7B-807 or enter a consent order in accordance with G.S. 7B-801. (2013-129, s. 18.)


§ 7B-801. Hearing.

(a) At any hearing authorized or required under this Subchapter, the court in its discretion shall determine whether the hearing or any part of the hearing shall be closed to the public. In determining whether to close the hearing or any part of the hearing, the court shall consider the circumstances of the case, including, but not limited to, the following factors:

(1)     The nature of the allegations against the juvenile's parent, guardian, custodian or caretaker;

(2)     The age and maturity of the juvenile;

(3)     The benefit to the juvenile of confidentiality;

(4)     The benefit to the juvenile of an open hearing; and

(5)     The extent to which the confidentiality afforded the juvenile's record pursuant to G.S. 132-1.4(l) and G.S. 7B-2901 will be compromised by an open hearing.

(b)     No hearing or part of a hearing shall be closed by the court if the juvenile requests that it remain open.

(b1)    Nothing in this Subchapter precludes the court in an abuse, neglect, or dependency proceeding from entering a consent adjudication order, disposition order, review order, or permanency planning order when each of the following apply:

(1)     All parties are present or represented by counsel, who is present and authorized to consent.

(2)     The juvenile is represented by counsel.

(3)     The court makes sufficient findings of fact.

(c)     The adjudicatory hearing shall be held in the district at such time and place as the chief district court judge shall designate, but no later than 60 days from the filing of the petition unless the judge pursuant to G.S. 7B-803 orders that it be held at a later time. (1979, c. 815, s. 1; 1998-202, s. 6; 1998-229, ss. 5, 22; 1999-456, s. 60; 2011-295, s. 5.)


§ 7B-802. Conduct of hearing.

The adjudicatory hearing shall be a judicial process designed to adjudicate the existence or nonexistence of any of the conditions alleged in a petition. In the adjudicatory hearing, the court shall protect the rights of the juvenile and the juvenile's parent to assure due process of law. (1979, c. 815, s. 1; 1998-202, s. 6; 1999-456, s. 60.)

§ 7B-803. Continuances.

The court may, for good cause, continue the hearing for as long as is reasonably required to receive additional evidence, reports, or assessments that the court has requested, or other information needed in the best interests of the juvenile and to allow for a reasonable time for the parties to conduct expeditious discovery. Otherwise, continuances shall be granted only in extraordinary circumstances when necessary for the proper administration of justice or in the best interests of the juvenile. Resolution of a pending criminal charge against a respondent arising out of the same transaction or occurrence as the juvenile petition shall not be the sole extraordinary circumstance for granting a continuance. (1979, c. 815, s. 1; 1987 (Reg. Sess., 1988), c. 1090, s. 9; 1998-202, s. 6; 1999-456, s. 60; 2013-129, s. 19.)

§ 7B-804. Rules of evidence.

Where the juvenile is alleged to be abused, neglected, or dependent, the rules of evidence in civil cases shall apply. (1979, c. 815, s. 1; 1981, c. 469, s. 17; 1998-202, s. 6; 1999-456, s. 60.)

§ 7B-805. Quantum of proof in adjudicatory hearing.

The allegations in a petition alleging that a juvenile is abused, neglected, or dependent shall be proved by clear and convincing evidence. (1979, c. 815, s. 1; 1998-202, s. 6; 1999-456, s. 60; 2010-90, s. 12; 2013-129, s. 20.)

§ 7B-806. Record of proceedings.

All adjudicatory and dispositional hearings shall be recorded by stenographic notes or by electronic or mechanical means. Records shall be reduced to a written transcript only when timely notice of appeal has been given. The court may order that other hearings be recorded. (1979, c. 815, s. 1; 1998-202, s. 6; 1999-456, s. 60.)

§ 7B-807. Adjudication.

(a)     If the court finds from the evidence, including stipulations by a party, that the allegations in the petition have been proven by clear and convincing evidence, the court shall so state. A record of specific stipulated adjudicatory facts shall be made by either reducing the facts to a writing, signed by each party stipulating to them and submitted to the court; or by reading the facts into the record, followed by an oral statement of agreement from each party stipulating to them. If the court finds that the allegations have not been proven, the court shall dismiss the petition with prejudice, and if the juvenile is in nonsecure custody, the juvenile shall be released to the parent, guardian, custodian, or caretaker.

(a1)    Repealed by Session Laws 2013-129, s. 21, effective October 1, 2013, and applicable to actions filed or pending on or after that date.

(b)     The adjudicatory order shall be in writing and shall contain appropriate findings of fact and conclusions of law. The order shall be reduced to writing, signed, and entered no later than 30 days following the completion of the hearing. If the order is not entered within 30 days following completion of the hearing, the clerk of court for juvenile matters shall schedule a subsequent hearing at the first session of court scheduled for the hearing of juvenile matters following the 30-day period to determine and explain the reason for the delay and to obtain any needed clarification as to the contents of the order. The order shall be entered within 10 days of the subsequent hearing required by this subsection. (1979, c. 815, s. 1; 1998-202, s. 6; 1999-456, s. 60; 2001-208, s. 17; 2001-487, s. 101; 2005-398, s. 3; 2010-90, s. 13; 2011-295, s. 6; 2013-129, s. 21.)


§ 7B-808. Predisposition report.

(a)     The court shall proceed to the dispositional hearing upon receipt of sufficient social, medical, psychiatric, psychological, and educational information. No predisposition report shall be submitted to or considered by the court prior to the completion of the adjudicatory hearing. The court may proceed with the dispositional hearing without receiving a predisposition report if the court makes a written finding that a report is not necessary.

(b)     The director of the department of social services shall prepare the predisposition report for the court containing the results of any mental health evaluation under G.S. 7B-503, a placement plan, and a treatment plan the director deems appropriate to meet the juvenile's needs.

(c) The chief district court judge may adopt local rules or make an administrative order addressing the sharing of the reports among parties, including an order that prohibits disclosure of the report to the juvenile if the court determines that disclosure would not be in the best interest of the juvenile. Such local rules or administrative order may not:

(1) Prohibit a party entitled by law to receive confidential information from receiving that information.

(2) Allow disclosure of any confidential source protected by statute. (1979, c. 815, s. 1; 1998-202, s. 6; 1999-456, s. 60; 2003-140, s. 2; 2004-203, s. 17.)

Article 9.

Dispositions.

§ 7B-900. Purpose.

The purpose of dispositions in juvenile actions is to design an appropriate plan to meet the needs of the juvenile and to achieve the objectives of the State in exercising jurisdiction. If possible, the initial approach should involve working with the juvenile and the juvenile's family in their own home so that the appropriate community resources may be involved in care, supervision, and treatment according to the needs of the juvenile. Thus, the court should arrange for appropriate community-level services to be provided to the juvenile and the juvenile's family in order to strengthen the home situation. (1979, c. 815, s. 1; 1995 (Reg. Sess., 1996), c. 609, s. 1; 1998-202, s. 6; 1999-456, s. 60.)

§ 7B-900.1. Post adjudication venue.

(a) At any time after adjudication, the court on its own motion or motion of any party may transfer venue to a different county, regardless of whether the action could have been commenced in that county, if the court finds that the forum is inconvenient, that transfer of the action to the other county is in the best interest of the juvenile, and that the rights of the parties are not prejudiced by the change of venue.

(b)     Before ordering that a case be transferred to another county, the court shall find that the director of the department of social services in the county in which the action is pending and the director in the county to which transfer is contemplated have communicated about the case and that:

(1)     The two directors are in agreement with respect to each county's responsibility for providing financial support for the juvenile and services for the juvenile and the juvenile's family; or

(2)     The Director of the Division of Social Services or the Director's designee has made that determination pursuant to G.S. 153A-257(d).

(c)     When the court transfers a case to a different county, the court shall join or substitute as a party to the action the director of the department of social services in the county to which the case is being transferred and, if the juvenile is in the custody of the department of social services in the county in which the action is pending, shall transfer custody to the department of social services in the county to which the case is being transferred. The director of the department of social services in the county to which the case is being transferred must be given notice and an opportunity to be heard before the court enters an order pursuant to this subsection. However, the director may waive the right to notice and a hearing.

(d)     Before ordering that a case be transferred to a different district, the court shall communicate with the chief district court judge or a judge presiding in juvenile court in the district to which the transfer is contemplated explaining the reasons for the proposed transfer. If the judge in the district to which the transfer is proposed makes a timely objection to the transfer, either verbally or in writing, the court shall order the transfer only after making detailed findings of fact that support a conclusion that the juvenile's best interests require that the case be transferred.

(e)     Before ordering that a case be transferred to another county, the court shall consider relevant factors, which may include:

(1)     The current residences of the juvenile and the parent, guardian, or custodian and the extent to which those residences have been and are likely to be stable.

(2) The reunification plan or other permanent plan for the juvenile and the likely effect of a change in venue on efforts to achieve permanence for the juvenile expeditiously.

(3) The nature and location of services and service providers necessary to achieve the reunification plan or other permanent plan for the juvenile.

(4) The impact upon the juvenile of the potential disruption of an existing therapeutic relationship.

(5) The nature and location of witnesses and evidence likely to be required in future hearings.

(6) The degree to which the transfer would cause inconvenience to one or more parties.

(7) Any agreement of the parties as to which forum is most convenient.

(8) The familiarity of the departments of social services, the courts, and the local offices of the guardian ad litem with the juvenile and the juvenile's family.

(9) Any other factor the court considers relevant.

(f) The order transferring venue shall be in writing, signed, and entered no later than 30 days from completion of the hearing. The order shall identify the next court action and specify the date within which the next hearing shall be held. If the order is not entered within 30 days following completion of the hearing, the clerk of court for juvenile matters shall schedule a subsequent hearing at the first session of court scheduled for the hearing of juvenile matters following the 30-day period to determine and explain the reason for the delay and to obtain any needed clarification as to the contents of the order. The order shall be entered within 10 days of the subsequent hearing required by this subsection.

(g) The clerk shall transmit to the court in the county to which the case is being transferred a copy of the complete record of the case within three business days after entry of the order transferring venue.

Upon receiving a case that has been transferred from another county, the clerk shall promptly satisfy the following:

(1)   Assign an appropriate file number to the case.

(2)   Ensure that any necessary appointments of new attorneys or guardians ad litem are made.

(3)   Calendar the next court action as set forth in the order transferring venue and give appropriate notice to all parties. (2009-311, s. 5.)

§ 7B-901.  Dispositional hearing.

The dispositional hearing shall take place immediately following the adjudicatory hearing and shall be concluded within 30 days of the conclusion of the adjudicatory hearing. The dispositional hearing may be informal and the court may consider written reports or other evidence concerning the needs of the juvenile. The juvenile and the juvenile's parent, guardian, or custodian shall have the right to present evidence, and they may advise the court concerning the disposition they believe to be in the best interests of the juvenile. The court may consider any evidence, including hearsay evidence as defined in G.S. 8C-1, Rule 801, including testimony or evidence from any person who is not a party, that the court finds to be relevant, reliable, and necessary to determine the needs of the juvenile and the most appropriate disposition. The court may exclude the public from the hearing unless the juvenile moves that the hearing be open, which motion shall be granted.

At the dispositional hearing, the court shall inquire as to the identity and location of any missing parent and whether paternity is at issue. The court shall include findings of the efforts undertaken to locate the missing parent and to serve that parent and efforts undertaken to establish paternity when paternity is an issue. The order may provide for specific efforts in determining the identity and location of any missing parent and specific efforts in establishing paternity. The court shall also inquire about efforts made to identify and notify relatives as potential resources for placement or support. (1979, c. 815, s. 1; 1981, c. 469, s. 18; 1998-202, s. 6; 1999-456, s. 60; 2003-62, s. 1; 2005-398, s. 4; 2007-276, s. 2; 2011-295, s. 7; 2013-129, s. 22.)

§ 7B-902: Repealed by Session Laws 2011-295, s. 8, effective October 1, 2011, and applicable to actions filed on or pending on or after that date.

§ 7B-903. Dispositional alternatives for abused, neglected, or dependent juvenile.

(a)     The following alternatives for disposition shall be available to any court exercising jurisdiction, and the court may combine any of the applicable alternatives when the court finds the disposition to be in the best interests of the juvenile:

(1)     The court may dismiss the case or continue the case in order to allow the parent, guardian, custodian, caretaker or others to take appropriate action.

(2)     In the case of any juvenile who needs more adequate care or supervision or who needs placement, the court may:

a.     Require that the juvenile be supervised in the juvenile's own home by the department of social services in the juvenile's county, or by other personnel as may be available to the court, subject to conditions applicable to the parent, guardian, custodian, or caretaker as the court may specify; or

b.     Place the juvenile in the custody of a parent, relative, private agency offering placement services, or some other suitable person; or

c.     Place the juvenile in the custody of the department of social services in the county of the juvenile's residence, or in the case of a juvenile who has legal residence outside the State, in the physical custody of the department of social services in the county where the juvenile is found so that agency may return the juvenile to the responsible authorities in the juvenile's home state. The director may, unless otherwise ordered by the court, arrange for, provide, or consent to, needed routine or emergency medical or surgical care or treatment. In the case where the parent is unknown, unavailable, or unable to act on behalf of the juvenile, the director may, unless otherwise ordered by the court, arrange for, provide, or consent to any psychiatric, psychological, educational, or other remedial evaluations or treatment for the juvenile placed by a court or the court's designee in the custody or physical custody of a county department of social services under the authority of this or any other Chapter of the General Statutes. Prior to exercising this authority, the director shall make reasonable efforts to obtain consent from a parent or guardian of the affected juvenile. If the director cannot obtain such consent, the director shall promptly notify the parent or guardian that care or treatment has been provided and shall give the parent frequent status reports on the circumstances of the juvenile. Upon request of a parent or guardian of the affected juvenile, the results or records of the aforementioned evaluations, findings, or treatment shall be made available to such parent or guardian by the director unless prohibited by G.S. 122C-53(d). If a juvenile is removed from the home and placed in custody or placement responsibility of a county department of social services, the director shall not allow unsupervised visitation with, or return physical custody of the juvenile to, the parent, guardian, custodian, or caretaker without a hearing at which the court finds that the juvenile will receive proper care and supervision in a safe home.

In placing a juvenile in out-of-home care under this section, the court shall first consider whether a relative of the juvenile is willing and able to provide proper care and supervision of the juvenile in a safe home. If the court finds that the relative is willing and able to provide proper care and supervision in a safe home, then the court shall order placement of the juvenile with the relative unless the court finds that the placement is contrary to the best interests of the juvenile. In placing a juvenile in out-of-home care under this section, the court shall also consider whether it is in the juvenile's best interest to remain in the juvenile's community of residence. Placement of a juvenile with a relative outside of this State must be in accordance with the Interstate Compact on the Placement of Children.

(3)     In any case, the court may order that the juvenile be examined by a physician, psychiatrist, psychologist, or other qualified expert as may be needed for the court to determine the needs of the juvenile:

a.     Upon completion of the examination, the court shall conduct a hearing to determine whether the juvenile is in need of medical, surgical, psychiatric, psychological, or other treatment and who should pay the cost of the treatment. The county manager, or such person who shall be designated by the chairman of the county commissioners, of the juvenile's residence shall be notified of the hearing, and allowed to be heard. If the court finds the juvenile to be in need of medical, surgical, psychiatric, psychological, or other treatment, the court shall permit the parent or other responsible persons to arrange for treatment. If the parent declines or is unable to make necessary arrangements, the court may order the needed treatment, surgery, or care, and the court may order the parent to pay the cost of the care pursuant to G.S. 7B-904. If the court finds the parent is unable to pay the cost of treatment, the court shall order the county to arrange for treatment of the juvenile and to pay for the cost of the treatment. The county department of social services shall recommend the facility that will provide the juvenile with treatment.

b.  If the court believes, or if there is evidence presented to the effect that the juvenile is mentally ill or is developmentally disabled, the court shall refer the juvenile to the area mental health, developmental disabilities, and substance abuse services director for appropriate action. A juvenile shall not be committed directly to a State hospital or mental retardation center; and orders purporting to commit a juvenile directly to a State hospital or mental retardation center except for an examination to determine capacity to proceed shall be void and of no effect. The area mental health, developmental disabilities, and substance abuse director shall be responsible for arranging an interdisciplinary evaluation of the juvenile and mobilizing resources to meet the juvenile's needs. If institutionalization is determined to be the best service for the juvenile, admission shall be with the voluntary consent of the parent or guardian. If the parent, guardian, custodian, or caretaker refuses to consent to a mental hospital or retardation center admission after such institutionalization is recommended by the area mental health, developmental disabilities, and substance abuse director, the signature and consent of the court may be substituted for that purpose. In all cases in which a regional mental hospital refuses admission to a juvenile referred for admission by a court and an area mental health, developmental disabilities, and substance abuse director or discharges a juvenile previously admitted on court referral prior to completion of treatment, the hospital shall submit to the court a written report setting out the reasons for denial of admission or discharge and setting out the juvenile's diagnosis, indications of mental illness, indications of need for treatment, and a statement as to the location of any facility known to have a treatment program for the juvenile in question.

(b)  When the court has found that a juvenile has suffered physical abuse and that the individual responsible for the abuse has a history of violent behavior against people, the court shall consider the opinion of the mental health professional who performed an evaluation under G.S. 7B-503(b) before returning the juvenile to the custody of that individual.

(c)  If the court determines that the juvenile shall be placed in the custody of an individual other than the parents, the court shall verify that the person receiving custody of the juvenile understands the legal significance of the placement and will have adequate resources to care appropriately for the juvenile. (1979, c. 815, s. 1; 1981, c. 469, s. 19; 1985, c. 589, s. 5; c. 777, s. 1; 1985 (Reg. Sess., 1986), c. 863, s. 2; 1991, c. 636, s. 19(a); 1995 (Reg. Sess., 1996), c. 609, s. 3; 1997-516, s. 1A; 1998-202, s. 6; 1998-229, ss. 6, 23; 1999-318, s. 6; 1999-456, s. 60; 2002-164, s. 4.8; 2003-140, s. 9(b).)

§ 7B-904.  Authority over parents of juvenile adjudicated as abused, neglected, or dependent.

(a)     If the court orders medical, surgical, psychiatric, psychological, or other treatment pursuant to G.S. 7B-903, the court may order the parent or other responsible parties to pay the cost of the treatment or care ordered.

(b)     At the dispositional hearing or a subsequent hearing if the court finds that it is in the best interests of the juvenile for the parent, guardian, custodian, stepparent, adult member of the juvenile's household, or adult relative entrusted with the juvenile's care to be directly involved in the juvenile's treatment, the court may order the parent, guardian, custodian, stepparent, adult member of the juvenile's household, or adult relative entrusted with the juvenile's care to participate in medical, psychiatric, psychological, or other treatment of the juvenile. The cost of the treatment shall be paid pursuant to G.S. 7B-903.

(c)     At the dispositional hearing or a subsequent hearing the court may determine whether the best interests of the juvenile require that the parent, guardian, custodian, stepparent, adult member of the juvenile's household, or adult relative entrusted with the juvenile's care undergo psychiatric, psychological, or other treatment or counseling directed toward remediating or remedying behaviors or conditions that led to or contributed to the juvenile's adjudication or to the court's decision to remove custody of the juvenile from the parent, guardian, custodian, stepparent, adult member of the juvenile's household, or adult relative entrusted with the juvenile's care. If the court finds that the best interests of the juvenile require the parent, guardian, custodian, stepparent, adult member of the juvenile's household, or adult relative entrusted with the juvenile's care undergo treatment, it may order that individual to comply with a plan of treatment approved by the court or condition legal custody or physical placement of the juvenile with the parent, guardian, custodian, stepparent, adult member of the juvenile's household, or adult relative entrusted with the juvenile's care upon that individual's compliance with the plan of treatment. The court may order the parent, guardian, custodian, stepparent, adult member of the juvenile's household, or adult relative entrusted with the juvenile's care to pay the cost of treatment ordered pursuant to this subsection. In cases in which the court has conditioned legal custody or physical placement of the juvenile with the parent, guardian, custodian, stepparent, adult member of the juvenile's household, or adult relative entrusted with the juvenile's care upon compliance with a plan of treatment, the court may charge the cost of the treatment to the county of the juvenile's residence if the court finds the parent, guardian, custodian, stepparent, adult member of the juvenile's household, or adult relative entrusted with the juvenile's care is unable to pay the cost of the treatment. In all other cases, if the court finds the parent, guardian, custodian, stepparent, adult member of the juvenile's household, or adult relative entrusted with the juvenile's care is unable to pay the cost of the treatment ordered pursuant to this subsection, the court may order that individual to receive treatment currently available from the area mental health program that serves the parent's catchment area.

(d) At the dispositional hearing or a subsequent hearing, when legal custody of a juvenile is vested in someone other than the juvenile's parent, if the court finds that the parent is able to do so, the court may order that the parent pay a reasonable sum that will cover, in whole or in part, the support of the juvenile after the order is entered. If the court requires the payment of child support, the amount of the payments shall be determined as provided in G.S. 50-13.4(c). If the court places a juvenile in the custody of a county department of social services and if the court finds that the parent is unable to pay the cost of the support required by the juvenile, the cost shall be paid by the county department of social services in whose custody the juvenile is placed, provided the juvenile is not receiving care in an institution owned or operated by the State or federal government or any subdivision thereof.

(d1) At the dispositional hearing or a subsequent hearing, the court may order the parent, guardian, custodian, or caretaker served with a copy of the summons pursuant to G.S. 7B-407 to do any of the following:

(1) Attend and participate in parental responsibility classes if those classes are available in the judicial district in which the parent, guardian, custodian, or caretaker resides.

(2) Provide, to the extent that person is able to do so, transportation for the juvenile to keep appointments for medical, psychiatric, psychological, or other treatment ordered by the court if the juvenile remains in or is returned to the home.

(3) Take appropriate steps to remedy conditions in the home that led to or contributed to the juvenile's adjudication or to the court's decision to remove custody of the juvenile from the parent, guardian, custodian, or caretaker.

(e) Upon motion of a party or upon the court's own motion, the court may issue an order directing the parent, guardian, custodian, or caretaker served with a copy of the summons pursuant to G.S. 7B-407 to appear and show cause why the parent, guardian, custodian, or caretaker should not be found or held in civil or criminal contempt for willfully failing to comply with an order of the court. Chapter 5A of the General Statutes shall govern contempt proceedings initiated pursuant to this section. (1979, c. 815, s. 1; 1983, c. 837, ss. 2, 3; 1987, c. 598, s. 2; 1989, c. 218; c. 529, s. 7; 1995, c. 328, s. 2; 1995 (Reg. Sess., 1996), c. 609, s. 4; 1997-456, s. 1; 1998-202, s. 6; 1999-318, s. 7; 1999-456, s. 60; 2001-208, s. 3; 2001-487, s. 101.)

§ 7B-905. Dispositional order.

(a) The dispositional order shall be in writing, signed, and entered no later than 30 days from the completion of the hearing, and shall contain appropriate findings of fact and conclusions of law. The court shall state with particularity, both orally and in the written order of disposition, the precise terms of the disposition including the kind, duration, and the person who is responsible for carrying out the disposition and the person or agency in whom custody is vested. If the order is not entered within 30 days following completion of the hearing, the clerk of court for juvenile matters shall schedule a subsequent hearing at the first session of court scheduled for the hearing of juvenile matters following the 30-day period to determine and explain the reason for the delay and to obtain any needed clarification as to the contents of the order. The order shall be entered within 10 days of the subsequent hearing required by this subsection.

(b) A dispositional order under which a juvenile is removed from the custody of a parent, guardian, custodian, or caretaker shall direct that the review hearing required by G.S. 7B-906.1 be held within 90 days from of the date of the dispositional hearing and, if practicable, shall set the date and time for the review hearing.

(c) Any dispositional order shall comply with the requirements of G.S. 7B-507.

(d) When a county department of social services having custody or placement responsibility of a juvenile intends to change the juvenile's placement, the department shall give the guardian ad litem for the juvenile notice of its intention unless precluded by emergency circumstances from doing so. Where emergency circumstances exist, the department of social services shall notify the guardian ad litem or the attorney advocate within 72 hours of the placement change, unless local rules require notification within a shorter time period. (1979, c. 815, s. 1; 1987 (Reg. Sess., 1988), c. 1090, s. 10; 1991, c. 434, s. 1; 1997-390, s. 8; 1998-202, s. 6; 1998-229, s. 24; 1999-456, s. 60; 2001-208, ss. 4, 18; 2001-487, s. 101; 2005-398, s. 5; 2011-295, s. 9; 2013-129, s. 23.)

§ 7B-905.1. Visitation.

(a)     An order that removes custody of a juvenile from a parent, guardian, or custodian or that continues the juvenile's placement outside the home shall provide for appropriate visitation as may be in the best interests of the juvenile consistent with the juvenile's health and safety. The court may specify in the order conditions under which visitation may be suspended.

(b)     If the juvenile is placed or continued in the custody or placement responsibility of a county department of social services, the court may order the director to arrange, facilitate, and supervise a visitation plan expressly approved or ordered by the court. The plan shall indicate the minimum frequency and length of visits and whether the visits shall be supervised. Unless the court orders otherwise, the director shall have discretion to determine who will supervise visits when supervision is required, to determine the location of visits, and to change the day and time of visits in response to scheduling conflicts, illness of the child or party, or extraordinary circumstances. The director shall promptly communicate a limited and temporary change in the visitation schedule to the affected party. Any ongoing change in the visitation schedule shall be communicated to the party in writing and state the reason for the change.

If the director makes a good faith determination that the visitation plan is not consistent with the juvenile's health and safety, the director may temporarily suspend all or part of the visitation plan. The director shall not be subject to any motion to show cause for this suspension but shall expeditiously file a motion for review.

(c)     If the juvenile is placed or continued in the custody or guardianship of a relative or other suitable person, any order providing for visitation shall specify the minimum frequency and length of the visits and whether the visits shall be supervised. The court may authorize additional visitation as agreed upon by the respondent and custodian or guardian.

(d)     If the court retains jurisdiction, all parties shall be informed of the right to file a motion for review of any visitation plan entered pursuant to this section.

Upon motion of any party and after proper notice and a hearing, the court may establish, modify, or enforce a visitation plan that is in the juvenile's best interest. Prior to or at the hearing, the court may order the department and guardian ad litem to investigate and make written recommendations as to appropriate visitation and give testimony concerning its recommendations. For resolution of issues related to visitation, the court may order the parents, guardian, or custodian to participate in custody mediation where there is a program established pursuant to G.S. 7A-494. In referring a case to custody mediation, the court shall specify the issue or issues for mediation, including, but not limited to, whether or not visitation shall be supervised and whether overnight visitation may occur. Custody mediation shall not permit the participants to consent to a change in custody. A copy of any agreement reached in custody mediation shall be provided to all parties and counsel and shall be approved by the court. The provisions of G.S. 50-13.1(d) through (f) apply to this section. (2013-129, s. 24.)

§ 7B-906: Repealed by Session Laws 2013-129, s. 25, effective October 1, 2013, and applicable to actions filed or pending on or after that date.

§ 7B-906.1. Review and permanency planning hearings.

(a)     In any case where custody is removed from a parent, guardian, or custodian, the court shall conduct a review hearing within 90 days from the date of the dispositional hearing and shall conduct a review hearing within six months thereafter. Within 12 months of the date of the initial order removing custody, there shall be a review hearing designated as a permanency planning hearing. Review hearings after the initial permanency planning hearing shall be designated as subsequent permanency planning hearings. The subsequent permanency planning hearings shall be held at least every six months thereafter or earlier as set by the court to review the progress made in finalizing the permanent plan for the juvenile, or if necessary, to make a new permanent plan for the juvenile.

(b)     The director of social services shall make a timely request to the clerk to calendar each hearing at a session of court scheduled for the hearing of juvenile matters. The clerk shall give 15 days' notice of the hearing and its purpose to (i) the parents, (ii) the juvenile if 12 years of age or more, (iii) the guardian, (iv) the person providing care for the juvenile, (v) the custodian or agency with custody, (vi) the guardian ad litem, and (vii) any other person or agency the court may specify. The department of social services shall either provide to the clerk the name and address of the person providing care for the juvenile for notice under this subsection or file written documentation with the clerk that the juvenile's current care provider was sent notice of hearing. Nothing in this subsection shall be construed to make the person providing care for the juvenile a party to the proceeding solely based on receiving notice and the right to be heard.

(c) At each hearing, the court shall consider information from the parents, the juvenile, the guardian, any person providing care for the juvenile, the custodian or agency with custody, the guardian ad litem, and any other person or agency that will aid in the court's review. The court may consider any evidence, including hearsay evidence as defined in G.S. 8C-1, Rule 801, or testimony or evidence from any person that is not a party, that the court finds to be relevant, reliable, and necessary to determine the needs of the juvenile and the most appropriate disposition.

(d) At each hearing, the court shall consider the following criteria and make written findings regarding those that are relevant:

(1) Services which have been offered to reunite the juvenile with either parent whether or not the juvenile resided with the parent at the time of removal or the guardian or custodian from whom the child was removed.

(2) Reports on visitation that has occurred and whether there is a need to create, modify, or enforce an appropriate visitation plan in accordance with G.S. 7B-905.1.

(3) Whether efforts to reunite the juvenile with either parent clearly would be futile or inconsistent with the juvenile's safety and need for a safe, permanent home within a reasonable period of time. The court shall consider efforts to reunite regardless of whether the juvenile resided with the parent, guardian, or custodian at the time of removal. If the court determines efforts would be futile or inconsistent, the court shall consider a permanent plan of care for the juvenile.

(4) Reports on the placements the juvenile has had, the appropriateness of the juvenile's current foster care placement, and the goals of the juvenile's foster care plan, including the role the current foster parent will play in the planning for the juvenile.

(5) If the juvenile is 16 or 17 years of age, a report on an independent living assessment of the juvenile and, if appropriate, an independent living plan developed for the juvenile.

(6) When and if termination of parental rights should be considered.

(7) Any other criteria the court deems necessary.

(e) At any permanency planning hearing where the juvenile is not placed with a parent, the court shall additionally consider the following criteria and make written findings regarding those that are relevant:

(1) Whether it is possible for the juvenile to be placed with a parent within the next six months and, if not, why such placement is not in the juvenile's best interests.

(2) Where the juvenile's placement with a parent is unlikely within six months, whether legal guardianship or custody with a relative or some other suitable person should be established and, if so, the rights and responsibilities that should remain with the parents.

(3) Where the juvenile's placement with a parent is unlikely within six months, whether adoption should be pursued and, if so, any barriers to the juvenile's adoption.

(4) Where the juvenile's placement with a parent is unlikely within six months, whether the juvenile should remain in the current placement, or be placed in another permanent living arrangement and why.

(5) Whether the county department of social services has since the initial permanency plan hearing made reasonable efforts to implement the permanent plan for the juvenile.

(6) Any other criteria the court deems necessary.

(f) In the case of a juvenile who is in the custody or placement responsibility of a county department of social services and has been in placement outside the home for 12 of the most recent 22 months, or a court of competent jurisdiction has determined that the parent (i) has abandoned the child, (ii) has committed murder or voluntary manslaughter of another child of the parent, or (iii) has aided, abetted, attempted, conspired, or solicited to commit murder or voluntary manslaughter of the child or another child of the parent, the director of the department of social services shall initiate a proceeding to terminate the parental rights of the parent unless the court finds any of the following:

(1)     The permanent plan for the juvenile is guardianship or custody with a relative or some other suitable person.

(2)     The court makes specific findings as to why the filing of a petition for termination of parental rights is not in the best interests of the child.

(3)     The department of social services has not provided the juvenile's family with services the department deems necessary when reasonable efforts are still required to enable the juvenile's return to a safe home.

(g)     At the conclusion of each permanency planning hearing, the judge shall make specific findings as to the best plan of care to achieve a safe, permanent home for the juvenile within a reasonable period of time.

(h)     The order shall be reduced to writing, signed, and entered no later than 30 days following the completion of the hearing. If the order is not entered within 30 days following completion of the hearing, the clerk of court for juvenile matters shall schedule a subsequent hearing at the first session of court scheduled for the hearing of juvenile matters following the 30-day period to determine and explain the reason for the delay and to obtain any needed clarification as to the contents of the order. The order shall be entered within 10 days of the subsequent hearing required by this subsection.

(i)      The court may maintain the juvenile's placement under review or order a different placement, appoint a guardian of the person for the juvenile pursuant to G.S. 7B-600, or order any disposition authorized by G.S. 7B-903, including the authority to place the child in the custody of either parent or any relative found by the court to be suitable and found by the court to be in the best interests of the juvenile.

(j)      If the court determines that the juvenile shall be placed in the custody of an individual other than a parent or appoints an individual guardian of the person pursuant to G.S. 7B-600, the court shall verify that the person receiving custody or being appointed as guardian of the juvenile understands the legal significance of the placement or appointment and will have adequate resources to care appropriately for the juvenile.

(k)     If at any time custody is placed with a parent or findings are made in accordance with subsection (n) of this section, the court shall be relieved of the duty to conduct periodic judicial reviews of the placement.

(l)     If the court continues the juvenile's placement in the custody or placement responsibility of a county department of social services, the provisions of G.S. 7B-507 shall apply to any order entered under this section.

(m)     If the court finds that a proceeding to terminate the parental rights of the juvenile's parents is necessary in order to perfect the permanent plan for the juvenile, the director of the department of social services shall file a petition to terminate parental rights within 60 calendar days from the date of the entry of the order unless the court makes written findings regarding why the petition cannot be filed within 60 days. If the court makes findings to the contrary, the court shall specify the time frame in which any needed petition to terminate parental rights shall be filed.

(n)     Notwithstanding other provisions of this Article, the court may waive the holding of hearings required by this section, may require written reports to the court by the agency or person holding custody in lieu of review hearings, or order that review hearings be held less often than every six months if the court finds by clear, cogent, and convincing evidence each of the following:

(1)     The juvenile has resided in the placement for a period of at least one year.

(2)     The placement is stable and continuation of the placement is in the juvenile's best interests.

(3)     Neither the juvenile's best interests nor the rights of any party require that review hearings be held every six months.

(4)     All parties are aware that the matter may be brought before the court for review at any time by the filing of a motion for review or on the court's own motion.

(5)     The court order has designated the relative or other suitable person as the juvenile's permanent custodian or guardian of the person.

The court may not waive or refuse to conduct a review hearing if a party files a motion seeking the review. However, if a guardian of the person has been appointed for the juvenile and the court has also made findings in accordance with subsection (n) of this section that guardianship is the permanent plan for the juvenile, the court shall proceed in accordance with G.S. 7B-600(b). (2013-129, s. 26.)

§ 7B-907: Repealed by Session Laws 2013-129, s. 25, effective October 1, 2013, and applicable to actions filed or pending on or after that date.

§ 7B-908. Post termination of parental rights' placement court review.

(a) The purpose of each placement review is to ensure that every reasonable effort is being made to provide for a permanent placement plan for the juvenile who has been placed in the custody of a county director or licensed child-placing agency, which is consistent with the juvenile's best interests. At each review hearing the court may consider information from the department of social services, the licensed child-placing agency, the guardian ad litem, the child, the person providing care for the child, and any other person or agency the court determines is likely to aid in the review. The court may consider any evidence, including hearsay evidence as defined in G.S. 8C-1, Rule 801, that the court finds to be relevant, reliable, and necessary to determine the needs of the juvenile and the most appropriate disposition.

(b) The court shall conduct a placement review not later than six months from the date of the termination hearing when parental rights have been terminated by a petition brought by any person or agency designated in G.S. 7B-1103(2) through (5) and a county director or licensed child-placing agency has custody of the juvenile. The court shall conduct reviews every six months thereafter until the juvenile is the subject of a decree of adoption:

(1) No more than 30 days and no less than 15 days prior to each review, the clerk shall give notice of the review to the juvenile if the juvenile is at least 12 years of age, the legal custodian of the juvenile, the person providing care for the juvenile, the guardian ad litem, if any, and any other person or agency the court may specify. The department of social services shall either provide to the clerk the name and address of the person providing care for the child for notice under this subsection or file written documentation with the clerk that the child's current care provider was sent notice of hearing. Only the juvenile, if the juvenile is at least 12 years of age, the legal custodian of the juvenile, the person providing care for the juvenile, and the guardian ad litem shall attend the review

hearings, except as otherwise directed by the court. Nothing in this subdivision shall be construed to make the person a party to the proceeding solely based on receiving notice and the right to be heard. Any individual whose parental rights have been terminated shall not be considered a party to the proceeding unless an appeal of the order terminating parental rights is pending, and a court has stayed the order pending the appeal.

(2) If a guardian ad litem for the juvenile has not been appointed previously by the court in the termination proceeding, the court, at the initial six-month review hearing, may appoint a guardian ad litem to represent the juvenile. The court may continue the case for such time as is necessary for the guardian ad litem to become familiar with the facts of the case.

(c) The court shall consider at least the following in its review and make written findings regarding the following that are relevant:

(1) The adequacy of the plan developed by the county department of social services or a licensed child-placing agency for a permanent placement relative to the juvenile's best interests and the efforts of the department or agency to implement such plan.

(2) Whether the juvenile has been listed for adoptive placement with the North Carolina Adoption Resource Exchange, the North Carolina Photo Adoption Listing Service (PALS), or any other specialized adoption agency.

(3) The efforts previously made by the department or agency to find a permanent home for the juvenile.

(4) Whether the current placement is in the juvenile's best interest.

(d) The court, after making findings of fact, shall do one of the following:

(1) Affirm the county department's or child-placing agency's plans.

(2) If a juvenile is not placed with prospective adoptive parents as selected in G.S. 7B-1112.1, order a placement or different plan the court finds to be in the juvenile's best interest after considering the department's recommendations.

In either case, the court may require specific additional steps that are necessary to accomplish a permanent placement that is in the best interests of the juvenile.

(e)     If the juvenile is the subject of a decree of adoption prior to the date scheduled for the review, within 10 days of receiving notice that the adoption decree has been entered, the department of social services shall file with the court and serve on any guardian ad litem for the juvenile written notice of the entry. The adoption decree shall not be filed in the court file. The review hearing shall be cancelled with notice of said cancellation given by the clerk to all persons previously notified.

(f)     Repealed by Session Laws 2011-295, s. 10, effective October 1, 2011, and applicable to actions filed or pending on or after that date. (1983, c. 607, s. 1; 1993, c. 537, s. 2; 1998-202, s. 6; 1998-229, ss. 9, 26; 1999-456, s. 60; 2003-62, s. 4; 2005-398, s. 8; 2007-276, s. 5; 2009-311, s. 8; 2011-295, s. 10; 2013-129, s. 27.)

7B-909.  Review of agency's plan for placement.

(a)     The director of social services or the director of the licensed private child-placing agency shall promptly notify the clerk to calendar the case for review of the department's or agency's plan for the juvenile at a session of court scheduled for the hearing of juvenile matters if the juvenile is in the custody of the department or agency and has not become the subject of a decree of adoption within six months following relinquishment of the juvenile for adoption by a parent, guardian, or guardian ad litem under the provisions of Part 7 of Article 3 of Chapter 48 of the General Statutes.

(b)     Repealed by Session Laws 2007-276, s. 6, effective October 1, 2007.

(b1)    If the court finds on motion of a department of social services or licensed child-placing agency that a consent or relinquishment for adoption necessary for the juvenile to be adopted cannot be obtained, and that no further steps are being taken to terminate the parental rights of the parent from whom consent or relinquishment has not been obtained, the court may order, upon finding that it is in the juvenile's best interest, that any relinquishment for adoption signed by a parent who has surrendered the child for adoption shall be voided pursuant to G.S. 48-3-707(a)(4). Before voiding any relinquishment under this subsection, the court shall require the county department of social services or licensed child-placing agency to give at least 15 days' notice to the relinquishing parent whose rights will be restored. The relinquishing parent shall have the right to be heard on (i) whether the relinquishment should be voided and (ii) the parent's plan to provide for the juvenile if the relinquishment is voided. If after due diligence the relinquishing parent cannot be located, the notice of hearing shall be deposited in the United States mail, return receipt requested, and sent to the address of the parent given in the relinquishment. The date of receipt of the notice is deemed the date of delivery or last attempted delivery.

(c) Notification of the court under this section shall be by a petition for review or motion for review, if the court is exercising jurisdiction over the juvenile. The review shall be conducted within 30 days following the filing of the petition for review unless the court shall otherwise direct. The court shall conduct reviews every six months until the juvenile is the subject of a decree of adoption. However, further reviews are not required after the voiding of a relinquishment under subsection (b1) of this section. The initial review and all subsequent reviews, except a review hearing under subsection (b1) of this section, shall be conducted pursuant to G.S. 7B-908. Any individual whose parental rights have been terminated or who has relinquished the juvenile for adoption under the provisions of Part 7 of Article 3 of Chapter 48 of the General Statutes shall not be considered a party to the review unless an appeal of the order terminating parental rights is pending, and a court has stayed the order pending the appeal. (1983, c. 607, s. 2; 1993, c. 537, s. 4; 1995, c. 457, s. 6; 1998-202, s. 6; 1998-229, s. 9; 1999-456, s. 60; 2005-398, s. 9; 2007-276, s. 6; 2013-129, s. 28; 2013-236, s. 1; 2013-410, s. 27.)

§ 7B-910. Review of voluntary foster care placements.

(a) The court shall review the placement of any juvenile in foster care made pursuant to a voluntary agreement between the juvenile's parents or guardian and a county department of social services and shall make findings from evidence presented at a review hearing with regard to:

(1) The voluntariness of the placement;

(2) The appropriateness of the placement;

(3) Whether the placement is in the best interests of the juvenile; and

(4) The services that have been or should be provided to the parents, guardian, foster parents, and juvenile, as the case may be, either (i) to improve the placement or (ii) to eliminate the need for the placement.

(b)     The court may approve the continued placement of the juvenile in foster care on a voluntary agreement basis, disapprove the continuation of the voluntary placement, or direct the department of social services to petition the court for legal custody if the placement is to continue.

(c)     An initial review hearing shall be held not more than 90 days after the juvenile's placement and shall be calendared by the clerk for hearing within such period upon timely request by the director of social services. An additional review hearing shall be held 90 days thereafter and any review hearings at such times as the court shall deem appropriate and shall direct, either upon its own motion or upon written request of the parents, guardian, foster parents, or director of social services. A juvenile placed under a voluntary agreement between the juvenile's parent or guardian and the county department of social services shall not remain in placement more than six months without the filing of a petition alleging abuse, neglect, or dependency.

(d)     The clerk shall give at least 15 days' advance written notice of the initial and subsequent review hearings to the parents or guardian of the juvenile, to the juvenile if 12 or more years of age, to the director of social services, and to any other persons whom the court may specify. (1983, c. 607, s. 2; 1993, c. 537, s. 4; 1995, c. 457, s. 6; 1998-202, s. 6; 1999-456, s. 60; 2001-208, s. 21; 2001-487, s. 101.)

§ 7B-911. Civil child custody order.

(a)     Upon placing custody with a parent or other appropriate person, the court shall determine whether or not jurisdiction in the juvenile proceeding should be terminated and custody of the juvenile awarded to a parent or other appropriate person pursuant to G.S. 50-13.1, 50-13.2, 50-13.5, and 50-13.7.

(b)     When the court enters a custody order under this section, the court shall either cause the order to be filed in an existing civil action relating to the custody of the juvenile or, if there is no other civil action, instruct the clerk to treat the order as the initiation of a civil action for custody.

If the order is filed in an existing civil action and the person to whom the court is awarding custody is not a party to that action, the court shall order that the person be joined as a party and that the caption of the case be changed accordingly. The order shall resolve any pending claim for custody and shall constitute a modification of any custody order previously entered in the action.

If the court's order initiates a civil action, the court shall designate the parties to the action and determine the most appropriate caption for the case. The civil filing fee is waived unless the court orders one or more of the parties to pay the filing fee for a civil action into the office of the clerk of superior court. The order shall constitute a custody determination, and any motion to enforce or modify the custody order shall be filed in the newly created civil action in accordance with the provisions of Chapter 50 of the General Statutes. The Administrative Office of the Courts may adopt rules and shall develop and make available appropriate forms for establishing a civil file to implement this section.

(c) When entering an order under this section, the court shall satisfy the following:

(1) Make findings and conclusions that support the entry of a custody order in an action under Chapter 50 of the General Statutes or, if the juvenile is already the subject of a custody order entered pursuant to Chapter 50, makes findings and conclusions that support modification of that order pursuant to G.S. 50-13.7.

(2) Make the following findings:

a. There is not a need for continued State intervention on behalf of the juvenile through a juvenile court proceeding.

b. At least six months have passed since the court made a determination that the juvenile's placement with the person to whom the court is awarding custody is the permanent plan for the juvenile, though this finding is not required if the court is awarding custody to a parent or to a person with whom the child was living when the juvenile petition was filed. (2005-320, s. 4; 2013-129, s. 29.)

ARTICLE 10.

Modification and Enforcement of Dispositional Orders; Appeals

§ 7B-1000. Authority to modify or vacate.

(a) Upon motion in the cause or petition, and after notice, the court may conduct a review hearing to determine whether the order of the court is in the best interests of the juvenile, and the court may modify or vacate the order in light of changes in circumstances or the needs of the juvenile. Notwithstanding the provision of this subsection, if a guardian of the person has been appointed for the juvenile and the court has also made findings that guardianship is the permanent plan for the juvenile, the court shall proceed in accordance with G.S. 7B-600(b).

(b) In any case where the court finds the juvenile to be abused, neglected, or dependent, the jurisdiction of the court to modify any order or disposition made in the case shall continue during the minority of the juvenile, until terminated by order of the court, or until the juvenile is otherwise emancipated. (1979, c. 815, s. 1; 1998-202, s. 6; 1999-456, s. 60; 2000-124, s. 3; 2013-129, s. 30.)

§ 7B-1001. Right to appeal.

(a) In a juvenile matter under this Subchapter, appeal of a final order of the court in a juvenile matter shall be made directly to the Court of Appeals. Only the following juvenile matters may be appealed:

(1) Any order finding absence of jurisdiction.

(2) Any order, including the involuntary dismissal of a petition, which in effect determines the action and prevents a judgment from which appeal might be taken.

(3) Any initial order of disposition and the adjudication order upon which it is based.

(4) Any order, other than a nonsecure custody order, that changes legal custody of a juvenile.

(5) An order entered under G.S. 7B-507(c) with rights to appeal properly preserved, as follows:

a. The Court of Appeals shall review the order to cease reunification together with an appeal of the termination of parental rights order if all of the following apply:

1. A motion or petition to terminate the parent's rights is heard and granted.

2. The order terminating parental rights is appealed in a proper and timely manner.

3. The order to cease reunification is identified as an issue in the record on appeal of the termination of parental rights.

b. A party who is a parent shall have the right to appeal the order if no termination of parental rights petition or motion is filed within 180 days of the order.

c. A party who is a custodian or guardian shall have the right to immediately appeal the order.

(6) Any order that terminates parental rights or denies a petition or motion to terminate parental rights.

(b) Notice of appeal and notice to preserve the right to appeal shall be given in writing by a proper party as defined in G.S. 7B-1002 and shall be made within 30 days after entry and service of the order in accordance with G.S. 1A-1, Rule 58.

(c) Notice of appeal shall be signed by both the appealing party and counsel for the appealing party, if any. In the case of an appeal by a juvenile, notice of appeal shall be signed by the guardian ad litem attorney advocate. (1979, c. 815, s. 1; 1998-202, s. 6; 1999-456, s. 60; 2001-208, s. 25; 2001-487, s. 101; 2005-398, s. 10; 2011-295, s. 11; 2013-129, s. 31.)

§ 7B-1002. Proper parties for appeal.

Appeal from an order permitted under G.S. 7B-1001 may be taken by:

(1) A juvenile acting through the juvenile's guardian ad litem previously appointed under G.S. 7B-601.

(2) A juvenile for whom no guardian ad litem has been appointed under G.S. 7B-601. If such an appeal is made, the court shall appoint a guardian ad litem pursuant to G.S. 1A-1, Rule 17 for the juvenile for the purposes of that appeal.

(3) A county department of social services.

(4) A parent, a guardian appointed under G.S. 7B-600 or Chapter 35A of the General Statutes, or a custodian as defined in G.S. 7B-101 who is a nonprevailing party.

(5) Any party that sought but failed to obtain termination of parental rights. (1979, c. 815, s. 1; 1998-202, s. 6; 1999-456, s. 60; 2005-398, s. 11.)

§ 7B-1003. Disposition pending appeal.

(a) During an appeal of an order entered under this Subchapter, the trial court may enforce the order unless the trial court or an appellate court orders a stay.

(b) Pending disposition of an appeal, unless directed otherwise by an appellate court or subsection (c) of this section applies, the trial court shall:

(1) Continue to exercise jurisdiction and conduct hearings under this Subchapter with the exception of Article 11 of the General Statutes; and

(2) Enter orders affecting the custody or placement of the juvenile as the court finds to be in the best interests of the juvenile.

(c) Pending disposition of an appeal of an order entered under Article 11 of this Chapter where the petition for termination of parental rights was not filed as a motion in a juvenile matter initiated under Article 4 of this Chapter, the court may enter a temporary order affecting the custody or placement of the juvenile as the court finds to be in the best interests of the juvenile. Upon the affirmation of the order of adjudication or disposition of the court in a juvenile case by the Court of Appeals, or by the Supreme Court in the event of an appeal, the court shall have authority to modify or alter its original order of adjudication or disposition as the court finds to be in the best interests of the juvenile to reflect any adjustment made by the juvenile or change in circumstances during the period of time the case on appeal was pending, provided that if the modifying order be entered ex parte, the court shall give notice to interested parties to show cause, if there be any, within 10 days thereafter, as to why the modifying order should be vacated or altered.

(d) When the court has found that a juvenile has suffered physical abuse and that the individual responsible for the abuse has a history of violent behavior, the court shall consider the opinion of the mental health professional who performed the evaluation under G.S. 7B-503(b) before returning the juvenile to the custody of that individual pending resolution of an appeal.

(e) The provisions of subsections (b), (c), and (d) of G.S. 7B-905 shall apply to any order entered during an appeal that provides for the placement or continued placement of a juvenile in foster care. (1979, c. 815, s. 1; 1987 (Reg. Sess., 1988), c. 1090, s. 12; 1998-202, s. 6; 1999-318, s. 8; 1999-456, s. 60; 2001-208, s. 27; 2001-487, s. 101; 2003-140, s. 8; 2005-398, s. 12.)

§ 7B-1004. Disposition after appeal.

When an order of the court is affirmed by the Court of Appeals or by the Supreme Court, the trial court may modify or alter the original order as the court finds to be in the best interests of the juvenile to reflect any change in circumstances during the period of time the appeal was pending. If the modifying order is entered ex parte, the court shall give notice to interested parties to show cause within 10 days thereafter as to why the modifying order should be vacated or altered. (1979, c. 815, s. 1; 1998-202, s. 6; 1999-456, s. 60; 2005-398, s. 13.)

Article 11.

Termination of Parental Rights.

§ 7B-1100. Legislative intent; construction of Article.

The General Assembly hereby declares as a matter of legislative policy with respect to termination of parental rights:

(1) The general purpose of this Article is to provide judicial procedures for terminating the legal relationship between a juvenile and the juvenile's biological or legal parents when the parents have demonstrated that they will not provide the degree of care which promotes the healthy and orderly physical and emotional well-being of the juvenile.

(2) It is the further purpose of this Article to recognize the necessity for any juvenile to have a permanent plan of care at the earliest possible age, while at the same time recognizing the need to protect all juveniles from the unnecessary severance of a relationship with biological or legal parents.

(3) Action which is in the best interests of the juvenile should be taken in all cases where the interests of the juvenile and those of the juvenile's parents or other persons are in conflict.

(4) This Article shall not be used to circumvent the provisions of Chapter 50A of the General Statutes, the Uniform Child-Custody Jurisdiction and Enforcement Act. (1977, c. 879, s. 8; 1979, c. 110, s. 6; 1998-202, s. 6; 1999-223, s. 5; 1999-456, s. 60.)

§ 7B-1101. Jurisdiction.

The court shall have exclusive original jurisdiction to hear and determine any petition or motion relating to termination of parental rights to any juvenile who resides in, is found in, or is in the legal or actual custody of a county department of social services or licensed child-placing agency in the district at the time of filing of the petition or motion. The court shall have jurisdiction to terminate the parental rights of any parent irrespective of the age of the parent. Provided, that before exercising jurisdiction under this Article, the court shall find that it has jurisdiction to make a child-custody determination under the provisions of G.S. 50A-201, 50A-203, or 50A-204. The court shall have jurisdiction to terminate the parental rights of any parent irrespective of the state of residence of the parent. Provided, that before exercising jurisdiction under this Article regarding the parental rights of a nonresident parent, the court shall find that it has jurisdiction to make a child-custody determination under the provisions of G.S. 50A-201 or G.S. 50A-203, without regard to G.S. 50A-204 and that process was served on the nonresident parent pursuant to G.S. 7B-1106. Provided, further, that the clerk of superior court shall have jurisdiction for adoptions under Chapter 48 of the General Statutes. (1977, c. 879, s. 8; 1979, c. 110, s. 7; 1979, 2nd Sess., c. 1206, s. 1; 1981, c. 996, s. 1; 1983, c. 89, s. 1; 1995, c. 457, s. 3; 1998-202, s. 6; 1999-223, s. 6; 1999-456, s. 60; 2000-144, s. 18; 2000-183, s. 2; 2003-140, s. 4; 2005-398, s. 14; 2007-152, s. 1.)

§ 7B-1101.1. Parent's right to counsel; guardian ad litem.

(a) The parent has the right to counsel, and to appointed counsel in cases of indigency, unless the parent waives the right. The fees of appointed counsel shall be borne by the Office of Indigent Defense Services. When a petition is filed, unless the parent is already represented by counsel, the clerk shall appoint provisional counsel for each respondent parent named in the petition in accordance with rules adopted by the Office of Indigent Defense Services and shall indicate the appointment on the juvenile summons. At the first hearing after service upon the respondent parent, the court shall dismiss the provisional counsel if the respondent parent:

(1) Does not appear at the hearing;

(2) Does not qualify for court-appointed counsel;

(3) Has retained counsel; or

(4) Waives the right to counsel.

The court shall confirm the appointment of counsel if subdivisions (1) through (4) of this subsection are not applicable to the respondent parent. The court may reconsider a parent's eligibility and desire for appointed counsel at any stage of the proceeding.

(a1) A parent qualifying for appointed counsel may be permitted to proceed without the assistance of counsel only after the court examines the parent and makes findings of fact sufficient to show that the waiver is knowing and voluntary. This examination shall be reported as provided in G.S. 7B-806.

(b) In addition to the right to appointed counsel under subsection (a) of this section, a guardian ad litem shall be appointed in accordance with G.S. 1A-1, Rule 17, to represent any parent who is under the age of 18 years and who is not married or otherwise emancipated.

(c) On motion of any party or on the court's own motion, the court may appoint a guardian ad litem for a parent who is incompetent in accordance with G.S. 1A-1, Rule 17.

(d) The parent's counsel shall not be appointed to serve as the guardian ad litem and the guardian ad litem shall not act as the parent's attorney. Communications between the guardian ad litem appointed under this section and the parent and between the guardian ad litem and the parent's counsel shall be privileged and confidential to the same extent that communications between the parent and the parent's counsel are privileged and confidential.

(e) Repealed by Session Laws 2013-129, s. 32, effective October 1, 2013, and applicable to actions filed or pending on or after that date.

(f) The fees of a guardian ad litem appointed pursuant to this section shall be borne by the Office of Indigent Defense Services when the court finds that the respondent is indigent. In other cases, the fees of the court-appointed guardian ad litem shall be a proper charge against the respondent if the respondent does not secure private legal counsel. (2005-398, s. 15; 2009-311, s. 9; 2011-326, s. 12(b); 2012-194, s. 41; 2013-129, s. 32.)

§ 7B-1102. Pending child abuse, neglect, or dependency proceedings.

(a) When the district court is exercising jurisdiction over a juvenile and the juvenile's parent in an abuse, neglect, or dependency proceeding, a person or agency specified in G.S. 7B-1103(a) may file in that proceeding a motion for termination of the parent's rights in relation to the juvenile.

(b) A motion pursuant to subsection (a) of this section and the notice required by G.S. 7B-1106.1 shall be served in accordance with G.S. 1A-1, Rule 5(b), except:

(1) Service must be in accordance with G.S. 1A-1, Rule 4, if one of the following applies:

a. The person or agency to be served was not served originally with summons.

b. The person or agency to be served was served originally by publication that did not include notice substantially in conformity with the notice required by G.S. 7B-406(b)(4)e.

c. Two years has elapsed since the date of the original action.

(2) In any case, the court may order that service of the motion and notice be made pursuant to G.S. 1A-1, Rule 4.

For purposes of this section, the parent of the juvenile shall not be deemed to be under disability even though the parent is a minor.

(b1)    If a parent who is served under G.S. 1A-1, Rule 4, with a motion under this section has an attorney of record, a copy of the motion and the notice served upon the parent shall also be sent to the parent's attorney.

(c)    When a petition for termination of parental rights is filed in the same district in which there is pending an abuse, neglect, or dependency proceeding involving the same juvenile, the court on its own motion or motion of a party may consolidate the action pursuant to G.S. 1A-1, Rule 42.  (1998-229, ss. 9.1, 26.1; 1999-456, s. 60; 2000-183, s. 3; 2011-332, s. 4.1.)

§ 7B-1103.  Who may file a petition or motion.

(a)    A petition or motion to terminate the parental rights of either or both parents to his, her, or their minor juvenile may only be filed by one or more of the following:

(1)    Either parent seeking termination of the right of the other parent.

(2)    Any person who has been judicially appointed as the guardian of the person of the juvenile.

(3)    Any county department of social services, consolidated county human services agency, or licensed child-placing agency to whom custody of the juvenile has been given by a court of competent jurisdiction.

(4)    Any county department of social services, consolidated county human services agency, or licensed child-placing agency to which the juvenile has been surrendered for adoption by one of the parents or by the guardian of the person of the juvenile, pursuant to G.S. 48-3-701.

(5)    Any person with whom the juvenile has resided for a continuous period of two years or more next preceding the filing of the petition or motion.

(6)    Any guardian ad litem appointed to represent the minor juvenile pursuant to G.S. 7B-601 who has not been relieved of this responsibility.

(7)    Any person who has filed a petition for adoption pursuant to Chapter 48 of the General Statutes.

(b) Any person or agency that may file a petition under subsection (a) of this section may intervene in a pending abuse, neglect, or dependency proceeding for the purpose of filing a motion to terminate parental rights.

(c) No person whose actions resulted in a conviction under G.S. 14-27.2 or G.S. 14-27.3 and the conception of the juvenile may file a petition to terminate the parental rights of another with respect to that juvenile. (1977, c. 879, s. 8; 1983, c. 870, s. 1; 1985, c. 758, s. 1; 1987, c. 371, s. 2; 1995 (Reg. Sess., 1996), c. 690, s. 4; 1998-202, s. 6; 1998-229, s. 9.1; 1999-456, s. 60; 2000-183, s. 4; 2004-128, s. 13.)

§ 7B-1104. Petition or motion.

The petition, or motion pursuant to G.S. 7B-1102, shall be verified by the petitioner or movant and shall be entitled "In Re (last name of juvenile), a minor juvenile", who shall be a party to the action, and shall set forth such of the following facts as are known; and with respect to the facts which are unknown the petitioner or movant shall so state:

(1) The name of the juvenile as it appears on the juvenile's birth certificate, the date and place of birth, and the county where the juvenile is presently residing.

(2) The name and address of the petitioner or movant and facts sufficient to identify the petitioner or movant as one authorized by G.S. 7B-1103 to file a petition or motion.

(3) The name and address of the parents of the juvenile. If the name or address of one or both parents is unknown to the petitioner or movant, the petitioner or movant shall set forth with particularity the petitioner's or movant's efforts to ascertain the identity or whereabouts of the parent or parents. The information may be contained in an affidavit attached to the petition or motion and incorporated therein by reference. A person whose actions resulted in a conviction under G.S. 14-27.2 or G.S. 14-27.3 and the conception of the juvenile need not be named in the petition.

(4) The name and address of any person who has been judicially appointed as guardian of the person of the juvenile.

(5) The name and address of any person or agency to whom custody of the juvenile has been given by a court of this or any other state; and a copy of the custody order shall be attached to the petition or motion.

(6) Facts that are sufficient to warrant a determination that one or more of the grounds for terminating parental rights exist.

(7) That the petition or motion has not been filed to circumvent the provisions of Article 2 of Chapter 50A of the General Statutes, the Uniform Child-Custody Jurisdiction and Enforcement Act. (1977, c. 879, s. 8; 1979, c. 110, s. 8; 1981, c. 469, s. 23; 1987, c. 550, s. 15; 1998-202, s. 6; 1999-223, s. 7; 1999-456, s. 60; 2000-183, s. 5; 2004-128, s. 14; 2009-38, s. 2.)

§ 7B-1105. Preliminary hearing; unknown parent.

(a) If either the name or identity of any parent whose parental rights the petitioner seeks to terminate is not known to the petitioner, the court shall, within 10 days from the date of filing of the petition, or during the next term of court in the county where the petition is filed if there is no court in the county in that 10-day period, conduct a preliminary hearing to ascertain the name or identity of such parent.

(b) The court may, in its discretion, inquire of any known parent of the juvenile concerning the identity of the unknown parent and may order the petitioner to conduct a diligent search for the parent. Should the court ascertain the name or identity of the parent, it shall enter a finding to that effect; and the parent shall be summoned to appear in accordance with G.S. 7B-1106.

(c) Notice of the preliminary hearing need be given only to the petitioner who shall appear at the hearing, but the court may cause summons to be issued to any person directing the person to appear and testify.

(d) If the court is unable to ascertain the name or identity of the unknown parent, the court shall order publication of notice of the termination proceeding and shall specifically order the place or places of publication and the contents of the notice which the court concludes is most likely to identify the juvenile to such unknown parent. The notice shall be published in a newspaper qualified for legal advertising in accordance with G.S. 1-597 and G.S. 1-598 and published in the counties directed by the court, once a week for three successive weeks. Provided, further, the notice shall:

(1) Designate the court in which the petition is pending;

(2) Be directed to "the father (mother) (father and mother) of a male (female) juvenile born on or about_____ in

(date)

       County,    ,

       (city)

_____, respondent";

(State)

(3) Designate the docket number and title of the case (the court may direct the actual name of the title be eliminated and the words "In Re Doe" substituted therefor);

(4) State that a petition seeking to terminate the parental rights of the respondent has been filed;

(5) Direct the respondent to answer the petition within 30 days after a date stated in the notice, exclusive of such date, which date so stated shall be the date of first publication of notice and be substantially in the form as set forth in G.S. 1A-1, Rule 4(j1); and

(6) State that the respondent's parental rights to the juvenile will be terminated upon failure to answer the petition within the time prescribed.

Upon completion of the service, an affidavit of the publisher shall be filed with the court.

(e) The court shall issue the order required by subsections (b) and (d) of this section within 30 days from the date of the preliminary hearing unless the court shall determine that additional time for investigation is required.

(f) Upon the failure of the parent served by publication pursuant to subsection (d) of this section to answer the petition within the time prescribed, the court shall issue an order terminating all parental rights of the unknown parent. (1977, c. 879, s. 8; 1987, c. 282, s. 1; 1998-202, s. 6; 1999-456, s. 60; 2011-295, s. 12.)

§ 7B-1106. Issuance of summons.

(a)     Except as provided in G.S. 7B-1105, upon the filing of the petition, the court shall cause a summons to be issued. The summons shall be directed to the following persons or agency, not otherwise a party petitioner, who shall be named as respondents:

(1)     The parents of the juvenile. However, a summons does not need to be directed to or served upon any parent who, under Chapter 48 of the General Statutes, has irrevocably relinquished the juvenile to a county department of social services or licensed child-placing agency or to any parent who has consented to the adoption of the juvenile by the petitioner.

(2)     Any person who has been judicially appointed as guardian of the person of the juvenile.

(3)     The custodian of the juvenile appointed by a court of competent jurisdiction.

(4)     Any county department of social services or licensed child-placing agency to whom a juvenile has been released by one parent pursuant to Part 7 of Article 3 of Chapter 48 of the General Statutes or any county department of social services to whom placement responsibility for the child has been given by a court of competent jurisdiction.

(5)     Repealed by Session Laws 2009-38, s. 3, effective May 27, 2009.

The summons shall notify the respondents to file a written answer within 30 days after service of the summons and petition. Service of the summons shall be completed as provided under the procedures established by G.S. 1A-1, Rule 4(j). But the parent of the juvenile shall not be deemed to be under a disability even though the parent is a minor.

(a1)    If a guardian ad litem has been appointed for the juvenile pursuant to G.S. 7B-601 and has not been relieved of responsibility or if the court appoints a guardian ad litem for the juvenile after the petition is filed, a copy of all pleadings and other papers required to be served shall be served on the juvenile's guardian ad litem or attorney advocate pursuant to procedures established under G.S. 1A-1, Rule 5.

(a2)    If an attorney has been appointed for a respondent pursuant to G.S. 7B-602 and has not been relieved of responsibility, a copy of all pleadings and other papers required to be served on the respondent shall be served on the respondent's attorney pursuant to procedures established under G.S. 1A-1, Rule 5.

(b)    The summons shall be issued for the purpose of terminating parental rights pursuant to the provisions of subsection (a) of this section and shall include:

(1)    The name of the minor juvenile;

(2)    Notice that a written answer to the petition must be filed with the clerk who signed the petition within 30 days after service of the summons and a copy of the petition, or the parent's rights may be terminated;

(3)    Notice that any counsel appointed previously and still representing the parent in an abuse, neglect, or dependency proceeding shall continue to represent the parent unless otherwise ordered by the court;

(4)    Notice that if the parent is indigent and is not already represented by appointed counsel, the parent is entitled to appointed counsel, that provisional counsel has been appointed, and that the appointment of provisional counsel shall be reviewed by the court at the first hearing after service;

(5)    Notice that the date, time, and place of any pretrial hearing pursuant to G.S. 7B-1108.1 and the hearing on the petition will be mailed by the petitioner upon filing of the answer or 30 days from the date of service if no answer is filed; and

(6)    Notice of the purpose of the hearing and notice that the parents may attend the termination hearing.

(c)    If a county department of social services, not otherwise a party petitioner, is served with a petition alleging that the parental rights of the parent should be terminated pursuant to G.S. 7B-1111, the department shall file a written answer and shall be deemed a party to the proceeding. (1977, c. 879, s. 8; 1981, c. 966, s. 2; 1983, c. 581, ss. 1, 2; 1995, c. 457, s. 4; 1998-202, s. 6;

1998-229, ss. 10, 27; 1999-456, s. 60; 2000-183, s. 13; 2001-208, s. 28; 2001-487, s. 101; 2009-38, s. 3; 2009-311, s. 10; 2011-295, s. 13; 2013-129, s. 33.)

§ 7B-1106.1. Notice in pending child abuse, neglect, or dependency cases.

(a)     Upon the filing of a motion pursuant to G.S. 7B-1102, the movant shall prepare a notice directed to each of the following persons or agency, not otherwise a movant:

(1)     The parents of the juvenile. However, notice does not need to be directed to or served upon any parent who, under Chapter 48 of the General Statutes, has irrevocably relinquished the juvenile to a county department of social services or licensed child-placing agency or to any parent who has consented to the adoption of the juvenile by the movant.

(2)     Any person who has been judicially appointed as guardian of the person of the juvenile.

(3)     The custodian of the juvenile appointed by a court of competent jurisdiction.

(4)     Any county department of social services or licensed child-placing agency to whom a juvenile has been released by one parent pursuant to Part 7 of Article 3 of Chapter 48 of the General Statutes or any county department of social services to whom placement responsibility for the juvenile has been given by a court of competent jurisdiction.

(5)     The juvenile's guardian ad litem or attorney advocate, if one has been appointed pursuant to G.S. 7B-601 and has not been relieved of responsibility.

(6)     Repealed by Session Laws 2009-38, s. 4, effective May 27, 2009.

The notice shall notify the person or agency to whom it is directed to file a written response within 30 days after service of the motion and notice. Service of the motion and notice shall be completed as provided under G.S. 7B-1102(b).

(b)     The notice required by subsection (a) of this section shall include all of the following:

(1)     The name of the minor juvenile.

(2) Notice that a written response to the motion must be filed with the clerk within 30 days after service of the motion and notice, or the parent's rights may be terminated.

(3) Notice that any counsel appointed previously and still representing the parent in an abuse, neglect, or dependency proceeding will continue to represent the parents unless otherwise ordered by the court.

(4) Notice that if the parent is indigent, the parent is entitled to appointed counsel and if the parent is not already represented by appointed counsel the parent may contact the clerk immediately to request counsel.

(5) Notice that the date, time, and place of any pretrial hearing pursuant to G.S. 7B-1108.1 and the hearing on the motion will be mailed by the moving party upon filing of the response or 30 days from the date of service if no response is filed.

(6) Notice of the purpose of the hearing and notice that the parents may attend the termination hearing.

(c) If a county department of social services, not otherwise a movant, is served with a motion seeking termination of a parent's rights, the director shall file a written response and shall be deemed a party to the proceeding. (2000-183, s. 6; 2009-38, s. 4; 2009-311, s. 11.)

§ 7B-1107. Failure of parent to answer or respond.

Upon the failure of a respondent parent to file written answer to the petition or written response to the motion within 30 days after service of the summons and petition or notice and motion, or within the time period established for a defendant's reply by G.S. 1A-1, Rule 4(j1) if service is by publication, the court may issue an order terminating all parental and custodial rights of that parent with respect to the juvenile; provided the court shall order a hearing on the petition or motion and may examine the petitioner or movant or others on the facts alleged in the petition or motion. (1977, c. 879, s. 8; 1979, c. 525, s. 3; 1987, c. 282, s. 2; 1998-202, s. 6; 1998-229, s. 10; 1999-456, s. 60; 2000-183, s. 7.)

§ 7B-1108. Answer or response of parent; appointment of guardian ad litem for juvenile.

(a) Any respondent may file a written answer to the petition or written response to the motion. Only a district court judge may grant an extension of time in which to answer or respond. The answer or response shall admit or deny the allegations of the petition or motion and shall set forth the name and address of the answering respondent or the respondent's attorney.

(b) If an answer or response denies any material allegation of the petition or motion, the court shall appoint a guardian ad litem for the juvenile to represent the best interests of the juvenile, unless the petition or motion was filed by the guardian ad litem pursuant to G.S. 7B-1103, or a guardian ad litem has already been appointed pursuant to G.S. 7B-601. A licensed attorney shall be appointed to assist those guardians ad litem who are not attorneys licensed to practice in North Carolina. The appointment, duties, and payment of the guardian ad litem shall be the same as in G.S. 7B-601 and G.S. 7B-603, but in no event shall a guardian ad litem who is trained and supervised by the guardian ad litem program be appointed to any case unless the juvenile is or has been the subject of a petition for abuse, neglect, or dependency or with good cause shown the local guardian ad litem program consents to the appointment.

(c) In proceedings under this Article, the appointment of a guardian ad litem shall not be required except, as provided above, in cases in which an answer or response is filed denying material allegations, or as required under G.S. 7B-1101; but the court may, in its discretion, appoint a guardian ad litem for a juvenile, either before or after determining the existence of grounds for termination of parental rights, in order to assist the court in determining the best interests of the juvenile.

(d) If a guardian ad litem has previously been appointed for the juvenile under G.S. 7B-601, and the appointment of a guardian ad litem could also be made under this section, the guardian ad litem appointed under G.S. 7B-601, and any attorney appointed to assist that guardian, shall also represent the juvenile in all proceedings under this Article and shall have the duties and payment of a guardian ad litem appointed under this section, unless the court determines that the best interests of the juvenile require otherwise. (1977, c. 879, s. 8; 1981 (Reg. Sess., 1982), c. 1331, s. 3; 1983, c. 870, s. 2; 1989 (Reg. Sess., 1990), c. 851, s. 1; 1998-202, s. 6; 1999-456, s. 60; 2000-183, s. 8; 2003-140, s. 7; 2009-311, s. 12; 2011-295, s. 14.)

§ 7B-1108.1. Pretrial hearing.

(a) The court shall conduct a pretrial hearing. However, the court may combine the pretrial hearing with the adjudicatory hearing on termination in which case no separate pretrial hearing order is required. At the pretrial hearing, the court shall consider the following:

(1) Retention or release of provisional counsel.

(2) Whether a guardian ad litem should be appointed for the juvenile, if not previously appointed.

(3) Whether all summons, service of process, and notice requirements have been met.

(4) Any pretrial motions.

(5) Any issues raised by any responsive pleading, including any affirmative defenses.

(6) Any other issue which can be properly addressed as a preliminary matter.

(b) Written notice of the pretrial hearing shall be in accordance with G.S. 7B-1106 and G.S. 7B-1106.1. (2009-311, s. 13.)

§ 7B-1109. Adjudicatory hearing on termination.

(a) The hearing on the termination of parental rights shall be conducted by the court sitting without a jury and shall be held in the district at such time and place as the chief district court judge shall designate, but no later than 90 days from the filing of the petition or motion unless the judge pursuant to subsection (d) of this section orders that it be held at a later time. Reporting of the hearing shall be as provided by G.S. 7A-198 for reporting civil trials.

(b) The court shall inquire whether the juvenile's parents are present at the hearing and, if so, whether they are represented by counsel. If the parents are not represented by counsel, the court shall inquire whether the parents desire counsel but are indigent. In the event that the parents desire counsel but are indigent as defined in G.S. 7A-450(a) and are unable to obtain counsel to represent them, counsel shall be appointed to represent them in accordance with rules adopted by the Office of Indigent Defense Services. The court shall grant the parents such an extension of time as is reasonable to permit their appointed counsel to prepare their defense to the termination petition or motion.

(c) The court may, upon finding that reasonable cause exists, order the juvenile to be examined by a psychiatrist, a licensed clinical psychologist, a physician, a public or private agency, or any other expert in order that the juvenile's psychological or physical condition or needs may be ascertained or, in the case of a parent whose ability to care for the juvenile is at issue, the court may order a similar examination of any parent of the juvenile.

(d) The court may for good cause shown continue the hearing for up to 90 days from the date of the initial petition in order to receive additional evidence including any reports or assessments that the court has requested, to allow the parties to conduct expeditious discovery, or to receive any other information needed in the best interests of the juvenile. Continuances that extend beyond 90 days after the initial petition shall be granted only in extraordinary circumstances when necessary for the proper administration of justice, and the court shall issue a written order stating the grounds for granting the continuance.

(e) The court shall take evidence, find the facts, and shall adjudicate the existence or nonexistence of any of the circumstances set forth in G.S. 7B-1111 which authorize the termination of parental rights of the respondent. The adjudicatory order shall be reduced to writing, signed, and entered no later than 30 days following the completion of the termination of parental rights hearing. If the order is not entered within 30 days following completion of the hearing, the clerk of court for juvenile matters shall schedule a subsequent hearing at the first session of court scheduled for the hearing of juvenile matters following the 30-day period to determine and explain the reason for the delay and to obtain any needed clarification as to the contents of the order. The order shall be entered within 10 days of the subsequent hearing required by this subsection.

(f) The burden in such proceedings shall be upon the petitioner or movant and all findings of fact shall be based on clear, cogent, and convincing evidence. The rules of evidence in civil cases shall apply. No husband-wife or physician-patient privilege shall be grounds for excluding any evidence regarding the existence or nonexistence of any circumstance authorizing the termination of parental rights. (1977, c. 879, s. 8; 1979, c. 669, s. 1; 1981, c. 966, s. 3; (Reg. Sess., 1982), c. 1331, s. 3; 1983, c. 870, s. 2; 1989 (Reg. Sess.,

1990), c. 851, s. 1; 1998-202, s. 6; 1999-456, s. 60; 2000-144, s. 19; 2000-183, s. 9; 2001-208, ss. 7, 22; 2001-487, s. 101; 2003-304, s. 2; 2005-398, s. 16; 2011-295, s. 15; 2013-129, s. 34.)

§ 7B-1110. Determination of best interests of the juvenile.

(a) After an adjudication that one or more grounds for terminating a parent's rights exist, the court shall determine whether terminating the parent's rights is in the juvenile's best interest. The court may consider any evidence, including hearsay evidence as defined in G.S. 8C-1, Rule 801, that the court finds to be relevant, reliable, and necessary to determine the best interests of the juvenile. In each case, the court shall consider the following criteria and make written findings regarding the following that are relevant:

(1) The age of the juvenile.

(2) The likelihood of adoption of the juvenile.

(3) Whether the termination of parental rights will aid in the accomplishment of the permanent plan for the juvenile.

(4) The bond between the juvenile and the parent.

(5) The quality of the relationship between the juvenile and the proposed adoptive parent, guardian, custodian, or other permanent placement.

(6) Any relevant consideration.

Any order shall be reduced to writing, signed, and entered no later than 30 days following the completion of the termination of parental rights hearing. If the order is not entered within 30 days following completion of the hearing, the clerk of court for juvenile matters shall schedule a subsequent hearing at the first session of court scheduled for the hearing of juvenile matters following the 30-day period to determine and explain the reason for the delay and to obtain any needed clarification as to the contents of the order. The order shall be entered within 10 days of the subsequent hearing required by this subsection.

(b) Should the court conclude that, irrespective of the existence of one or more circumstances authorizing termination of parental rights, the best interests of the juvenile require that rights should not be terminated, the court shall dismiss the petition or deny the motion, but only after setting forth the facts and conclusions upon which the dismissal or denial is based.

(c)     Should the court determine that circumstances authorizing termination of parental rights do not exist, the court shall dismiss the petition or deny the motion, making appropriate findings of fact and conclusions.

(d)     Counsel for the petitioner or movant shall serve a copy of the termination of parental rights order upon the guardian ad litem for the juvenile, if any, and upon the juvenile if the juvenile is 12 years of age or older.

(e)     The court may tax the cost of the proceeding to any party. (1977, c. 879, s. 8; 1981 (Reg. Sess., 1982), c. 1131, s. 1; 1983, c. 581, s. 3; c. 607, s. 3; 1998-202, s. 6; 1999-456, s. 60; 2000-183, s. 10; 2001-208, s. 23; 2001-487, s. 101; 2005-398, s. 17; 2011-295, s. 16.)


§ 7B-1111.  Grounds for terminating parental rights.

(a)     The court may terminate the parental rights upon a finding of one or more of the following:

(1)     The parent has abused or neglected the juvenile. The juvenile shall be deemed to be abused or neglected if the court finds the juvenile to be an abused juvenile within the meaning of G.S. 7B-101 or a neglected juvenile within the meaning of G.S. 7B-101.

(2)     The parent has willfully left the juvenile in foster care or placement outside the home for more than 12 months without showing to the satisfaction of the court that reasonable progress under the circumstances has been made in correcting those conditions which led to the removal of the juvenile. Provided, however, that no parental rights shall be terminated for the sole reason that the parents are unable to care for the juvenile on account of their poverty.

(3)     The juvenile has been placed in the custody of a county department of social services, a licensed child-placing agency, a child-caring institution, or a foster home, and the parent, for a continuous period of six months next preceding the filing of the petition or motion, has willfully failed for such period to pay a reasonable portion of the cost of care for the juvenile although physically and financially able to do so.

(4) One parent has been awarded custody of the juvenile by judicial decree or has custody by agreement of the parents, and the other parent whose parental rights are sought to be terminated has for a period of one year or more next preceding the filing of the petition or motion willfully failed without justification to pay for the care, support, and education of the juvenile, as required by said decree or custody agreement.

(5) The father of a juvenile born out of wedlock has not, prior to the filing of a petition or motion to terminate parental rights, done any of the following:

a. Filed an affidavit of paternity in a central registry maintained by the Department of Health and Human Services; provided, the petitioner or movant shall inquire of the Department of Health and Human Services as to whether such an affidavit has been so filed and the Department's certified reply shall be submitted to and considered by the court.

b. Legitimated the juvenile pursuant to provisions of G.S. 49-10, G.S. 49-12.1, or filed a petition for this specific purpose.

c. Legitimated the juvenile by marriage to the mother of the juvenile.

d. Provided substantial financial support or consistent care with respect to the juvenile and mother.

e. Established paternity through G.S. 49-14, 110-132, 130A-101, 130A-118, or other judicial proceeding.

(6) That the parent is incapable of providing for the proper care and supervision of the juvenile, such that the juvenile is a dependent juvenile within the meaning of G.S. 7B-101, and that there is a reasonable probability that such incapability will continue for the foreseeable future. Incapability under this subdivision may be the result of substance abuse, mental retardation, mental illness, organic brain syndrome, or any other cause or condition that renders the parent unable or unavailable to parent the juvenile and the parent lacks an appropriate alternative child care arrangement.

(7) The parent has willfully abandoned the juvenile for at least six consecutive months immediately preceding the filing of the petition or motion, or the parent has voluntarily abandoned an infant pursuant to G.S. 7B-500 for at least 60 consecutive days immediately preceding the filing of the petition or motion.

(8) The parent has committed murder or voluntary manslaughter of another child of the parent or other child residing in the home; has aided, abetted, attempted, conspired, or solicited to commit murder or voluntary manslaughter of the child, another child of the parent, or other child residing in the home; has committed a felony assault that results in serious bodily injury to the child, another child of the parent, or other child residing in the home; or has committed murder or voluntary manslaughter of the other parent of the child. The petitioner has the burden of proving any of these offenses in the termination of parental rights hearing by (i) proving the elements of the offense or (ii) offering proof that a court of competent jurisdiction has convicted the parent of the offense, whether or not the conviction was by way of a jury verdict or any kind of plea. If the parent has committed the murder or voluntary manslaughter of the other parent of the child, the court shall consider whether the murder or voluntary manslaughter was committed in self-defense or in the defense of others, or whether there was substantial evidence of other justification.

(9) The parental rights of the parent with respect to another child of the parent have been terminated involuntarily by a court of competent jurisdiction and the parent lacks the ability or willingness to establish a safe home.

(10) Where the juvenile has been relinquished to a county department of social services or a licensed child-placing agency for the purpose of adoption or placed with a prospective adoptive parent for adoption; the consent or relinquishment to adoption by the parent has become irrevocable except upon a showing of fraud, duress, or other circumstance as set forth in G.S. 48-3-609 or G.S. 48-3-707; termination of parental rights is a condition precedent to adoption in the jurisdiction where the adoption proceeding is to be filed; and the parent does not contest the termination of parental rights.

(11) The parent has been convicted of a sexually related offense under Chapter 14 of the General Statutes that resulted in the conception of the juvenile.

(b) The burden in such proceedings shall be upon the petitioner or movant to prove the facts justifying such termination by clear and convincing evidence. (1977, c. 879, s. 8; 1979, c. 669, s. 2; 1979, 2nd Sess., c. 1088, s. 2; c. 1206, s. 2; 1983, c. 89, s. 2; c. 512; 1985, c. 758, ss. 2, 3; c. 784; 1991 (Reg. Sess., 1992), c. 941, s. 1; 1997-390, ss. 1, 2; 1997-443, s. 11A.118(a); 1998-202, s. 6; 1998-229, ss. 11, 28; 1999-456, s. 60; 2000-183, s. 11; 2001-208, s. 6; 2001-

291, s. 3; 2001-487, s. 101; 2003-140, s. 3; 2005-146, s. 1; 2007-151, s. 1; 2007-484, s. 26(a); 2012-40, s. 1; 2013-129, s. 35.)

§ 7B-1112. Effects of termination order.

An order terminating the parental rights completely and permanently terminates all rights and obligations of the parent to the juvenile and of the juvenile to the parent arising from the parental relationship, except that the juvenile's right of inheritance from the juvenile's parent shall not terminate until a final order of adoption is issued. The parent is not thereafter entitled to notice of proceedings to adopt the juvenile and may not object thereto or otherwise participate therein:

(1) If the juvenile had been placed in the custody of or released for adoption by one parent to a county department of social services or licensed child-placing agency and is in the custody of the agency at the time of the filing of the petition or motion, including a petition or motion filed pursuant to G.S. 7B-1103(a)(6), that agency shall, upon entry of the order terminating parental rights, acquire all of the rights for placement of the juvenile, except as otherwise provided in G.S. 7B-908(d), as the agency would have acquired had the parent whose rights are terminated released the juvenile to that agency pursuant to the provisions of Part 7 of Article 3 of Chapter 48 of the General Statutes, including the right to consent to the adoption of the juvenile.

(2) Except as provided in subdivision (1) above, upon entering an order terminating the parental rights of one or both parents, the court may place the juvenile in the custody of the petitioner or movant, or some other suitable person, or in the custody of the department of social services or licensed child-placing agency, as may appear to be in the best interests of the juvenile. (1977, c. 879, s. 8; 1983, c. 870, s. 3; 1995, c. 457, s. 5; 1998-202, s. 6; 1998-229, s. 11; 1999-456, s. 60; 2000-183, s. 12; 2011-295, s. 17; 2012-194, s. 2.)

§ 7B-1112.1. Selection of adoptive parents.

The process of selection of specific adoptive parents shall be the responsibility of and within the discretion of the county department of social services or licensed child-placing agency. In selecting the adoptive parents, any current placement provider wanting to adopt the child shall be considered. The guardian ad litem may request information from and consult with the county department or child-placing agency concerning the selection process. If the guardian ad litem requests information about the selection process, the county shall provide the information within five business days. The county department of social services shall notify the guardian ad litem and the foster parents of the selection of prospective adoptive parents within 10 days of the selection and before the filing of the adoption petition. If the guardian ad litem disagrees with the selection of adoptive parents or the foster parents want to adopt the juvenile and were not selected as adoptive parents, the guardian ad litem or foster parents shall file a motion within 10 days of the department's notification and schedule the case for hearing on the next juvenile calendar. The department shall not change the juvenile's placement to the prospective adoptive parents unless the time period for filing a motion has expired and no motion has been filed. The Department shall provide a copy of a motion for judicial review of adoption selection to the foster parents not selected. Nothing in this section shall be construed to make the foster parents a party to the proceeding solely based on receiving notification and the right to be heard by filing a motion. In hearing any motion, the court shall consider the recommendations of the agency and the guardian ad litem and other facts related to the selection of adoptive parents. The court shall then determine whether the proposed adoptive placement is in the juvenile's best interests. (2011-295, s. 18; 2013-129, s. 36.)

§ 7B-1113: Repealed by Session Laws 2005-398, s. 18, effective October 1, 2005.

§ 7B-1114. Reinstatement of parental rights.

(a) A juvenile whose parent's rights have been terminated, the guardian ad litem attorney, or a county department of social services with custody of the juvenile may file a motion to reinstate the parent's rights if all of the following conditions are satisfied:

(1) The juvenile is at least 12 years of age or, if the juvenile is younger than 12, the motion alleges extraordinary circumstances requiring consideration of the motion.

(2) The juvenile does not have a legal parent, is not in an adoptive placement, and is not likely to be adopted within a reasonable period of time.

(3) The order terminating parental rights was entered at least three years before the filing of the motion, unless the court has found or the juvenile's

attorney advocate and the county department of social services with custody of the juvenile stipulate that the juvenile's permanent plan is no longer adoption.

(b)     If a motion could be filed under subsection (a) of this section and the parent whose rights have been terminated contacts the county department of social services with custody of the juvenile or the juvenile's guardian ad litem regarding reinstatement of the parent's rights, the department or the guardian ad litem shall notify the juvenile that the juvenile has a right to file a motion for reinstatement of parental rights.

(c)     If a motion to reinstate parental rights is filed and the juvenile does not have a guardian ad litem appointed pursuant to G.S. 7B-601, the court shall appoint a guardian ad litem to represent the best interests of the juvenile. The appointment, duties, and payment of the guardian ad litem and the guardian ad litem attorney shall be the same as in G.S. 7B-601 and G.S. 7B-603.

(d)     The party filing a motion to reinstate parental rights shall serve the motion on each of the following who is not the movant:

(1)     The juvenile.

(2)     The juvenile's guardian ad litem or the guardian ad litem attorney.

(3)     The county department of social services with custody of the juvenile.

(4)     The former parent whose rights the motion seeks to have reinstated.

A former parent who is served under this subsection is not a party to the proceeding and is not entitled to appointed counsel but may retain counsel at the former parent's own expense.

(e)     The movant shall ask the clerk to calendar the case for a preliminary hearing on the motion for reinstatement of parental rights within 60 days of the filing of the motion at a session of court scheduled for the hearing of juvenile matters. The movant shall give at least 15 days' notice of the hearing and state its purpose to the persons listed in subdivisions (d)(1) through (d)(4) of this section. In addition, the movant shall send a notice of the hearing to the juvenile's placement provider. Nothing in this section shall be construed to make the former parent or the juvenile's placement provider a party to the proceeding based solely on being served with the motion or receiving notice and the right to be heard.

(f) At least seven days before the preliminary hearing, the department of social services and the juvenile's guardian ad litem shall provide to the court, the other parties, and the former parent reports that address the factors specified in subsection (g) of this section.

(g) At the preliminary hearing and any subsequent hearing on the motion, the court shall consider information from the county department of social services with custody of the juvenile, the juvenile, the juvenile's guardian ad litem, the juvenile's former parent whose parental rights are the subject of the motion, the juvenile's placement provider, and any other person or agency that may aid the court in its review. The court may consider any evidence, including hearsay evidence as defined in G.S. 8C-1, Rule 801, that the court finds to be relevant, reliable, and necessary to determine the needs of the juvenile and whether reinstatement is in the juvenile's best interest. The court shall consider the following criteria and make written findings regarding the following that are relevant:

(1) What efforts were made to achieve adoption or a permanent guardianship.

(2) Whether the parent whose rights the motion seeks to have reinstated has remedied the conditions that led to the juvenile's removal and termination of the parent's rights.

(3) Whether the juvenile would receive proper care and supervision in a safe home if placed with the parent.

(4) The age and maturity of the child and the ability of the child to express the child's preference.

(5) The parent's willingness to resume contact with the juvenile and to have parental rights reinstated.

(6) The juvenile's willingness to resume contact with the parent and to have parental rights reinstated.

(7) Services that would be needed by the juvenile and the parent if the parent's rights were reinstated.

(8) Any other criteria the court deems necessary.

(h) At the conclusion of the preliminary hearing, the court shall either dismiss the motion or order that the juvenile's permanent plan become reinstatement of parental rights. If the court does not dismiss the motion, the court shall conduct interim hearings at least every six months until the motion is granted or dismissed. Interim hearings may be combined with posttermination of parental rights review hearings required by G.S. 7B-908. At each interim hearing, the court shall assess whether the plan of reinstatement of parental rights continues to be in the juvenile's best interest and whether the department of social services has made reasonable efforts to achieve the permanent plan.

(i) At any hearing under this section, after making proper findings of fact and conclusions of law, the court may do one of the following:

(1) Enter an order for visitation in accordance with G.S. 7B-905.1.

(2) Order that the juvenile be placed in the former parent's home and supervised by the department of social services either directly or, when the former parent lives in a different county, through coordination with the county department of social services in that county, or by other personnel as may be available to the court, subject to conditions applicable to the former parent as the court may specify. Any order authorizing placement with the former parent shall specify that the juvenile's placement and care remain the responsibility of the county department of social services with custody of the juvenile and that the department is to provide or arrange for the placement of the juvenile.

(j) The court shall either dismiss or grant a motion for reinstatement of parental rights within 12 months from the date the motion was filed, unless the court makes written findings why a final determination cannot be made within that time. If the court makes such findings, the court shall specify the time frame in which a final order shall be entered.

(k) An order reinstating parental rights restores all rights, powers, privileges, immunities, duties, and obligations of the parent as to the juvenile, including those relating to custody, control, and support of the juvenile. If a parent's rights are reinstated, the court shall be relieved of the duty to conduct periodic reviews.

(l) An order shall be entered no later than 30 days following the completion of any hearing pursuant to this section. If the order is not entered within 30 days following completion of the hearing, the clerk of court for juvenile matters shall schedule a subsequent hearing at the first session of court scheduled for the hearing of juvenile matters following the 30-day period to determine and explain the reason for the delay and to obtain any needed clarification as to the contents of the order. The order shall be entered within 10 days of the subsequent hearing required by this subsection.

(m)     The granting of a motion for reinstatement of parental rights does not vacate or otherwise affect the validity of the original order terminating parental rights.

(n)     A parent whose rights are reinstated pursuant to this section is not liable for child support or the costs of any services provided to the juvenile for the period from the date of the order terminating the parent's rights to the date of the order reinstating the parent's rights. (2011-295, s. 18; 2013-129, s. 37.)

Article 12.

Guardian ad Litem Program.

§ 7B-1200.  Office of Guardian ad Litem Services established.

There is established within the Administrative Office of the Courts an Office of Guardian ad Litem Services to provide services in accordance with G.S. 7B-601 to abused, neglected, or dependent juveniles involved in judicial proceedings and to assure that all participants in these proceedings are adequately trained to carry out their responsibilities. Each local program shall consist of volunteer guardians ad litem, at least one program attorney, a program coordinator who is a paid State employee, and any clerical staff as the Administrative Office of the Courts in consultation with the local program deems necessary. The Administrative Office of the Courts shall adopt rules and regulations necessary and appropriate for the administration of the program. (1983, c. 761, s. 160; 1987 (Reg. Sess., 1988), c. 1037, s. 32; c. 1090, s. 7; 1998-202, s. 6.)

§ 7B-1201.  Implementation and administration.

(a)     Local Programs. - The Administrative Office of the Courts shall, in cooperation with each chief district court judge and other personnel in the district, implement and administer the program mandated by this Article. Where a local program has not yet been established in accordance with this Article, the district court district shall operate a guardian ad litem program approved by the Administrative Office of the Courts.

(b)     Advisory Committee Established. - The Director of the Administrative Office of the Courts shall appoint a Guardian ad Litem Advisory Committee consisting of at least five members to advise the Office of Guardian ad Litem Services in matters related to this program. The members of the Advisory Committee shall receive the same per diem and reimbursement for travel expenses as members of State boards and commissions generally. (1983, c. 761, s. 160; 1987 (Reg. Sess., 1988), c. 1037, s. 33; 1998-202, s. 6.)

§ 7B-1202. Conflict of interest or impracticality of implementation.

If a conflict of interest prohibits a local program from providing representation to an abused, neglected, or dependent juvenile, the court may appoint any member of the district bar to represent the juvenile. If the Administrative Office of the Courts determines that within a particular district court district the implementation of a local program is impractical, or that an alternative plan meets the conditions of G.S. 7B-1203, the Administrative Office of the Courts shall waive the establishment of the program within the district. (1983, c. 761, s. 160; 1987 (Reg. Sess., 1988), c. 1037, s. 34; c. 1090, s. 8; 1998-202, s. 6.)

§ 7B-1203. Alternative plans.

A district court district shall be granted a waiver from the implementation of a local program if the Administrative Office of the Courts determines that the following conditions are met:

(1)     An alternative plan has been developed to provide adequate guardian ad litem services for every juvenile consistent with the duties stated in G.S. 7B-601; and

(2)     The proposed alternative plan will require no greater proportion of State funds than the district court district's abuse and neglect caseload represents to the State's abuse and neglect caseload. Computation of abuse and neglect caseloads shall include such factors as the juvenile population, number of substantiated abuse and neglect reports, number of abuse and neglect petitions, number of abused and neglected juveniles in care to be reviewed

pursuant to G.S. 7B-906.1, nature of the district's district court caseload, and number of petitions to terminate parental rights.

When an alternative plan is approved pursuant to this section, the Administrative Office of the Courts shall retain authority to monitor implementation of the said plan in order to assure compliance with the requirements of this Article and G.S. 7B-601. In any district court district where the Administrative Office of the Courts determines that implementation of an alternative plan is not in compliance with the requirements of this section, the Administrative Office of the Courts may implement and administer a program authorized by this Article. (1983, c. 761, s. 160; 1987 (Reg. Sess., 1988), c. 1037, s. 35; 1998-202, s. 6; 2013-129, s. 38.)

§ 7B-1204.  Civil liability of volunteers.

Any volunteer participating in a judicial proceeding pursuant to the program authorized by this Article shall not be civilly liable for acts or omissions committed in connection with the proceeding if the volunteer acted in good faith and was not guilty of gross negligence. (1983, c. 761, s. 160; 1998-202, s. 6.)

Article 13.

Prevention of Abuse and Neglect.

§ 7B-1300.  Purpose.

It is the expressed intent of this Article to make the prevention of abuse and neglect, as defined in G.S. 7B-101, a priority of this State and to establish the Children's Trust Fund as a means to that end. (1983, c. 894, s. 1; 1998-202, s. 6.)

§ 7B-1301.  Program on Prevention of Abuse and Neglect.

(a)     The Department of Health and Human Services, through the Division of Social Services, shall implement the Program on Prevention of Abuse and Neglect. The Division of Social Services shall provide the staff and support services for implementing this program.

(b) In order to carry out the purposes of this Article:

(1) Repealed by Session Laws 2009-451, s. 10.43(b), effective July 1, 2009.

(2) The Division of Social Services shall review applications and contract with public or private nonprofit organizations, agencies, schools, or with qualified individuals to operate community-based educational and service programs designed to prevent the occurrence of abuse and neglect. Every contract entered into by the Division of Social Services shall contain provisions that at least twenty-five percent (25%) of the total funding required for a program be provided by the administering organization in the form of in-kind or other services and that a mechanism for evaluation of services provided under the contract be included in the services to be performed. In addition, every proposal to the Division of Social Services for funding under this Article shall include assurances that the proposal has been forwarded to the local department of social services for comment so that the Division of Social Services may consider coordination and duplication of effort on the local level.

(3) The Division of Social Services shall develop appropriate guidelines and criteria for awarding contracts under this Article. These criteria shall include, but are not limited to: documentation of need within the proposed geographical impact area; diversity of geographical areas of programs funded under this Article; demonstrated effectiveness of the proposed strategy or program for preventing abuse and neglect; reasonableness of implementation plan for achieving stated objectives; utilization of community resources including volunteers; provision for an evaluation component that will provide outcome data; plan for dissemination of the program for implementation in other communities; and potential for future funding from private sources.

(4) The Division of Social Services shall develop guidelines for regular monitoring of contracts awarded under this Article in order to maximize the investments in prevention programs by the Children's Trust Fund and to establish appropriate accountability measures for administration of contracts.

(5) The Division of Social Services shall develop a State plan for the prevention of abuse and neglect for submission to the Governor, the President of the Senate, and the Speaker of the House of Representatives.

(c) To assist in implementing this Article, the Division of Social Services may accept contributions, grants, or gifts in cash or otherwise from persons, associations, or corporations. All monies received by the Division of Social Services from contributions, grants, or gifts and not through appropriation by the General Assembly shall be deposited in the Children's Trust Fund. Disbursements of the funds shall be on the authorization of the Department of Health and Human Services. In order to maintain an effective expenditure and revenue control, the funds are subject in all respects to State law and regulations, but no appropriation is required to permit expenditure of the funds.

(d)     Programs contracted for under this Article are intended to prevent abuse and neglect of juveniles. Abuse and neglect prevention programs are defined to be those programs and services which impact on juveniles and families before any substantiated incident of abuse or neglect has occurred. These programs may include, but are not limited to:

(1)     Community-based educational programs on prenatal care, perinatal bonding, child development, basic child care, care of children with special needs, and coping with family stress; and

(2)     Community-based programs relating to crisis care, aid to parents, and support groups for parents and their children experiencing stress within the family unit.

(e)     No more than twenty percent (20%) of each year's total awards may be utilized for funding State-level programs to coordinate community-based programs. (1983, c. 894, s. 1; 1993 (Reg. Sess., 1994), c. 677, s. 1; 1998-202, s. 6; 2009-451, s. 10.43(b).)

§ 7B-1302.  Children's Trust Fund.

(a)     There is established a fund to be known as the "Children's Trust Fund," in the Department of Health and Human Services, Division of Social Services, which shall be funded by a portion of the marriage license fee under G.S. 161-11.1 and a portion of the special license plate fee under G.S. 20-81.12. The money in the Fund shall be used by the Division of Social Services to fund abuse and neglect prevention programs so authorized by this Article.

(b)     The Department of Health and Human Services shall report annually on revenues and expenditures of the Children's Trust Fund to the Joint Legislative Commission on Governmental Operations. (1983, c. 894, s. 1; 1998-202, s. 6;

1999-277, s. 5; 2004-124, s. 7.33(b); 2009-451, s. 10.43(c); 2010-31, s. 10.20A(a).)

Article 14.

North Carolina Child Fatality Prevention System.

§ 7B-1400. Declaration of public policy.

The General Assembly finds that it is the public policy of this State to prevent the abuse, neglect, and death of juveniles. The General Assembly further finds that the prevention of the abuse, neglect, and death of juveniles is a community responsibility; that professionals from disparate disciplines have responsibilities for children or juveniles and have expertise that can promote their safety and well-being; and that multidisciplinary reviews of the abuse, neglect, and death of juveniles can lead to a greater understanding of the causes and methods of preventing these deaths. It is, therefore, the intent of the General Assembly, through this Article, to establish a statewide multidisciplinary, multiagency child fatality prevention system consisting of the State Team established in G.S. 7B-1404 and the Local Teams established in G.S. 7B-1406. The purpose of the system is to assess the records of selected cases in which children are being served by child protective services and the records of all deaths of children in North Carolina from birth to age 18 in order to (i) develop a communitywide approach to the problem of child abuse and neglect, (ii) understand the causes of childhood deaths, (iii) identify any gaps or deficiencies that may exist in the delivery of services to children and their families by public agencies that are designed to prevent future child abuse, neglect, or death, and (iv) make and implement recommendations for changes to laws, rules, and policies that will support the safe and healthy development of our children and prevent future child abuse, neglect, and death. (1991, c. 689, s. 233(a); 1993, c. 321, s. 285(a); 1998-202, s. 6.)

§ 7B-1401. Definitions.

The following definitions apply in this Article:

(1)     Additional Child Fatality. - Any death of a child that did not result from suspected abuse or neglect and about which no report of abuse or neglect had

been made to the county department of social services within the previous 12 months.

(2) Local Team. - A Community Child Protection Team or a Child Fatality Prevention Team.

(3) State Team. - The North Carolina Child Fatality Prevention Team.

(4) Task Force. - The North Carolina Child Fatality Task Force.

(5) Team Coordinator. - The Child Fatality Prevention Team Coordinator. (1991, c. 689, s. 233(a); 1993, c. 321, s. 285(a); 1998-202, s. 6.)

§ 7B-1402. Task Force - creation; membership; vacancies.

(a) There is created the North Carolina Child Fatality Task Force within the Department of Health and Human Services for budgetary purposes only.

(b) The Task Force shall be composed of 35 members, 11 of whom shall be ex officio members, four of whom shall be appointed by the Governor, 10 of whom shall be appointed by the Speaker of the House of Representatives, and 10 of whom shall be appointed by the President Pro Tempore of the Senate. The ex officio members other than the Chief Medical Examiner shall be nonvoting members and may designate representatives from their particular departments, divisions, or offices to represent them on the Task Force. The members shall be as follows:

(1) The Chief Medical Examiner;

(2) The Attorney General;

(3) The Director of the Division of Social Services;

(4) The Director of the State Bureau of Investigation;

(5) The Director of the Division of Maternal and Child Health of the Department of Health and Human Services;

(6) The Director of the Governor's Youth Advocacy and Involvement Office;

(7)     The Superintendent of Public Instruction;

(8)     The Chairman of the State Board of Education;

(9)     The Director of the Division of Mental Health, Developmental Disabilities, and Substance Abuse Services;

(10)    The Secretary of the Department of Health and Human Services;

(11)    The Director of the Administrative Office of the Courts;

(12)    A director of a county department of social services, appointed by the Governor upon recommendation of the President of the North Carolina Association of County Directors of Social Services;

(13)    A representative from a Sudden Infant Death Syndrome counseling and education program, appointed by the Governor upon recommendation of the Director of the Division of Maternal and Child Health of the Department of Health and Human Services;

(14)    A representative from the North Carolina Child Advocacy Institute, appointed by the Governor upon recommendation of the President of the Institute;

(15)    A director of a local department of health, appointed by the Governor upon the recommendation of the President of the North Carolina Association of Local Health Directors;

(16)    A representative from a private group, other than the North Carolina Child Advocacy Institute, that advocates for children, appointed by the Speaker of the House of Representatives upon recommendation of private child advocacy organizations;

(17)    A pediatrician, licensed to practice medicine in North Carolina, appointed by the Speaker of the House of Representatives upon recommendation of the North Carolina Pediatric Society;

(18)    A representative from the North Carolina League of Municipalities, appointed by the Speaker of the House of Representatives upon recommendation of the League;

(18a)    A representative from the North Carolina Domestic Violence Commission, appointed by the Speaker of the House of Representatives upon recommendation of the Director of the Commission;

(19)    One public member, appointed by the Speaker of the House of Representatives;

(20)    A county or municipal law enforcement officer, appointed by the President Pro Tempore of the Senate upon recommendation of organizations that represent local law enforcement officers;

(21)    A district attorney, appointed by the President Pro Tempore of the Senate upon recommendation of the President of the North Carolina Conference of District Attorneys;

(22)    A representative from the North Carolina Association of County Commissioners, appointed by the President Pro Tempore of the Senate upon recommendation of the Association;

(22a)    A representative from the North Carolina Coalition Against Domestic Violence, appointed by the President Pro Tempore of the Senate upon recommendation of the Executive Director of the Coalition;

(23)    One public member, appointed by the President Pro Tempore of the Senate; and

(24)    Five members of the Senate, appointed by the President Pro Tempore of the Senate, and five members of the House of Representatives, appointed by the Speaker of the House of Representatives.

(c)    All members of the Task Force are voting members. Vacancies in the appointed membership shall be filled by the appointing officer who made the initial appointment. Terms shall be two years. The members shall elect a chair who shall preside for the duration of the chair's term as member. In the event a vacancy occurs in the chair before the expiration of the chair's term, the members shall elect an acting chair to serve for the remainder of the unexpired term. (1991, c. 689, s. 233(a); 1991 (Reg. Sess., 1992), c. 900, s. 169(b); 1993, c. 321, s. 285(a); 1993 (Reg. Sess., 1994), c. 769, s. 27.8(d); 1996, 2nd Ex. Sess., c. 17, s. 3.2; 1997-443, s. 11A.98; 1997-456, s. 27; 1998-202, s. 6; 1998-212, s. 12.44(a), (b); 2004-186, s. 5.1.)

§ 7B-1403. Task Force - duties.

The Task Force shall:

(1)     Undertake a statistical study of the incidences and causes of child deaths in this State and establish a profile of child deaths. The study shall include (i) an analysis of all community and private and public agency involvement with the decedents and their families prior to death, and (ii) an analysis of child deaths by age, cause, and geographic distribution;

(2)     Develop a system for multidisciplinary review of child deaths. In developing such a system, the Task Force shall study the operation of existing Local Teams. The Task Force shall also consider the feasibility and desirability of local or regional review teams and, should it determine such teams to be feasible and desirable, develop guidelines for the operation of the teams. The Task Force shall also examine the laws, rules, and policies relating to confidentiality of and access to information that affect those agencies with responsibilities for children, including State and local health, mental health, social services, education, and law enforcement agencies, to determine whether those laws, rules, and policies inappropriately impede the exchange of information necessary to protect children from preventable deaths, and, if so, recommend changes to them;

(3)     Receive and consider reports from the State Team; and

(4)     Perform any other studies, evaluations, or determinations the Task Force considers necessary to carry out its mandate. (1991, c. 689, s. 233(a); 1996, 2nd Ex. Sess., c. 17, s. 3.2; 1998-202, s. 6; 1998-212, s. 12.44(a), (c).)


§ 7B-1404. State Team - creation; membership; vacancies.

(a)     There is created the North Carolina Child Fatality Prevention Team within the Department of Health and Human Services for budgetary purposes only.

(b)     The State Team shall be composed of the following 11 members of whom nine members are ex officio and two are appointed:

(1)     The Chief Medical Examiner, who shall chair the State Team;

(2) The Attorney General;

(3) The Director of the Division of Social Services, Department of Health and Human Services;

(4) The Director of the State Bureau of Investigation;

(5) The Director of the Division of Maternal and Child Health of the Department of Health and Human Services;

(6) The Superintendent of Public Instruction;

(7) The Director of the Division of Mental Health, Developmental Disabilities, and Substance Abuse Services, Department of Health and Human Services;

(8) The Director of the Administrative Office of the Courts;

(9) The pediatrician appointed pursuant to G.S. 7B-1402(b) to the Task Force;

(10) A public member, appointed by the Governor; and

(11) The Team Coordinator.

The ex officio members other than the Chief Medical Examiner may designate a representative from their departments, divisions, or offices to represent them on the State Team.

(c) All members of the State Team are voting members. Vacancies in the appointed membership shall be filled by the appointing officer who made the initial appointment. (1991, c. 689, s. 233(a); 1993, c. 321, s. 285(a); 1997-443, s. 11A.99; 1997-456, s. 27; 1998-202, s. 6.)


§ 7B-1405. State Team - duties.

The State Team shall:

(1) Review current deaths of children when those deaths are attributed to child abuse or neglect or when the decedent was reported as an abused or neglected juvenile pursuant to G.S. 7B-301 at any time before death;

(2) Report to the Task Force during the existence of the Task Force, in the format and at the time required by the Task Force, on the State Team's activities and its recommendations for changes to any law, rule, and policy that would promote the safety and well-being of children;

(3) Upon request of a Local Team, provide technical assistance to the Team;

(4) Periodically assess the operations of the multidisciplinary child fatality prevention system and make recommendations for changes as needed;

(5) Work with the Team Coordinator to develop guidelines for selecting child deaths to receive detailed, multidisciplinary death reviews by Local Teams that review cases of additional child fatalities; and

(6) Receive reports of findings and recommendations from Local Teams that review cases of additional child fatalities and work with the Team Coordinator to implement recommendations. (1991, c. 689, s. 233(a); 1993, c. 321, s. 285(a); 1997-443, s. 11A.99; 1997-456, s. 27; 1998-202, s. 6.)


§ 7B-1406. Community Child Protection Teams; Child Fatality Prevention Teams; creation and duties.

(a) Community Child Protection Teams are established in every county of the State. Each Community Child Protection Team shall:

(1) Review, in accordance with the procedures established by the director of the county department of social services under G.S. 7B-1409:

a. Selected active cases in which children are being served by child protective services; and

b. Cases in which a child died as a result of suspected abuse or neglect, and

1. A report of abuse or neglect has been made about the child or the child's family to the county department of social services within the previous 12 months, or

2. The child or the child's family was a recipient of child protective services within the previous 12 months.

(2) Submit annually to the board of county commissioners recommendations, if any, and advocate for system improvements and needed resources where gaps and deficiencies may exist.

In addition, each Community Child Protection Team may review the records of all additional child fatalities and report findings in connection with these reviews to the Team Coordinator.

(b) Any Community Child Protection Team that determines it will not review additional child fatalities shall notify the Team Coordinator. In accordance with the plan established under G.S. 7B-1408(1), a separate Child Fatality Prevention Team shall be established in that county to conduct these reviews. Each Child Fatality Prevention Team shall:

(1) Review the records of all cases of additional child fatalities.

(2) Submit annually to the board of county commissioners recommendations, if any, and advocate for system improvements and needed resources where gaps and deficiencies may exist.

(3) Report findings in connection with these reviews to the Team Coordinator.

(c) All reports to the Team Coordinator under this section shall include:

(1) A listing of the system problems identified through the review process and recommendations for preventive actions;

(2) Any changes that resulted from the recommendations made by the Local Team;

(3) Information about each death reviewed; and

(4)     Any additional information requested by the Team Coordinator. (1993, c. 321, s. 285(a); 1998-202, s. 6.)

§ 7B-1407.  Local Teams; composition.

(a)     Each Local Team shall consist of representatives of public and nonpublic agencies in the community that provide services to children and their families and other individuals who represent the community. No single team shall encompass a geographic or governmental area larger than one county.

(b)     Each Local Team shall consist of the following persons:

(1)     The director of the county department of social services and a member of the director's staff;

(2)     A local law enforcement officer, appointed by the board of county commissioners;

(3)     An attorney from the district attorney's office, appointed by the district attorney;

(4)     The executive director of the local community action agency, as defined by the Department of Health and Human Services, or the executive director's designee;

(5)     The superintendent of each local school administrative unit located in the county, or the superintendent's designee;

(6)     A member of the county board of social services, appointed by the chair of that board;

(7)     A local mental health professional, appointed by the director of the area authority established under Chapter 122C of the General Statutes;

(8)     The local guardian ad litem coordinator, or the coordinator's designee;

(9)     The director of the local department of public health; and

(10)    A local health care provider, appointed by the local board of health.

(c) In addition, a Local Team that reviews the records of additional child fatalities shall include the following five additional members:

(1) An emergency medical services provider or firefighter, appointed by the board of county commissioners;

(2) A district court judge, appointed by the chief district court judge in that district;

(3) A county medical examiner, appointed by the Chief Medical Examiner;

(4) A representative of a local child care facility or Head Start program, appointed by the director of the county department of social services; and

(5) A parent of a child who died before reaching the child's eighteenth birthday, to be appointed by the board of county commissioners.

(d) The Team Coordinator shall serve as an ex officio member of each Local Team that reviews the records of additional child fatalities. The board of county commissioners may appoint a maximum of five additional members to represent county agencies or the community at large to serve on any Local Team. Vacancies on a Local Team shall be filled by the original appointing authority.

(e) Each Local Team shall elect a member to serve as chair at the Team's pleasure.

(f) Each Local Team shall meet at least four times each year.

(g) The director of the local department of social services shall call the first meeting of the Community Child Protection Team. The director of the local department of health, upon consultation with the Team Coordinator, shall call the first meeting of the Child Fatality Prevention Team. Thereafter, the chair of each Local Team shall schedule the time and place of meetings, in consultation with these directors, and shall prepare the agenda. The chair shall schedule Team meetings no less often than once per quarter and often enough to allow adequate review of the cases selected for review. Within three months of election, the chair shall participate in the appropriate training developed under this Article. (1993, c. 321, s. 285(a); 1997-443, s. 11A.100; 1997-456, s. 27; 1997-506, s. 52; 1998-202, s. 6.)

§ 7B-1408.  Child Fatality Prevention Team Coordinator; duties.

The Child Fatality Prevention Team Coordinator shall serve as liaison between the State Team and the Local Teams that review records of additional child fatalities and shall provide technical assistance to these Local Teams. The Team Coordinator shall:

(1)     Develop a plan to establish Local Teams that review the records of additional child fatalities in each county.

(2)     Develop model operating procedures for these Local Teams that address when public meetings should be held, what items should be addressed in public meetings, what information may be released in written reports, and any other information the Team Coordinator considers necessary.

(3)     Provide structured training for these Local Teams at the time of their establishment, and continuing technical assistance thereafter.

(4)     Provide statistical information on all child deaths occurring in each county to the appropriate Local Team, and assure that all child deaths in a county are assessed through the multidisciplinary system.

(5)     Monitor the work of these Local Teams.

(6)     Receive reports of findings, and other reports that the Team Coordinator may require, from these Local Teams.

(7)     Report the aggregated findings of these Local Teams to each Local Team that reviews the records of additional child fatalities and to the State Team.

(8)     Evaluate the impact of local efforts to identify problems and make changes. (1993, c. 321, s. 285(a); 1998-202, s. 6.)

§ 7B-1409.  Community Child Protection Teams; duties of the director of the county department of social services.

In addition to any other duties as a member of the Community Child Protection Team, and in connection with the reviews under G.S. 7B-1406(a)(1), the director of the county department of social services shall:

(1) Assure the development of written operating procedures in connection with these reviews, including frequency of meetings, confidentiality policies, training of members, and duties and responsibilities of members;

(2) Assure that the Team defines the categories of cases that are subject to its review;

(3) Determine and initiate the cases for review;

(4) Bring for review any case requested by a Team member;

(5) Provide staff support for these reviews;

(6) Maintain records, including minutes of all official meetings, lists of participants for each meeting of the Team, and signed confidentiality statements required under G.S. 7B-1413, in compliance with applicable rules and law; and

(7) Report quarterly to the county board of social services, or as required by the board, on the activities of the Team. (1993, c. 321, s. 285(a); 1998-202, s. 6.)

§ 7B-1410. Local Teams; duties of the director of the local department of health.

In addition to any other duties as a member of the Local Team and in connection with reviews of additional child fatalities, the director of the local department of health shall:

(1) Distribute copies of the written procedures developed by the Team Coordinator under G.S. 7B-1408 to the administrators of all agencies represented on the Local Team and to all members of the Local Team;

(2) Maintain records, including minutes of all official meetings, lists of participants for each meeting of the Local Team, and signed confidentiality statements required under G.S. 7B-1413, in compliance with applicable rules and law;

(3) Provide staff support for these reviews; and

(4) Report quarterly to the local board of health, or as required by the board, on the activities of the Local Team. (1993, c. 321, s. 285(a); 1998-202, s. 6.)

§ 7B-1411. Community Child Protection Teams; responsibility for training of team members.

The Division of Social Services, Department of Health and Human Services, shall develop and make available, on an ongoing basis, for the members of Local Teams that review active cases in which children are being served by child protective services, training materials that address the role and function of the Local Team, confidentiality requirements, an overview of child protective services law and policy, and Team record keeping. (1993, c. 321, s. 285(a); 1997-443, s. 11A.118(a); 1998-202, s. 6.)

§ 7B-1412. Task Force - reports.

The Task Force shall report annually to the Governor and General Assembly, within the first week of the convening or reconvening of the General Assembly. The report shall contain at least a summary of the conclusions and recommendations for each of the Task Force's duties, as well as any other recommendations for changes to any law, rule, or policy that it has determined will promote the safety and well-being of children. Any recommendations of changes to law, rule, or policy shall be accompanied by specific legislative or policy proposals and detailed fiscal notes setting forth the costs to the State. (1991, c. 689, s. 233(a); 1991 (Reg. Sess., 1992), c. 900, s. 169(a); 1993 (Reg. Sess., 1994), c. 769, s. 27.8(a); 1996, 2nd Ex. Sess., c. 17, ss. 3.1, 3.2; 1998-202, s. 6; 1998-212, s. 12.44(a), (d).)

§ 7B-1413. Access to records.

(a) The State Team, the Local Teams, and the Task Force during its existence, shall have access to all medical records, hospital records, and records maintained by this State, any county, or any local agency as necessary to carry out the purposes of this Article, including police investigations data, medical examiner investigative data, health records, mental health records, and social services records. The State Team, the Task Force, and the Local Teams shall not, as part of the reviews authorized under this Article, contact, question, or interview the child, the parent of the child, or any other family member of the child whose record is being reviewed. Any member of a Local Team may share, only in an official meeting of that Local Team, any information available to that member that the Local Team needs to carry out its duties.

(b) Meetings of the State Team and the Local Teams are not subject to the provisions of Article 33C of Chapter 143 of the General Statutes. However, the Local Teams may hold periodic public meetings to discuss, in a general manner not revealing confidential information about children and families, the findings of their reviews and their recommendations for preventive actions. Minutes of all public meetings, excluding those of executive sessions, shall be kept in compliance with Article 33C of Chapter 143 of the General Statutes. Any minutes or any other information generated during any closed session shall be sealed from public inspection.

(c) All otherwise confidential information and records acquired by the State Team, the Local Teams, and the Task Force during its existence, in the exercise of their duties are confidential; are not subject to discovery or introduction into evidence in any proceedings; and may only be disclosed as necessary to carry out the purposes of the State Team, the Local Teams, and the Task Force. In addition, all otherwise confidential information and records created by a Local Team in the exercise of its duties are confidential; are not subject to discovery or introduction into evidence in any proceedings; and may only be disclosed as necessary to carry out the purposes of the Local Team. No member of the State Team, a Local Team, nor any person who attends a meeting of the State Team or a Local Team, may testify in any proceeding about what transpired at the meeting, about information presented at the meeting, or about opinions formed by the person as a result of the meetings. This subsection shall not, however, prohibit a person from testifying in a civil or criminal action about matters within that person's independent knowledge.

(d) Each member of a Local Team and invited participant shall sign a statement indicating an understanding of and adherence to confidentiality requirements, including the possible civil or criminal consequences of any breach of confidentiality.

(e) Cases receiving child protective services at the time of review by a Local Team shall have an entry in the child's protective services record to indicate that the case was received by that Team. Additional entry into the record shall be at the discretion of the director of the county department of social services.

(f) The Social Services Commission shall adopt rules to implement this section in connection with reviews conducted by Community Child Protection Teams. The Commission for Public Health shall adopt rules to implement this section in connection with Local Teams that review additional child fatalities. In particular, these rules shall allow information generated by an executive session of a Local Team to be accessible for administrative or research purposes only. (1991, c. 689, s. 233(a); 1993, c. 321, s. 285(a); 1998-202, s. 6; 2007-182, s. 1.3.)

§ 7B-1414. Administration; funding.

(a) To the extent of funds available, the chairs of the Task Force and State Team may hire staff or consultants to assist the Task Force and the State Team in completing their duties.

(b) Members, staff, and consultants of the Task Force or State Team shall receive travel and subsistence expenses in accordance with the provisions of G.S. 138-5 or G.S. 138-6, as the case may be, paid from funds appropriated to implement this Article and within the limits of those funds.

(c) With the approval of the Legislative Services Commission, legislative staff and space in the Legislative Building and the Legislative Office Building may be made available to the Task Force. (1991, c. 689, s. 233(a); 1998-202, s. 6.)

SUBCHAPTER II. UNDISCIPLINED AND DELINQUENT JUVENILES.

Article 15.

Purposes; Definitions.

§ 7B-1500. Purpose.

This Subchapter shall be interpreted and construed so as to implement the following purposes and policies:

(1) To protect the public from acts of delinquency.

(2) To deter delinquency and crime, including patterns of repeat offending:

a. By providing swift, effective dispositions that emphasize the juvenile offender's accountability for the juvenile's actions; and

b. By providing appropriate rehabilitative services to juveniles and their families.

(3) To provide an effective system of intake services for the screening and evaluation of complaints and, in appropriate cases, where court intervention is not necessary to ensure public safety, to refer juveniles to community-based resources.

(4) To provide uniform procedures that assure fairness and equity; that protect the constitutional rights of juveniles, parents, and victims; and that encourage the court and others involved with juvenile offenders to proceed with all possible speed in making and implementing determinations required by this Subchapter. (1979, c. 815, s. 1; 1987 (Reg. Sess., 1988), c. 1090, s. 1; 1998-202, s. 6.)


§ 7B-1501. Definitions.

In this Subchapter, unless the context clearly requires otherwise, the following words have the listed meanings. The singular includes the plural, unless otherwise specified.

(1) Chief court counselor. - The person responsible for administration and supervision of juvenile intake, probation, and post-release supervision in each judicial district, operating under the supervision of the Division of Juvenile Justice of the Department of Public Safety.

(2) Clerk. - Any clerk of superior court, acting clerk, or assistant or deputy clerk.

(3) Community-based program. - A program providing nonresidential or residential treatment to a juvenile under the jurisdiction of the juvenile court in the community where the juvenile's family lives. A community-based program may include specialized foster care, family counseling, shelter care, and other appropriate treatment.

(4) Court. - The district court division of the General Court of Justice.

(5) Repealed by Session Laws 2001-490, s. 2.1, effective June 30, 2001.

(6) Custodian. - The person or agency that has been awarded legal custody of a juvenile by a court.

(7) Delinquent juvenile. - Any juvenile who, while less than 16 years of age but at least 6 years of age, commits a crime or infraction under State law or under an ordinance of local government, including violation of the motor vehicle laws, or who commits indirect contempt by a juvenile as defined in G.S. 5A-31.

(8) Detention. - The secure confinement of a juvenile under a court order.

(9) Detention facility. - A facility approved to provide secure confinement and care for juveniles. Detention facilities include both State and locally administered detention homes, centers, and facilities.

(10) District. - Any district court district as established by G.S. 7A-133.

(10a) Division. - The Division of Juvenile Justice of the Department of Public Safety created under Article 12 of Chapter 143B of the General Statutes.

(11) Holdover facility. - A place in a jail which has been approved by the Department of Health and Human Services as meeting the State standards for detention as required in G.S. 153A-221 providing close supervision where the juvenile cannot converse with, see, or be seen by the adult population.

(12) House arrest. - A requirement that the juvenile remain at the juvenile's residence unless the court or the juvenile court counselor authorizes the juvenile to leave for school, counseling, work, or other similar specific purposes, provided the juvenile is accompanied in transit by a parent, legal guardian, or other person approved by the juvenile court counselor.

(13) Intake. - The process of screening and evaluating a complaint alleging that a juvenile is delinquent or undisciplined to determine whether the complaint should be filed as a petition.

(14) Interstate Compact on Juveniles. - An agreement ratified by 50 states and the District of Columbia providing a formal means of returning a juvenile, who is an absconder, escapee, or runaway, to the juvenile's home state, and codified in Article 28 of this Chapter.

(15) Judge. - Any district court judge.

(16) Judicial district. - Any district court district as established by G.S. 7A-133.

(17) Juvenile. - Except as provided in subdivisions (7) and (27) of this section, any person who has not reached the person's eighteenth birthday and is not married, emancipated, or a member of the Armed Forces of the United States. Wherever the term "juvenile" is used with reference to rights and privileges, that term encompasses the attorney for the juvenile as well.

(18) Juvenile court. - Any district court exercising jurisdiction under this Chapter.

(18a) Juvenile court counselor. - A person responsible for intake services and court supervision services to juveniles under the supervision of the chief court counselor.

(19) Repealed by Session Laws 2000, c. 137, s. 2, effective July 20, 2000.

(20) Petitioner. - The individual who initiates court action by the filing of a petition or a motion for review alleging the matter for adjudication.

(21) Post-release supervision. - The supervision of a juvenile who has been returned to the community after having been committed to the Division for placement in a youth development center.

(22) Probation. - The status of a juvenile who has been adjudicated delinquent, is subject to specified conditions under the supervision of a juvenile court counselor, and may be returned to the court for violation of those conditions during the period of probation.

(23) Prosecutor. - The district attorney or an assistant district attorney.

(24) Protective supervision. - The status of a juvenile who has been adjudicated undisciplined and is under the supervision of a juvenile court counselor.

(25) Teen court program. - A community resource for the diversion of cases in which a juvenile has allegedly committed certain offenses for hearing by a

jury of the juvenile's peers, which may assign the juvenile to counseling, restitution, curfews, community service, or other rehabilitative measures.

(26) Repealed by Session Laws 2001-95, s. 1, effective May 18, 2001.

(27) Undisciplined juvenile. -

a. A juvenile who, while less than 16 years of age but at least 6 years of age, is unlawfully absent from school; or is regularly disobedient to and beyond the disciplinary control of the juvenile's parent, guardian, or custodian; or is regularly found in places where it is unlawful for a juvenile to be; or has run away from home for a period of more than 24 hours; or

b. A juvenile who is 16 or 17 years of age and who is regularly disobedient to and beyond the disciplinary control of the juvenile's parent, guardian, or custodian; or is regularly found in places where it is unlawful for a juvenile to be; or has run away from home for a period of more than 24 hours.

(28) Wilderness program. - A rehabilitative residential treatment program in a rural or outdoor setting.

(29) Youth development center. - A secure residential facility authorized to provide long-term treatment, education, and rehabilitative services for delinquent juveniles committed by the court to the Division. (1979, c. 815, s. 1; 1981, c. 336; c. 359, s. 2; c. 469, ss. 1-3; c. 716, s. 1; 1985, c. 648; c. 757, s. 156(q); 1985 (Reg. Sess., 1986), c. 852, s. 16; 1987, c. 162; c. 695; 1987 (Reg. Sess., 1988), c. 1037, ss. 36, 37; 1989 (Reg. Sess., 1990), c. 815, s. 1; 1991, c. 258, s. 3; c. 273, s. 11; 1991 (Reg. Sess., 1992), c. 1030, s. 3; 1993, c. 324, s. 1; c. 516, ss. 1-3; 1997-113, s. 1; 1997-390, ss. 3, 3.2; 1997-443, s. 11A.118(a); 1997-506, s. 30; 1998-202, s. 6; 1998-229, s. 1; 2000-137, s. 2; 2001-95, ss. 1, 2, 5; 2001-487, s. 3; 2001-490, s. 2.1; 2007-168, s. 2; 2009-545, s. 1; 2009-547, s. 1; 2011-145, s. 19.1(l); 2011-183, s. 4.)

Article 16.

Jurisdiction.

§ 7B-1600. Jurisdiction over undisciplined juveniles.

(a) The court has exclusive, original jurisdiction over any case involving a juvenile who is alleged to be undisciplined. For purposes of determining jurisdiction, the age of the juvenile at the time of the alleged offense governs.

(b) When the court obtains jurisdiction over a juvenile under this section, jurisdiction shall continue until terminated by order of the court, the juvenile reaches the age of 18 years, or the juvenile is emancipated.

(c) The court has jurisdiction over the parent, guardian, or custodian of a juvenile who is under the jurisdiction of the court pursuant to this section, if the parent, guardian, or custodian has been served with a summons pursuant to G.S. 7B-1805. (1979, c. 815, s. 1; 1983, c. 837, s. 1; 1985, c. 459, s. 2; 1987, c. 409, s. 2; 1995, c. 328, s. 3; c. 462, s. 2; 1996, 2nd Ex. Sess., c. 18, s. 23.2(c); 1998-202, s. 6.)

§ 7B-1601. Jurisdiction over delinquent juveniles.

(a) The court has exclusive, original jurisdiction over any case involving a juvenile who is alleged to be delinquent. For purposes of determining jurisdiction, the age of the juvenile at the time of the alleged offense governs.

(b) When the court obtains jurisdiction over a juvenile alleged to be delinquent, jurisdiction shall continue until terminated by order of the court or until the juvenile reaches the age of 18 years, except as provided otherwise in this Article.

(c) When delinquency proceedings cannot be concluded before the juvenile reaches the age of 18 years, the court retains jurisdiction for the sole purpose of conducting proceedings pursuant to Article 22 of this Chapter and either transferring the case to superior court for trial as an adult or dismissing the petition.

(d) When the court has not obtained jurisdiction over a juvenile before the juvenile reaches the age of 18, for a felony and any related misdemeanors the juvenile allegedly committed on or after the juvenile's thirteenth birthday and prior to the juvenile's sixteenth birthday, the court has jurisdiction for the sole purpose of conducting proceedings pursuant to Article 22 of this Chapter and either transferring the case to superior court for trial as an adult or dismissing the petition.

(e) The court has jurisdiction over delinquent juveniles in the custody of the Division and over proceedings to determine whether a juvenile who is under the post-release supervision of the juvenile court counselor has violated the terms of the juvenile's post-release supervision.

(f) The court has jurisdiction over persons 18 years of age or older who are under the extended jurisdiction of the juvenile court.

(g) The court has jurisdiction over the parent, guardian, or custodian of a juvenile who is under the jurisdiction of the court pursuant to this section if the parent, guardian, or custodian has been served with a summons pursuant to G.S. 7B-1805. (1979, c. 815, s. 1; 1983, c. 837, s. 1; 1985, c. 459, s. 2; 1987, c. 409, s. 2; 1995, c. 328, s. 3; c. 462, s. 2; 1996, 2nd Ex. Sess., c. 18, s. 23.2(c); 1998-202, s. 6; 2000-137, s. 3; 2001-490, s. 2.2; 2011-145, s. 19.1(l).)

§ 7B-1602. Extended jurisdiction over a delinquent juvenile under certain circumstances.

(a) When a juvenile is committed to the Division for placement in a youth development center for an offense that would be first degree murder pursuant to G.S. 14-17, first-degree rape pursuant to G.S. 14-27.2, or first-degree sexual offense pursuant to G.S. 14-27.4 if committed by an adult, jurisdiction shall continue until terminated by order of the court or until the juvenile reaches the age of 21 years, whichever occurs first.

(b) When a juvenile is committed to the Division for placement in a youth development center for an offense that would be a Class B1, B2, C, D, or E felony if committed by an adult, other than an offense set forth in subsection (a) of this section, jurisdiction shall continue until terminated by order of the court or until the juvenile reaches the age of 19 years, whichever occurs first. (1979, c. 815, s. 1; 1981, c. 469, s. 4; 1996, 2nd Ex. Sess., c. 18, s. 23.2(d); 1998-202, s. 6; 2000-137, s. 3; 2001-95, s. 5; 2011-145, s. 19.1(l).)

§ 7B-1603. Jurisdiction in certain circumstances.

The court has exclusive original jurisdiction of all of the following proceedings:

(1) Proceedings under the Interstate Compact on the Placement of Children set forth in Article 38 of this Chapter.

(2) Proceedings involving judicial consent for emergency surgical or medical treatment for a juvenile when the juvenile's parent, guardian, custodian, or person who has assumed the status and obligation of a parent without being awarded legal custody of the juvenile by a court refuses to consent for treatment to be rendered.

(3) Proceedings to determine whether a juvenile should be emancipated.

(4) Proceedings in which a juvenile has been ordered pursuant to G.S. 5A-32(b) to appear and show cause why the juvenile should not be held in contempt. (1979, c. 815, s. 1; 1983, c. 837, s. 1; 1985, c. 459, s. 2; 1987, c. 409, s. 2; 1995, c. 328, s. 3; c. 462, s. 2; 1996, 2nd Ex. Sess., c. 18, s. 23.2(c); 1998-202, s. 6; 2007-168, s. 3.)

§ 7B-1604. Limitations on juvenile court jurisdiction.

(a) Any juvenile, including a juvenile who is under the jurisdiction of the court, who commits a criminal offense on or after the juvenile's sixteenth birthday is subject to prosecution as an adult. A juvenile who is emancipated shall be prosecuted as an adult for the commission of a criminal offense.

(b) A juvenile who is transferred to and convicted in superior court shall be prosecuted as an adult for any criminal offense the juvenile commits after the superior court conviction. (1979, c. 815, s. 1; 1981, c. 469, s. 4; 1983, c. 837, s. 1; 1985, c. 459, s. 2; 1987, c. 409, s. 2; 1995, c. 328, s. 3; c. 462, s. 2; 1996, 2nd Ex. Sess., c. 18, s. 23.2(c); 1998-202, s. 6.)

Article 17.

Screening of Delinquency and Undisciplined Complaints.

§ 7B-1700. Intake services.

The chief court counselor, under the direction of the Division, shall establish intake services in each judicial district of the State for all delinquency and undisciplined cases.

The purpose of intake services shall be to determine from available evidence whether there are reasonable grounds to believe the facts alleged are true, to determine whether the facts alleged constitute a delinquent or undisciplined offense within the jurisdiction of the court, to determine whether the facts alleged are sufficiently serious to warrant court action, and to obtain assistance from community resources when court referral is not necessary. The juvenile court counselor shall not engage in field investigations to substantiate complaints or to produce supplementary evidence but may refer complainants to law enforcement agencies for those purposes. (1979, c. 815, s. 1; 1998-202, s. 6; 2000-137, s. 3; 2001-490, s. 2.3; 2011-145, s. 19.1(l).)

§ 7B-1700.1. Duty to report abuse, neglect, dependency.

Any time a juvenile court counselor or any person has cause to suspect that a juvenile is abused, neglected, or dependent, or has died as the result of maltreatment, the juvenile court counselor or the person shall make a report to the county department of social services as required by G.S. 7B-301. (2009-311, s. 14.)

§ 7B-1701. Preliminary inquiry.

When a complaint is received, the juvenile court counselor shall make a preliminary determination as to whether the juvenile is within the jurisdiction of the court as a delinquent or undisciplined juvenile. If the juvenile court counselor finds that the facts contained in the complaint do not state a case within the jurisdiction of the court, that legal sufficiency has not been established, or that the matters alleged are frivolous, the juvenile court counselor, without further inquiry, shall refuse authorization to file the complaint as a petition.

When requested by the juvenile court counselor, the prosecutor shall assist in determining the sufficiency of evidence as it affects the quantum of proof and the elements of offenses.

The juvenile court counselor, without further inquiry, shall authorize the complaint to be filed as a petition if the juvenile court counselor finds reasonable grounds to believe that the juvenile has committed one of the following nondivertible offenses:

(1)     Murder;

(2) First-degree rape or second degree rape;

(3) First-degree sexual offense or second degree sexual offense;

(4) Arson;

(5) Any violation of Article 5, Chapter 90 of the General Statutes that would constitute a felony if committed by an adult;

(6) First degree burglary;

(7) Crime against nature; or

(8) Any felony which involves the willful infliction of serious bodily injury upon another or which was committed by use of a deadly weapon. (1979, c. 815, s. 1; 1983, c. 251, s. 1; 1998-202, s. 6; 2001-490, s. 2.4.)

§ 7B-1702. Evaluation.

Upon a finding of legal sufficiency, except in cases involving nondivertible offenses set out in G.S. 7B-1701, the juvenile court counselor shall determine whether a complaint should be filed as a petition, the juvenile diverted pursuant to G.S. 7B-1706, or the case resolved without further action. In making the decision, the counselor shall consider criteria provided by the Department. The intake process shall include the following steps if practicable:

(1) Interviews with the complainant and the victim if someone other than the complainant;

(2) Interviews with the juvenile and the juvenile's parent, guardian, or custodian;

(3) Interviews with persons known to have relevant information about the juvenile or the juvenile's family.

Interviews required by this section shall be conducted in person unless it is necessary to conduct them by telephone. (1979, c. 815, s. 1; 1981, c. 469, s. 5; 1998-202, s. 6; 2000-137, s. 3; 2001-490, s. 2.5.)

§ 7B-1703. Evaluation decision.

(a) The juvenile court counselor shall complete evaluation of a complaint within 15 days of receipt of the complaint, with an extension for a maximum of 15 additional days at the discretion of the chief court counselor. The juvenile court counselor shall decide within this time period whether a complaint shall be filed as a juvenile petition.

(b) Except as provided in G.S. 7B-1706, if the juvenile court counselor determines that a complaint should be filed as a petition, the counselor shall file the petition as soon as practicable, but in any event within 15 days after the complaint is received, with an extension for a maximum of 15 additional days at the discretion of the chief court counselor. The juvenile court counselor shall assist the complainant when necessary with the preparation and filing of the petition, shall include on it the date and the words "Approved for Filing", shall sign it, and shall transmit it to the clerk of superior court.

(c) If the juvenile court counselor determines that a petition should not be filed, the juvenile court counselor shall notify the complainant immediately in writing with reasons for the decision and shall include notice of the complainant's right to have the decision reviewed by the prosecutor. The juvenile court counselor shall sign the complaint after indicating on it:

(1) The date of the determination;

(2) The words "Not Approved for Filing"; and

(3) Whether the matter is "Closed" or "Diverted and Retained".

Except as provided in G.S. 7B-1706, any complaint not approved for filing as a juvenile petition shall be destroyed by the juvenile court counselor after holding the complaint for a temporary period to allow review as provided in G.S. 7B-1705. (1979, c. 815, s. 1; 1998-202, s. 6; 2001-490, s. 2.6.)


§ 7B-1704. Request for review by prosecutor.

The complainant has five calendar days, from receipt of the juvenile court counselor's decision not to approve the filing of a petition, to request review by the prosecutor. The juvenile court counselor shall notify the prosecutor immediately of such request and shall transmit to the prosecutor a copy of the complaint. The prosecutor shall notify the complainant and the juvenile court counselor of the time and place for the review. (1979, c. 815, s. 1; 1998-202, s. 6; 2001-490, s. 2.7.)

§ 7B-1705. Review of determination that petition should not be filed.

No later than 20 days after the complainant is notified, the prosecutor shall review the juvenile court counselor's determination that a juvenile petition should not be filed. Review shall include conferences with the complainant and the juvenile court counselor. At the conclusion of the review, the prosecutor shall: (i) affirm the decision of the juvenile court counselor or direct the filing of a petition and (ii) notify the complainant of the prosecutor's action. (1979, c. 815, s. 1; 1981, c. 469, s. 6; 1998-202, s. 6; 2001-490, s. 2.8.)

§ 7B-1706. Diversion plans and referral.

(a) Unless the offense is one in which a petition is required by G.S. 7B-1701, upon a finding of legal sufficiency the juvenile court counselor may divert the juvenile pursuant to a diversion plan, which may include referring the juvenile to any of the following resources:

(1) An appropriate public or private resource;

(2) Restitution;

(3) Community service;

(4) Victim-offender mediation;

(5) Regimented physical training;

(6) Counseling;

(7) A teen court program, as set forth in subsection (c) of this section.

As part of a diversion plan, the juvenile court counselor may enter into a diversion contract with the juvenile and the juvenile's parent, guardian, or custodian.

(b) Unless the offense is one in which a petition is required by G.S. 7B-1701, upon a finding of legal sufficiency the juvenile court counselor may enter into a diversion contract with the juvenile and the parent, guardian, or custodian; provided, a diversion contract requires the consent of the juvenile and the juvenile's parent, guardian, or custodian. A diversion contract shall:

(1) State conditions by which the juvenile agrees to abide and any actions the juvenile agrees to take;

(2) State conditions by which the parent, guardian, or custodian agrees to abide and any actions the parent, guardian, or custodian agrees to take;

(3) Describe the role of the juvenile court counselor in relation to the juvenile and the parent, guardian, or custodian;

(4) Specify the length of the contract, which shall not exceed six months;

(5) Indicate that all parties understand and agree that:

a. The juvenile's violation of the contract may result in the filing of the complaint as a petition; and

b. The juvenile's successful completion of the contract shall preclude the filing of a petition.

After a diversion contract is signed by the parties, the juvenile court counselor shall provide copies of the contract to the juvenile and the juvenile's parent, guardian, or custodian. The juvenile court counselor shall notify any agency or other resource from which the juvenile or the juvenile's parent, guardian, or custodian will be seeking services or treatment pursuant to the terms of the contract. At any time during the term of the contract if the juvenile court counselor determines that the juvenile has failed to comply substantially with the terms of the contract, the juvenile court counselor may file the complaint as a petition. Unless the juvenile court counselor has filed the complaint as a petition, the juvenile court counselor shall close the juvenile's file in regard to the diverted matter within six months after the date of the contract.

(c) If a teen court program has been established in the district, the juvenile court counselor, upon a finding of legal sufficiency, may refer to a teen court program, any case in which a juvenile has allegedly committed an offense that would be an infraction or misdemeanor if committed by an adult. However, the juvenile court counselor shall not refer a case to a teen court program (i) if the juvenile has been referred to a teen court program previously, or (ii) if the juvenile is alleged to have committed any of the following offenses:

(1)     Driving while impaired under G.S. 20-138.1, 20-138.2, 20-138.3, 20-138.5, or 20-138.7, or any other motor vehicle violation;

(2)     A Class A1 misdemeanor;

(3)     An assault in which a weapon is used; or

(4)     A controlled substance offense under Article 5 of Chapter 90 of the General Statutes, other than simple possession of a Schedule VI drug or alcohol.

(d)     The juvenile court counselor shall maintain diversion plans and contracts entered into pursuant to this section to allow juvenile court counselors to determine when a juvenile has had a complaint diverted previously. Diversion plans and contracts are not public records under Chapter 132 of the General Statutes, shall not be included in the clerk's record pursuant to G.S. 7B-3000, and shall be withheld from public inspection or examination. Diversion plans and contracts shall be destroyed when the juvenile reaches the age of 18 years or when the juvenile is no longer under the jurisdiction of the court, whichever is longer.

(e)     No later than 60 days after the juvenile court counselor diverts a juvenile, the juvenile court counselor shall determine whether the juvenile and the juvenile's parent, guardian, or custodian have complied with the terms of the diversion plan or contract. In making this determination, the juvenile court counselor shall contact any referral resources to determine whether the juvenile and the juvenile's parent, guardian, or custodian complied with any recommendations for treatment or services made by the resource. If the juvenile and the juvenile's parent, guardian, or custodian have not complied, the juvenile court counselor shall reconsider the decision to divert and may authorize the filing of the complaint as a petition within 10 days after making the determination. If the juvenile court counselor does not file a petition, the juvenile court counselor may continue to monitor the case for up to six months from the date of the diversion plan or contract. At any point during that time period if the juvenile and the juvenile's parent, guardian, or custodian fail to comply, the juvenile court counselor shall reconsider the decision to divert and may authorize the filing of the complaint as a petition. After six months, the juvenile court counselor shall close the diversion plan or contract file. (1979, c. 815, s. 1; 1998-202, s. 6; 2001-490, s. 2.9.)

§ 7B-1707. Direct contempt by juvenile.

The preceding sections of this Article do not apply when a juvenile is ordered pursuant to G.S. 5A-32(b) to appear and show cause why the juvenile should not be held in contempt. (2007-168, s. 4.)

Article 18.

Venue; Petition; Summons.

§ 7B-1800. Venue.

(a) A proceeding in which a juvenile is alleged to be delinquent or undisciplined shall be commenced and adjudicated in the district in which the offense is alleged to have occurred. When a proceeding is commenced in a district other than that of the juvenile's residence, the court shall proceed to adjudication in that district and, if the juvenile is in residential treatment or foster care in that district, the court shall conduct the dispositional hearing in that district as well, unless the judge enters an order, supported by findings of fact, that a transfer would serve the ends of justice or is in the best interests of the juvenile.

(b) Except as provided in subsection (a) of this section, after adjudication, the following procedures shall be available to the court:

(1) The court may transfer the proceeding to the court in the district where the juvenile resides for disposition.

(2) Where the proceeding is not transferred under subdivision (1) of this section, the court shall immediately notify the chief district court judge in the district in which the juvenile resides. If the chief district court judge requests a transfer within five days after receipt of notification, the court shall transfer the proceeding.

(3) Where the proceeding is not transferred under subdivision (1) or (2) of this section, the court, upon motion of the juvenile, shall transfer the proceeding

to the court in the district where the juvenile resides for disposition. The court shall advise the juvenile of the juvenile's right to transfer under this section. (1979, c. 815, s. 1; 1998-202, s. 6; 2004-155, s. 1.)

§ 7B-1801. Pleading and process.

The pleading in a juvenile action is the petition. The process in a juvenile action is the summons. (1979, c. 815, s. 1; 1998-202, s. 6.)

§ 7B-1802. Petition.

The petition shall contain the name, date of birth, and address of the juvenile and the name and last known address of the juvenile's parent, guardian, or custodian. The petition shall allege the facts that invoke jurisdiction over the juvenile. The petition shall not contain information on more than one juvenile.

A petition in which delinquency is alleged shall contain a plain and concise statement, without allegations of an evidentiary nature, asserting facts supporting every element of a criminal offense and the juvenile's commission thereof with sufficient precision clearly to apprise the juvenile of the conduct which is the subject of the allegation.

Sufficient copies of the petition shall be prepared so that copies will be available for the juvenile, for each parent if living separate and apart, for the guardian or custodian if any, for the juvenile court counselor, for the prosecutor, and for any person determined by the court to be a necessary party. (1979, c. 815, s. 1; 1981, c. 469, s. 9; 1998-202, s. 6; 2001-490, s. 2.10.)

§ 7B-1803. Receipt of complaints; filing of petition.

(a)    All complaints concerning a juvenile alleged to be delinquent or undisciplined shall be referred to the juvenile court counselor for screening and evaluation. Thereafter, if the juvenile court counselor determines that a petition should be filed, the petition shall be drawn by the juvenile court counselor or the clerk, signed by the complainant, and verified before an official authorized to administer oaths. If the circumstances indicate a need for immediate attachment of jurisdiction and if the juvenile court counselor is out of the county or otherwise unavailable to receive a complaint and to draw a petition when it is needed, the clerk shall assist the complainant in communicating the complaint to the juvenile court counselor by telephone and, with the approval of the juvenile court counselor, shall draw a petition and file it when signed and verified. A copy of the complaint and petition shall be transmitted to the juvenile court counselor.

(b)     If review is requested pursuant to G.S. 7B-1704, the prosecutor shall review a complaint and any decision of the juvenile court counselor not to authorize that the complaint be filed as a petition. If the prosecutor, after review, authorizes a complaint to be filed as a petition, the prosecutor shall prepare the complaint to be filed by the clerk as a petition, recording the day of filing. (1979, c. 815, s. 1; 1981, c. 469, ss. 10, 11; 1998-202, s. 6; 2001-490, s. 2.11; 2012-172, s. 1.)

§ 7B-1804. Commencement of action.

(a)     An action is commenced by the filing of a petition in the clerk's office when that office is open, or by a magistrate's acceptance of a petition for filing pursuant to subsection (b) of this section when the clerk's office is closed.

(b)     When the office of the clerk is closed and the juvenile court counselor requests a petition alleging a juvenile to be delinquent or undisciplined, a magistrate may draw and verify the petition and accept it for filing, which acceptance shall constitute filing. The magistrate's authority under this subsection is limited to emergency situations when a petition is required in order to obtain a secure or nonsecure custody order. Any petition accepted for filing under this subsection shall be delivered to the clerk's office for processing as soon as that office is open for business. (1979, c. 815, s. 1; 1987, c. 409, s. 3; 1998-202, s. 6; 2001-490, s. 2.12.)

§ 7B-1805. Issuance of summons.

(a)     Immediately after a petition has been filed alleging that a juvenile is undisciplined or delinquent, the clerk shall issue a summons to the juvenile and to the parent, guardian, or custodian requiring them to appear for a hearing at the time and place stated in the summons. A copy of the petition shall be attached to each summons.

(b)     A summons shall be on a printed form supplied by the Administrative Office of the Courts and shall include:

(1) Notice of the nature of the proceeding and the purpose of the hearing scheduled on the summons.

(2) Notice of any right to counsel and information about how to seek the appointment of counsel prior to a hearing.

(3) Notice that, if the court determines at the adjudicatory hearing that the allegations of the petition are true, the court will conduct a dispositional hearing and will have jurisdiction to enter orders affecting substantial rights of the juvenile and of the parent, guardian, or custodian, including orders that:

a. Affect the juvenile's custody;

b. Impose conditions on the juvenile;

c. Require that the juvenile receive medical, psychiatric, psychological, or other treatment and that the parent participate in the treatment;

d. Require the parent to undergo psychiatric, psychological, or other treatment or counseling;

e. Order the parent to pay for treatment that is ordered for the juvenile or the parent; and

f. Order the parent to pay support for the juvenile for any period the juvenile does not reside with the parent or to pay attorneys' fees or other fees or expenses as ordered by the court.

(4) Notice that the parent, guardian, or custodian shall be required to attend scheduled hearings and that failure without reasonable cause to attend may result in proceedings for contempt of court.

(5) Notice that the parent, guardian, or custodian shall be responsible for bringing the juvenile before the court at any hearing the juvenile is required to attend and that failure without reasonable cause to bring the juvenile before the court may result in proceedings for contempt of court.

(c) The summons shall advise the parent, guardian, or custodian that upon service, jurisdiction over the parent, guardian, or custodian is obtained and that failure of the parent, guardian, or custodian to appear or bring the juvenile before the court without reasonable cause or to comply with any order of the court pursuant to Article 27 of this Chapter may cause the court to issue a show cause order for contempt. The summons shall contain the following language in bold type:

"TO THE PARENT(S), GUARDIAN(S), OR CUSTODIAN(S): YOUR FAILURE TO APPEAR IN COURT FOR A SCHEDULED HEARING OR TO COMPLY WITH AN ORDER OF THE COURT MAY RESULT IN A FINDING OF CRIMINAL CONTEMPT. A PERSON HELD IN CRIMINAL CONTEMPT MAY BE SUBJECT TO IMPRISONMENT OF UP TO 30 DAYS, A FINE NOT TO EXCEED FIVE HUNDRED DOLLARS ($500.00) OR BOTH."

(d) A summons shall be directed to the person summoned to appear and shall be delivered to any person authorized to serve process. (1979, c. 815, s. 1; 1987 (Reg. Sess., 1988), c. 1090, s. 2; 1995, c. 328, s. 1; 1998-202, s. 6.)

§ 7B-1806. Service of summons.

The summons and petition shall be personally served upon the parent, the guardian, or custodian and the juvenile not less than five days prior to the date of the scheduled hearing. The time for service may be waived in the discretion of the court.

If the parent, guardian, or custodian entitled to receive a summons cannot be found by a diligent effort, the court may authorize service of the summons and petition by mail or by publication. The cost of the service by publication shall be advanced by the petitioner and may be charged as court costs as the court may direct.

The court may issue a show cause order for contempt against a parent, guardian, or custodian who is personally served and fails without reasonable cause to appear and to bring the juvenile before the court.

The provisions of G.S. 15A-301(a), (c), (d), and (e) relating to criminal process apply to juvenile process; provided the period of time for return of an unserved summons is 30 days. (1979, c. 815, s. 1; 1998-202, s. 6.)

§ 7B-1807. Notice to parent and juvenile of scheduled hearings.

The clerk shall give to all parties, including both parents of the juvenile, the juvenile's guardian or custodian, and any other person who has assumed the status and obligation of a parent without being awarded legal custody of the juvenile by a court, five days' written notice of the date and time of all scheduled hearings unless the party is notified in open court or the court orders otherwise. (1998-202, s. 6.)

§ 7B-1808. First appearance for felony cases.

(a) A juvenile who is alleged in the petition to have committed an offense that would be a felony if committed by an adult shall be summoned to appear before the court for a first appearance within 10 days of the filing of the petition. If the juvenile is in secure or nonsecure custody, the first appearance shall take place at the initial hearing required by G.S. 7B-1906. Unless the juvenile is in secure or nonsecure custody, the court may continue the first appearance to a time certain for good cause.

(b) At the first appearance, the court shall:

(1) Inform the juvenile of the allegations set forth in the petition;

(2) Determine whether the juvenile has retained counsel or has been assigned counsel;

(3) If applicable, inform the juvenile of the date of the probable cause hearing, which shall be within 15 days of the first appearance; and

(4) Inform the parent, guardian, or custodian that the parent, guardian, or custodian is required to attend all hearings scheduled in the matter and may be held in contempt of court for failure to attend any scheduled hearing.

If the juvenile is not represented by counsel, counsel for the juvenile shall be appointed in accordance with rules adopted by the Office of Indigent Services. (1998-202, s. 6; 2000-144, s. 20; 2001-487, s. 4.)

Article 19.

Temporary Custody; Secure and Nonsecure Custody; Custody Hearings.

§ 7B-1900. Taking a juvenile into temporary custody.

Temporary custody means the taking of physical custody and providing personal care and supervision until a court order for secure or nonsecure custody can be obtained. A juvenile may be taken into temporary custody without a court order under the following circumstances:

(1) By a law enforcement officer if grounds exist for the arrest of an adult in identical circumstances under G.S. 15A-401(b).

(2) By a law enforcement officer or a juvenile court counselor if there are reasonable grounds to believe that the juvenile is an undisciplined juvenile.

(3) By a law enforcement officer, by a juvenile court counselor, by a member of the Black Mountain Center, Alcohol Rehabilitation Center, and Juvenile Evaluation Center Joint Security Force established pursuant to G.S. 122C-421, or by personnel of the Division if there are reasonable grounds to believe the juvenile is an absconder from any residential facility operated by the Division or from an approved detention facility. (1979, c. 815, s. 1; 1985, c. 408, s. 1; 1985 (Reg. Sess., 1986), c. 863, s. 1; 1994, Ex. Sess., c. 27, s. 2; 1995, c. 391, s. 1; 1997-443, s. 11A.118(a); 1998-202, s. 6; 2000-137, s. 3; 2001-490, s. 2.13; 2011-145, s. 19.1(l).)

§ 7B-1901. Duties of person taking juvenile into temporary custody.

(a) A person who takes a juvenile into custody without a court order under G.S. 7B-1900(1) or (2) shall proceed as follows:

(1) Notify the juvenile's parent, guardian, or custodian that the juvenile has been taken into temporary custody and advise the parent, guardian, or custodian of the right to be present with the juvenile until a determination is made as to the need for secure or nonsecure custody. Failure to notify the parent, guardian, or custodian that the juvenile is in custody shall not be grounds for release of the juvenile.

(2) Release the juvenile to the juvenile's parent, guardian, or custodian if the person having the juvenile in temporary custody decides that continued custody is unnecessary. In the case of a juvenile unlawfully absent from school, if continued custody is unnecessary, the person having temporary custody may deliver the juvenile to the juvenile's school or, if the local city or county

government and the local school board adopt a policy, to a place in the local school administrative unit.

(3)     If the juvenile is not released, request that a petition be drawn pursuant to G.S. 7B-1803 or G.S. 7B-1804. Once the petition has been drawn and verified, the person shall communicate with the juvenile court counselor. If the juvenile court counselor approves the filing of the petition, the juvenile court counselor shall contact the judge or the person delegated authority pursuant to G.S. 7B-1902 if other than the juvenile court counselor, for a determination of the need for continued custody.

(b)     A juvenile taken into temporary custody under this Article shall not be held for more than 12 hours, or for more than 24 hours if any of the 12 hours falls on a Saturday, Sunday, or legal holiday, unless a petition or motion for review has been filed and an order for secure or nonsecure custody has been entered.

(c)     A person who takes a juvenile into custody under G.S. 7B-1900(3), after receiving an order for secure custody, shall transport the juvenile to the nearest approved facility providing secure custody. The person then shall contact the administrator of the facility from which the juvenile absconded, who shall be responsible for returning the juvenile to that facility. (1979, c. 815, s. 1; 1981, c. 335, ss. 1, 2; 1994, Ex. Sess., c. 17, s. 1; c. 27, s. 3; 1995, c. 391, s. 2; 1998-202, s. 6; 2001-490, s. 2.14.)

§ 7B-1902.  Authority to issue custody orders; delegation.

In the case of any juvenile alleged to be within the jurisdiction of the court, when the court finds it necessary to place the juvenile in custody, the court may order that the juvenile be placed in secure or nonsecure custody pursuant to criteria set out in G.S. 7B-1903.

Any district court judge may issue secure and nonsecure custody orders pursuant to G.S. 7B-1903. The chief district court judge may delegate the court's authority to the chief court counselor or the chief court counselor's counseling staff by administrative order filed in the office of the clerk of superior court. The administrative order shall specify which persons may be contacted for approval of a secure or nonsecure custody order. The chief district court judge shall not delegate the court's authority to detain or house juveniles in holdover facilities pursuant to G.S. 7B-1905 or G.S. 7B-2513. (1979, c. 815, s. 1; 1981, c. 425; 1983, c. 590, s. 1; 1998-202, s. 6.)

§ 7B-1903. Criteria for secure or nonsecure custody.

(a) When a request is made for nonsecure custody, the court shall first consider release of the juvenile to the juvenile's parent, guardian, custodian, or other responsible adult. An order for nonsecure custody shall be made only when there is a reasonable factual basis to believe the matters alleged in the petition are true, and that:

(1) The juvenile is a runaway and consents to nonsecure custody; or

(2) The juvenile meets one or more of the criteria for secure custody, but the court finds it in the best interests of the juvenile that the juvenile be placed in a nonsecure placement.

(b) When a request is made for secure custody, the court may order secure custody only where the court finds there is a reasonable factual basis to believe that the juvenile committed the offense as alleged in the petition, and that one of the following circumstances exists:

(1) The juvenile is charged with a felony and has demonstrated that the juvenile is a danger to property or persons.

(2) The juvenile has demonstrated that the juvenile is a danger to persons and is charged with either (i) a misdemeanor at least one element of which is assault on a person or (ii) a misdemeanor in which the juvenile used, threatened to use, or displayed a firearm or other deadly weapon.

(2a) The juvenile has demonstrated that the juvenile is a danger to persons and is charged with a violation of G.S. 20-138.1 or G.S. 20-138.3.

(3) The juvenile has willfully failed to appear on a pending delinquency charge or on charges of violation of probation or post-release supervision, providing the juvenile was properly notified.

(4) A delinquency charge is pending against the juvenile, and there is reasonable cause to believe the juvenile will not appear in court.

(5) The juvenile is an absconder from (i) any residential facility operated by the Division or any detention facility in this State or (ii) any comparable facility in another state.

(6) There is reasonable cause to believe the juvenile should be detained for the juvenile's own protection because the juvenile has recently suffered or attempted self-inflicted physical injury. In such case, the juvenile must have been refused admission by one appropriate hospital, and the period of secure custody is limited to 24 hours to determine the need for inpatient hospitalization. If the juvenile is placed in secure custody, the juvenile shall receive continuous supervision and a physician shall be notified immediately.

(7) The juvenile is alleged to be undisciplined by virtue of the juvenile's being a runaway and is inappropriate for nonsecure custody placement or refuses nonsecure custody, and the court finds that the juvenile needs secure custody for up to 24 hours, excluding Saturdays, Sundays, and State holidays, to evaluate the juvenile's need for medical or psychiatric treatment or to facilitate reunion with the juvenile's parents, guardian, or custodian.

(8) The juvenile is alleged to be undisciplined and has willfully failed to appear in court after proper notice; the juvenile shall be brought to court as soon as possible and in no event should be held more than 24 hours, excluding Saturdays, Sundays, and State holidays.

(c) When a juvenile has been adjudicated delinquent, the court may order secure custody pending the dispositional hearing or pending placement of the juvenile pursuant to G.S. 7B-2506.

(d) The court may order secure custody for a juvenile who is alleged to have violated the conditions of the juvenile's probation or post-release supervision, but only if the juvenile is alleged to have committed acts that damage property or injure persons.

(e) If the criteria for secure custody as set out in subsection (b), (c), or (d) of this section are met, the court may enter an order directing an officer or other authorized person to assume custody of the juvenile and to take the juvenile to the place designated in the order. (1979, c. 815, s. 1; 1981, c. 426, ss. 1-4; c. 526; 1983, c. 590, ss. 2-6; 1987, c. 101; 1987 (Reg. Sess., 1988), c. 1090, s. 3; 1989, c. 550; 1998-202, s. 6; 2000-137, s. 3; 2001-158, s. 1; 2007-493, s. 31; 2011-145, s. 19.1(l); 2012-172, s. 3.)

§ 7B-1904. Order for secure or nonsecure custody.

The custody order shall be in writing and shall direct a law enforcement officer or other authorized person to assume custody of the juvenile and to make due return on the order. The official executing the order shall give a copy of the order to the juvenile's parent, guardian, or custodian. If the order is for nonsecure custody, the official executing the order shall also give a copy of the petition and order to the person or agency with whom the juvenile is being placed. If the order is for secure custody, copies of the petition and custody order shall accompany the juvenile to the detention facility or holdover facility of the jail. A message of the Division of Criminal Information, State Bureau of Investigation, stating that a juvenile petition and secure custody order relating to a specified juvenile are on file in a particular county shall be authority to detain the juvenile in secure custody until a copy of the juvenile petition and secure custody order can be forwarded to the juvenile detention facility. The copies of the juvenile petition and secure custody order shall be transmitted to the detention facility no later than 72 hours after the initial detention of the juvenile.

An officer receiving an order for custody which is complete and regular on its face may execute it in accordance with its terms and need not inquire into its regularity or continued validity, nor does the officer incur criminal or civil liability for its execution. (1979, c. 815, s. 1; 1989, c. 124; 1998-202, s. 6; 2009-311, s. 15.)

§ 7B-1905. Place of secure or nonsecure custody.

(a) A juvenile meeting the criteria set out in G.S. 7B-1903(a), may be placed in nonsecure custody with a department of social services or a person designated in the order for temporary residential placement in:

(1) A licensed foster home or a home otherwise authorized by law to provide such care;

(2) A facility operated by a department of social services; or

(3) Any other home or facility approved by the court and designated in the order.

In placing a juvenile in nonsecure custody, the court shall first consider whether a relative of the juvenile is willing and able to provide proper care and supervision of the juvenile. If the court finds that the relative is willing and able to provide proper care and supervision, the court shall order placement of the juvenile with the relative unless the court finds that placement with the relative would be contrary to the best interest of the juvenile. Placement of a juvenile outside of this State shall be in accordance with the Interstate Compact on the Placement of Children set forth in Article 38 of this Chapter.

(b) Pursuant to G.S. 7B-1903(b), (c), or (d), a juvenile may be temporarily detained in an approved detention facility which shall be separate from any jail, lockup, prison, or other adult penal institution, except as provided in subsection (c) of this section. It shall be unlawful for a county or any unit of government to operate a juvenile detention facility unless the facility meets the standards and rules adopted by the Department of Public Safety.

(c) A juvenile who has allegedly committed an offense that would be a Class A, B1, B2, C, D, or E felony if committed by an adult may be detained in secure custody in a holdover facility up to 72 hours, if the court, based on information provided by the juvenile court counselor, determines that no acceptable alternative placement is available and the protection of the public requires the juvenile be housed in a holdover facility. (1979, c. 815, s. 1; 1983, c. 639, ss. 1, 2; 1997-390, s. 4; 1997-443, s. 11A.118(a); 1998-202, s. 6; 1998-229, s. 3; 1999-423, s. 14; 2001-490, s. 2.15; 2012-172, s. 4.)

§ 7B-1906. Secure or nonsecure custody hearings.

(a) No juvenile shall be held under a secure custody order for more than five calendar days or under a nonsecure custody order for more than seven calendar days without a hearing on the merits or an initial hearing to determine the need for continued custody. A hearing conducted under this subsection may not be continued or waived. In every case in which an order has been entered by an official exercising authority delegated pursuant to G.S. 7B-1902, a hearing to determine the need for continued custody shall be conducted on the day of the next regularly scheduled session of district court in the city or county where the order was entered if the session precedes the expiration of the applicable time period set forth in this subsection. If the session does not precede the expiration of the time period, the hearing may be conducted at another regularly scheduled session of district court in the district where the order was entered.

(b) As long as the juvenile remains in secure or nonsecure custody, further hearings to determine the need for continued secure custody shall be held at intervals of no more than 10 calendar days. A subsequent hearing on continued nonsecure custody shall be held within seven business days, excluding Saturdays, Sundays, and legal holidays when the courthouse is closed for transactions, of the initial hearing required in subsection (a) of this section and hearings thereafter shall be held at intervals of no more than 30 calendar days. In the case of a juvenile alleged to be delinquent, further hearings may be waived only with the consent of the juvenile, through counsel for the juvenile.

(c) The court shall determine whether a juvenile who is alleged to be delinquent has retained counsel or has been assigned counsel; if the juvenile is not represented by counsel, counsel for the juvenile shall be appointed in accordance with rules adopted by the Office of Indigent Defense Services.

(d) At a hearing to determine the need for continued custody, the court shall receive testimony and shall allow the juvenile and the juvenile's parent, guardian, or custodian an opportunity to introduce evidence, to be heard in their own behalf, and to examine witnesses. The State shall bear the burden at every stage of the proceedings to provide clear and convincing evidence that restraints on the juvenile's liberty are necessary and that no less intrusive alternative will suffice. The court shall not be bound by the usual rules of evidence at the hearings.

(e) The court shall be bound by criteria set forth in G.S. 7B-1903 in determining whether continued custody is warranted.

(f) The court may impose appropriate restrictions on the liberty of a juvenile who is released from secure custody, including:

(1) Release on the written promise of the juvenile's parent, guardian, or custodian to produce the juvenile in court for subsequent proceedings;

(2) Release into the care of a responsible person or organization;

(3) Release conditioned on restrictions on activities, associations, residence, or travel if reasonably related to securing the juvenile's presence in court; or

(4) Any other conditions reasonably related to securing the juvenile's presence in court.

(g) If the court determines that the juvenile meets the criteria in G.S. 7B-1903 and should continue in custody, the court shall issue an order to that effect. The order shall be in writing with appropriate findings of fact. The findings of fact shall include the evidence relied upon in reaching the decision and the purposes which continued custody is to achieve.

(h) The hearing to determine the need to continue custody may be conducted by audio and video transmission which allows the court and the juvenile to see and hear each other. If the juvenile has counsel, the juvenile may communicate fully and confidentially with the juvenile's attorney during the proceeding. Prior to the use of audio and video transmission, the procedures and type of equipment for audio and video transmission shall be submitted to the Administrative Office of the Courts by the chief district court judge and approved by the Administrative Office of the Courts. (1979, c. 815, s. 1; 1981, c. 469, s. 13; 1987 (Reg. Sess., 1988), c. 1090, s. 4; 1994, Ex. Sess., c. 27, s. 1; 1997-390, ss. 5, 6; 1998-202, s. 6; 1998-229, s. 4; 2000-144, s. 21; 2003-337, s. 10.)

§ 7B-1907. Telephonic communication authorized.

All communications, notices, orders, authorizations, and requests authorized or required by G.S. 7B-1901, 7B-1903, and 7B-1904 may be made by telephone when other means of communication are impractical. All written orders pursuant to telephonic communication shall bear the name and the title of the person communicating by telephone, the signature and the title of the official entering the order, and the hour and the date of the authorization. (1979, c. 815, s. 1; 1998-202, s. 6.)

Article 20.

Basic Rights.

§ 7B-2000. Juvenile's right to counsel; presumption of indigence.

(a) A juvenile alleged to be within the jurisdiction of the court has the right to be represented by counsel in all proceedings. Counsel for the juvenile shall be appointed in accordance with rules adopted by the Office of Indigent Defense Services, unless counsel is retained for the juvenile, in any proceeding in which the juvenile is alleged to be (i) delinquent or (ii) in contempt of court when alleged or adjudicated to be undisciplined.

(b) All juveniles shall be conclusively presumed to be indigent, and it shall not be necessary for the court to receive from any juvenile an affidavit of indigency. (1979, c. 815, s. 1; 1998-202, s. 6; 2000-144, s. 22.)

§ 7B-2001. Appointment of guardian.

In any case when no parent, guardian, or custodian appears in a hearing with the juvenile or when the court finds it would be in the best interests of the juvenile, the court may appoint a guardian of the person for the juvenile. The guardian shall operate under the supervision of the court with or without bond and shall file only such reports as the court shall require. Unless the court orders otherwise, the guardian:

(1) Shall have the care, custody, and control of the juvenile or may arrange a suitable placement for the juvenile.

(2) May represent the juvenile in legal actions before any court.

(3) May consent to certain actions on the part of the juvenile in place of the parent or custodian, including (i) marriage, (ii) enlisting in the Armed Forces of the United States, and (iii) enrollment in school.

(4) May consent to any necessary remedial, psychological, medical, or surgical treatment for the juvenile.

The authority of the guardian shall continue until the guardianship is terminated by court order, until the juvenile is emancipated pursuant to Subchapter IV of this Chapter, or until the juvenile reaches the age of majority. (1979, c. 815, s. 1; 1997-390, s. 7; 1998-202, s. 6; 2011-183, s. 5.)

§ 7B-2002. Payment of court-appointed attorney.

An attorney appointed pursuant to G.S. 7B-2000 or pursuant to any other provision of this Subchapter shall be paid a reasonable fee in accordance with rules adopted by the Office of Indigent Defense Services. The court may require payment of the attorneys' fees from a person other than the juvenile as provided in G.S. 7A-450.1, 7A-450.2, and 7A-450.3. A person who does not comply with the court's order of payment may be found in civil contempt as provided in G.S. 5A-21. (1979, c. 815, s. 1; 1983, c. 726, ss. 2, 3; 1987 (Reg. Sess., 1988), c. 1090, s. 6; 1991, c. 575, s. 1; 1998-202, s. 6; 2000-144, s. 23.)

Article 21.

Law Enforcement Procedures in Delinquency Proceedings.

§ 7B-2100. Role of the law enforcement officer.

A law enforcement officer who takes a juvenile into temporary custody should select the most appropriate course of action to the situation, the needs of the juvenile, and the protection of the public safety. The officer may:

(1) Release the juvenile, with or without first counseling the juvenile;

(2) Release the juvenile to the juvenile's parent, guardian, or custodian;

(3) Refer the juvenile to community resources;

(4) Seek a petition; or

(5) Seek a petition and request a custody order. (1979, c. 815, s. 1; 1998-202, s. 6.)

§ 7B-2101. Interrogation procedures.

(a) Any juvenile in custody must be advised prior to questioning:

(1) That the juvenile has a right to remain silent;

(2) That any statement the juvenile does make can be and may be used against the juvenile;

(3) That the juvenile has a right to have a parent, guardian, or custodian present during questioning; and

(4) That the juvenile has a right to consult with an attorney and that one will be appointed for the juvenile if the juvenile is not represented and wants representation.

(b) When the juvenile is less than 14 years of age, no in-custody admission or confession resulting from interrogation may be admitted into evidence unless the confession or admission was made in the presence of the juvenile's parent, guardian, custodian, or attorney. If an attorney is not present, the parent, guardian, or custodian as well as the juvenile must be advised of the juvenile's rights as set out in subsection (a) of this section; however, a parent, guardian, or custodian may not waive any right on behalf of the juvenile.

(c) If the juvenile indicates in any manner and at any stage of questioning pursuant to this section that the juvenile does not wish to be questioned further, the officer shall cease questioning.

(d) Before admitting into evidence any statement resulting from custodial interrogation, the court shall find that the juvenile knowingly, willingly, and understandingly waived the juvenile's rights. (1979, c. 815, s. 1; 1998-202, s. 6.)

§ 7B-2102. Fingerprinting and photographing juveniles.

(a) A law enforcement officer or agency shall fingerprint and photograph a juvenile who was 10 years of age or older at the time the juvenile allegedly committed a nondivertible offense as set forth in G.S. 7B-1701, when a complaint has been prepared for filing as a petition and the juvenile is in physical custody of law enforcement or the Division.

(a1) A county juvenile detention facility shall photograph a juvenile who has been committed to that facility. The county detention facility shall release any photograph it makes or receives pursuant to this section to the Division, upon the Division's request. The duty of confidentiality in subsection (d) of this section applies to the Division, except as provided in G.S. 7B-3102.

(b) If a law enforcement officer or agency does not take the fingerprints or a photograph of the juvenile pursuant to subsection (a) of this section or the fingerprints or photograph have been destroyed pursuant to subsection (e) of this section, a law enforcement officer or agency shall fingerprint and photograph a juvenile who has been adjudicated delinquent if the juvenile was

10 years of age or older at the time the juvenile committed an offense that would be a felony if committed by an adult.

(c) A law enforcement officer, facility, or agency who fingerprints or photographs a juvenile pursuant to this section shall do so in a proper format for transfer to the State Bureau of Investigation and the Federal Bureau of Investigation. After the juvenile, who was 10 years of age or older at the time of the offense, is adjudicated delinquent of an offense that would be a felony if committed by an adult, fingerprints obtained pursuant to this section shall be transferred to the State Bureau of Investigation and placed in the Automated Fingerprint Identification System (AFIS) to be used for all investigative and comparison purposes. Photographs obtained pursuant to this section shall be placed in a format approved by the State Bureau of Investigation and may be used for all investigative or comparison purposes. The State Bureau of Investigation shall release any photograph it receives pursuant to this section to the Division, upon the Division's request. The duty of confidentiality in subsection (d) of this section applies to the Division, except as provided in G.S. 7B-3102.

(d) Fingerprints and photographs taken pursuant to this section are not public records under Chapter 132 of the General Statutes, shall not be included in the clerk's record pursuant to G.S. 7B-3000, shall be withheld from public inspection or examination, and shall not be eligible for expunction pursuant to G.S. 7B-3200. Fingerprints and photographs taken pursuant to this section shall be maintained separately from any juvenile record, other than the electronic file maintained by the State Bureau of Investigation.

(d1) Repealed by Session Laws 2007-458, s. 1, effective October 1, 2007.

(e) If a juvenile is fingerprinted and photographed pursuant to subsection (a) of this section, the custodian of records shall destroy all fingerprints and photographs at the earlier of the following:

(1) The juvenile court counselor or prosecutor does not file a petition against the juvenile within one year of fingerprinting and photographing the juvenile pursuant to subsection (a) of this section;

(2) The court does not find probable cause pursuant to G.S. 7B-2202; or

(3) The juvenile is not adjudicated delinquent of any offense that would be a felony or a misdemeanor if committed by an adult.

The chief court counselor shall notify the local custodian of records, and the local custodian of records shall notify any other record-holding agencies, when a decision is made not to file a petition, the court does not find probable cause, or the court does not adjudicate the juvenile delinquent. (1996, 2nd Ex. Sess., c. 18, s. 23.2(a); 1998-202, s. 6; 2000-137, s. 3; 2001-490, s. 2.16; 2003-297, s. 2; 2007-458, ss. 1, 3(a), (b); 2011-145, s. 19.1(l).)

§ 7B-2103. Authority to issue nontestimonial identification order where juvenile alleged to be delinquent.

Except as provided in G.S. 7B-2102, nontestimonial identification procedures shall not be conducted on any juvenile without a court order issued pursuant to this Article unless the juvenile has been charged as an adult or transferred to superior court for trial as an adult in which case procedures applicable to adults, as set out in Articles 14 and 23 of Chapter 15A of the General Statutes, shall apply. A nontestimonial identification order authorized by this Article may be issued by any judge of the district court or of the superior court upon request of a prosecutor. As used in this Article, "nontestimonial identification" means identification by fingerprints, palm prints, footprints, measurements, blood specimens, urine specimens, saliva samples, hair samples, or other reasonable physical examination, handwriting exemplars, voice samples, photographs, and lineups or similar identification procedures requiring the presence of a juvenile. (1979, c. 815, s. 1; 1981, c. 454, s. 1; 1998-202, s. 6.)

§ 7B-2104. Time of application for nontestimonial identification order.

A request for a nontestimonial identification order may be made prior to taking a juvenile into custody or after custody and prior to the adjudicatory hearing. (1979, c. 815, s. 1; 1981, c. 454, s. 2; 1998-202, s. 6.)

§ 7B-2105. Grounds for nontestimonial identification order.

(a)     Except as provided in subsection (b) of this section, a nontestimonial identification order may issue only on affidavit or affidavits sworn to before the court and establishing the following grounds for the order:

(1)     That there is probable cause to believe that an offense has been committed that would be a felony if committed by an adult;

(2) That there are reasonable grounds to suspect that the juvenile named or described in the affidavit committed the offense; and

(3) That the results of specific nontestimonial identification procedures will be of material aid in determining whether the juvenile named in the affidavit committed the offense.

(b) A nontestimonial identification order to obtain a blood specimen from a juvenile may issue only on affidavit or affidavits sworn to before the court and establishing the following grounds for the order:

(1) That there is probable cause to believe that an offense has been committed that would be a felony if committed by an adult;

(2) That there is probable cause to believe that the juvenile named or described in the affidavit committed the offense; and

(3) That there is probable cause to believe that obtaining a blood specimen from the juvenile will be of material aid in determining whether the juvenile named in the affidavit committed the offense. (1979, c. 815, s. 1; 1997-80, s. 11; 1998-202, s. 6.)

§ 7B-2106. Issuance of order.

Upon a showing that the grounds specified in G.S. 7B-2105 exist, the judge may issue an order following the same procedure as in the case of adults under G.S. 15A-274, 15A-275, 15A-276, 15A-277, 15A-278, 15A-279, 15A-280, and 15A-282. (1979, c. 815, s. 1; 1998-202, s. 6.)

§ 7B-2107. Nontestimonial identification order at request of juvenile.

A juvenile in custody for or charged with an offense which if committed by an adult would be a felony offense may request that nontestimonial identification procedures be conducted. If it appears that the results of specific nontestimonial identification procedures will be of material aid to the juvenile's defense, the judge to whom the request was directed must order the State to conduct the identification procedures. (1979, c. 815, s. 1; 1997-80, s. 12; 1998-202, s. 6.)

§ 7B-2108.  Destruction of records resulting from nontestimonial identification procedures.

The results of any nontestimonial identification procedures shall be retained or disposed of as follows:

(1)     If a petition is not filed against a juvenile who has been the subject of nontestimonial identification procedures, all records of the evidence shall be destroyed.

(2)     If the juvenile is not adjudicated delinquent or convicted in superior court following transfer, all records resulting from a nontestimonial order shall be destroyed. Further, in the case of a juvenile who is under 13 years of age and who is adjudicated delinquent for an offense that would be less than a felony if committed by an adult, all records shall be destroyed.

(3)     If a juvenile 13 years of age or older is adjudicated delinquent for an offense that would be a felony if committed by an adult, all records resulting from a nontestimonial order may be retained in the court file. Special precautions shall be taken to ensure that these records will be maintained in a manner and under sufficient safeguards to limit their use to inspection by law enforcement officers for comparison purposes in the investigation of a crime.

(4)     If the juvenile is transferred to and convicted in superior court, all records resulting from nontestimonial identification procedures shall be processed as in the case of an adult.

(5)     Any evidence seized pursuant to a nontestimonial order shall be retained by law enforcement officers until further order is entered by the court.

(6)     Destruction of nontestimonial identification records pursuant to this section shall be performed by the law enforcement agency having possession of the records. Following destruction, the law enforcement agency shall make written certification to the court of the destruction. (1979, c. 815, s. 1; 1994, Ex. Sess., c. 22, s. 28; 1998-202, s. 6.)


§ 7B-2109.  Penalty for willful violation.

Any person who willfully violates provisions of this Article which prohibit conducting nontestimonial identification procedures without an order issued by the court shall be guilty of a Class 1 misdemeanor. (1979, c. 815, s. 1; 1993, c. 539, s. 5; 1994, Ex. Sess., c. 24, s. 14(c); 1998-202, s. 6.)

Article 22.

Probable Cause Hearing and Transfer Hearing.

§ 7B-2200.  Transfer of jurisdiction of juvenile to superior court.

After notice, hearing, and a finding of probable cause the court may, upon motion of the prosecutor or the juvenile's attorney or upon its own motion, transfer jurisdiction over a juvenile to superior court if the juvenile was 13 years of age or older at the time the juvenile allegedly committed an offense that would be a felony if committed by an adult. If the alleged felony constitutes a Class A felony and the court finds probable cause, the court shall transfer the case to the superior court for trial as in the case of adults. (1979, c. 815, s. 1; 1991 (Reg. Sess., 1992), c. 842, s. 1; 1994, Ex. Sess., c. 22, s. 25; 1998-202, s. 6.)

§ 7B-2201.  Fingerprinting and DNA sample from juvenile transferred to superior court.

(a) When jurisdiction over a juvenile is transferred to the superior court, the juvenile shall be fingerprinted and the juvenile's fingerprints shall be sent to the State Bureau of Investigation.

(b) When jurisdiction over a juvenile is transferred to the superior court, a DNA sample shall be taken from the juvenile if any of the offenses for which the juvenile is transferred are included in the provisions of G.S. 15A-266.3A. (1981, c. 862, s. 2; 1998-202, s. 6; 2010-94, s. 13.)

§ 7B-2202.  Probable cause hearing.

(a) The court shall conduct a hearing to determine probable cause in all felony cases in which a juvenile was 13 years of age or older when the offense was allegedly committed. The hearing shall be conducted within 15 days of the date of the juvenile's first appearance. The court may continue the hearing for good cause.

(b) At the probable cause hearing:

(1) A prosecutor shall represent the State;

(2) The juvenile shall be represented by counsel;

(3) The juvenile may testify, call, and examine witnesses, and present evidence; and

(4) Each witness shall testify under oath or affirmation and be subject to cross-examination.

(c) The State shall by nonhearsay evidence, or by evidence that satisfies an exception to the hearsay rule, show that there is probable cause to believe that the offense charged has been committed and that there is probable cause to believe that the juvenile committed it, except:

(1) A report or copy of a report made by a physicist, chemist, firearms identification expert, fingerprint technician, or an expert or technician in some other scientific, professional, or medical field, concerning the results of an examination, comparison, or test performed in connection with the case in issue, when stated in a report by that person, is admissible in evidence;

(2) If there is no serious contest, reliable hearsay is admissible to prove value, ownership of property, possession of property in a person other than the juvenile, lack of consent of the owner, possessor, or custodian of property to the breaking or entering of premises, chain of custody, and authenticity of signatures.

(d) Counsel for the juvenile may waive in writing the right to the hearing and stipulate to a finding of probable cause.

(e) If probable cause is found and transfer to superior court is not required by G.S. 7B-2200, upon motion of the prosecutor or the juvenile's attorney or upon its own motion, the court shall either proceed to a transfer hearing or set a date for that hearing. If the juvenile has not received notice of the intention to seek transfer at least five days prior to the probable cause hearing, the court, at the request of the juvenile, shall continue the transfer hearing.

(f) If the court does not find probable cause for a felony offense, the court shall:

(1) Dismiss the proceeding, or

(2) If the court finds probable cause to believe that the juvenile committed a lesser included offense that would constitute a misdemeanor if committed by an adult, either proceed to an adjudicatory hearing or set a date for that hearing. (1979, c. 815, s. 1; 1981, c. 469, ss. 15, 16; 1994, Ex. Sess., c. 22, s. 26; 1998-202, s. 6.)

§ 7B-2203. Transfer hearing.

(a) At the transfer hearing, the prosecutor and the juvenile may be heard and may offer evidence, and the juvenile's attorney may examine any court or probation records, or other records the court may consider in determining whether to transfer the case.

(b) In the transfer hearing, the court shall determine whether the protection of the public and the needs of the juvenile will be served by transfer of the case to superior court and shall consider the following factors:

(1) The age of the juvenile;

(2) The maturity of the juvenile;

(3) The intellectual functioning of the juvenile;

(4) The prior record of the juvenile;

(5) Prior attempts to rehabilitate the juvenile;

(6) Facilities or programs available to the court prior to the expiration of the court's jurisdiction under this Subchapter and the likelihood that the juvenile would benefit from treatment or rehabilitative efforts;

(7) Whether the alleged offense was committed in an aggressive, violent, premeditated, or willful manner; and

(8) The seriousness of the offense and whether the protection of the public requires that the juvenile be prosecuted as an adult.

(c) Any order of transfer shall specify the reasons for transfer. When the case is transferred to superior court, the superior court has jurisdiction over that felony, any offense based on the same act or transaction or on a series of acts or transactions connected together or constituting parts of a single scheme or plan of that felony, and any greater or lesser included offense of that felony.

(d) If the court does not transfer the case to superior court, the court shall either proceed to an adjudicatory hearing or set a date for that hearing. (1979, c. 815, s. 1; 1983, c. 532, s. 1; 1994, Ex. Sess., c. 22, s. 27; 1998-202, s. 6.)

§ 7B-2204. Right to pretrial release; detention.

Once the order of transfer has been entered, the juvenile has the right to pretrial release as provided in G.S. 15A-533 and G.S 15A-534. The release order shall specify the person or persons to whom the juvenile may be released. Pending release, the court shall order that the juvenile be detained in a detention facility while awaiting trial. The court may order the juvenile to be held in a holdover facility at any time the presence of the juvenile is required in court for pretrial hearings or trial, if the court finds that it would be inconvenient to return the juvenile to the detention facility.

Should the juvenile be found guilty, or enter a plea of guilty or no contest to a criminal offense in superior court and receive an active sentence, then immediate transfer to the Division of Adult Correction of the Department of Public Safety shall be ordered. Until such time as the juvenile is transferred to the Division of Adult Correction of the Department of Public Safety, the juvenile may be detained in a holdover facility. The juvenile may not be detained in a detention facility pending transfer to the Division of Adult Correction of the Department of Public Safety.

The juvenile may be kept by the Division of Adult Correction of the Department of Public Safety as a safekeeper until the juvenile is placed in an appropriate correctional program. (1979, c. 815, s. 1; 1987, c. 144; 1991, c. 352, s. 1; 1998-202, s. 6; 2011-145, s. 19.1(h).)

Article 23.

Discovery.

§ 7B-2300. Disclosure of evidence by petitioner.

(a) Statement of the Juvenile. - Upon motion of a juvenile alleged to be delinquent, the court shall order the petitioner:

(1) To permit the juvenile to inspect and copy any relevant written or recorded statements within the possession, custody, or control of the petitioner made by the juvenile or any other party charged in the same action; and

(2) To divulge, in written or recorded form, the substance of any oral statement made by the juvenile or any other party charged in the same action.

(b) Names of Witnesses. - Upon motion of the juvenile, the court shall order the petitioner to furnish the names of persons to be called as witnesses. A copy of the record of witnesses under the age of 16 shall be provided by the petitioner to the juvenile upon the juvenile's motion if accessible to the petitioner.

(c) Documents and Tangible Objects. - Upon motion of the juvenile, the court shall order the petitioner to permit the juvenile to inspect and copy books, papers, documents, photographs, motion pictures, mechanical or electronic recordings, tangible objects, or portions thereof:

(1) Which are within the possession, custody, or control of the petitioner, the prosecutor, or any law enforcement officer conducting an investigation of the matter alleged; and

(2) Which are material to the preparation of the defense, are intended for use by the petitioner as evidence, or were obtained from or belong to the juvenile.

(d) Reports of Examinations and Tests. - Upon motion of a juvenile, the court shall order the petitioner to permit the juvenile to inspect and copy results of physical or mental examinations or of tests, measurements, or experiments made in connection with the case, within the possession, custody, or control of the petitioner. In addition upon motion of a juvenile, the court shall order the petitioner to permit the juvenile to inspect, examine, and test, subject to appropriate safeguards, any physical evidence or a sample of it or tests or experiments made in connection with the evidence in the case if it is available to the petitioner, the prosecutor, or any law enforcement officer conducting an investigation of the matter alleged, and if the petitioner intends to offer the evidence at trial.

(e) Except as provided in subsections (a) through (d) of this section, this Article does not require the production of reports, memoranda, or other internal documents made by the petitioner, law enforcement officers, or other persons acting on behalf of the petitioner in connection with the investigation or prosecution of the case or of statements made by witnesses or the petitioner to anyone acting on behalf of the petitioner.

(f) Nothing in this section prohibits a petitioner from making voluntary disclosures in the interest of justice. (1979, c. 815, s. 1; 1998-202, s. 6.)

§ 7B-2301. Disclosure of evidence by juvenile.

(a) Names of Witnesses. - Upon motion of the petitioner, the court shall order the juvenile to furnish to the petitioner the names of persons to be called as witnesses.

(b) Documents and Tangible Objects. - If the court grants any relief sought by the juvenile under G.S. 7B-2300, upon motion of the petitioner, the court shall order the juvenile to permit the petitioner to inspect and copy books, papers, documents, photographs, motion pictures, mechanical or electronic recordings, tangible objects, or portions thereof which are within the possession, custody, or control of the juvenile and which the juvenile intends to introduce in evidence.

(c) Reports of Examinations and Tests. - If the court grants any relief sought by the juvenile under G.S. 7B-2300, upon motion of the petitioner, the court shall order the juvenile to permit the petitioner to inspect and copy results of physical or mental examinations or of tests, measurements, or experiments made in connection with the case within the possession and control of the juvenile which the juvenile intends to introduce in evidence or which were prepared by a witness whom the juvenile intends to call if the results relate to the witness's testimony. In addition, upon motion of a petitioner, the court shall order the juvenile to permit the petitioner to inspect, examine, and test, subject to appropriate safeguards, any physical evidence or a sample of it if the juvenile intends to offer the evidence or tests or experiments made in connection with the evidence in the case. (1979, c. 815, s. 1; 1998-202, s. 6.)

§ 7B-2302. Regulation of discovery; protective orders.

(a) Upon written motion of a party and a finding of good cause, the court may at any time order that discovery or inspection be denied, restricted, or deferred.

(b) The court may permit a party seeking relief under subsection (a) of this section to submit supporting affidavits or statements to the court for in camera inspection. If thereafter the court enters an order granting relief under subsection (a) of this section, the material submitted in camera must be available to the Court of Appeals in the event of an appeal. (1979, c. 815, s. 1; 1998-202, s. 6.)

§ 7B-2303. Continuing duty to disclose.

If a party, subject to compliance with an order issued pursuant to this Article, discovers additional evidence prior to or during the hearing or decides to use additional evidence, and if the evidence is or may be subject to discovery or inspection under this Article, the party shall promptly notify the other party of the existence of the additional evidence or of the name of each additional witness. (1979, c. 815, s. 1; 1998-202, s. 6.)

Article 24.

Hearing Procedures.

§ 7B-2400. Amendment of petition.

The court may permit a petition to be amended when the amendment does not change the nature of the offense alleged. If a motion to amend is allowed, the juvenile shall be given a reasonable opportunity to prepare a defense to the amended allegations. (1979, c. 815, s. 1; 1998-202, s. 6.)

§ 7B-2401. Determination of incapacity to proceed; evidence; temporary commitment; temporary orders.

The provisions of G.S. 15A-1001, 15A-1002, and 15A-1003 apply to all cases in which a juvenile is alleged to be delinquent. No juvenile committed under this section may be placed in a situation where the juvenile will come in contact with adults committed for any purpose. (1979, c. 815, s. 1; 1998-202, s. 6.)

§ 7B-2402. Open hearings.

All hearings authorized or required pursuant to this Subchapter shall be open to the public unless the court closes the hearing or part of the hearing for good cause, upon motion of a party or its own motion. If the court closes the hearing or part of the hearing to the public, the court may allow any victim, member of a victim's family, law enforcement officer, witness or any other person directly involved in the hearing to be present at the hearing.

In determining good cause to close a hearing or part of a hearing, the court shall consider the circumstances of the case, including, but not limited to, the following factors:

(1)     The nature of the allegations against the juvenile;

(2)     The age and maturity of the juvenile;

(3)     The benefit to the juvenile of confidentiality;

(4)     The benefit to the public of an open hearing; and

(5)     The extent to which the confidentiality of the juvenile's file will be compromised by an open hearing.

No hearing or part of a hearing shall be closed by the court if the juvenile requests that it remain open. (1979, c. 815, s. 1; 1998-202, s. 6; 1998-229, s. 5.)

§ 7B-2402.1. Restraint of juveniles in courtroom.

At any hearing authorized or required by this Subchapter, the judge may subject a juvenile to physical restraint in the courtroom only when the judge finds the restraint to be reasonably necessary to maintain order, prevent the juvenile's escape, or provide for the safety of the courtroom. Whenever practical, the judge shall provide the juvenile and the juvenile's attorney an opportunity to be heard to contest the use of restraints before the judge orders the use of restraints. If restraints are ordered, the judge shall make findings of fact in support of the order. (2007-100, s. 1.)

§ 7B-2403. Adjudicatory hearing.

The adjudicatory hearing shall be held within a reasonable time in the district at the time and place the chief district court judge designates. (1979, c. 815, s. 1; 1998-202, s. 6; 1998-229, s. 5.)

§ 7B-2404. Participation of the prosecutor.

A prosecutor shall represent the State in contested delinquency hearings including first appearance, detention, probable cause, transfer, adjudicatory, dispositional, probation revocation, post-release supervision, and extended jurisdiction hearings. (1979, c. 815, s. 1; 1981, c. 469, s. 12; 1998-202, s. 6.)

§ 7B-2405. Conduct of the adjudicatory hearing.

The adjudicatory hearing shall be a judicial process designed to determine whether the juvenile is undisciplined or delinquent. In the adjudicatory hearing, the court shall protect the following rights of the juvenile and the juvenile's parent, guardian, or custodian to assure due process of law:

(1) The right to written notice of the facts alleged in the petition;

(2) The right to counsel;

(3) The right to confront and cross-examine witnesses;

(4) The privilege against self-incrimination;

(5) The right of discovery; and

(6) All rights afforded adult offenders except the right to bail, the right of self-representation, and the right of trial by jury. (1979, c. 815, s. 1; 1998-202, s. 6.)

§ 7B-2406. Continuances.

The court for good cause may continue the hearing for as long as is reasonably required to receive additional evidence, reports, or assessments that the court has requested, or other information needed in the best interests of the juvenile and to allow for a reasonable time for the parties to conduct expeditious discovery. Otherwise, continuances shall be granted only in extraordinary circumstances when necessary for the proper administration of justice or in the best interests of the juvenile. (1979, c. 815, s. 1; 1987 (Reg. Sess., 1988), c. 1090, s. 9; 1998-202, s. 6.)

§ 7B-2407. When admissions by juvenile may be accepted.

(a) The court may accept an admission from a juvenile only after first addressing the juvenile personally and:

(1) Informing the juvenile that the juvenile has a right to remain silent and that any statement the juvenile makes may be used against the juvenile;

(2) Determining that the juvenile understands the nature of the charge;

(3) Informing the juvenile that the juvenile has a right to deny the allegations;

(4) Informing the juvenile that by the juvenile's admissions the juvenile waives the juvenile's right to be confronted by the witnesses against the juvenile;

(5) Determining that the juvenile is satisfied with the juvenile's representation; and

(6) Informing the juvenile of the most restrictive disposition on the charge.

(b) By inquiring of the prosecutor, the juvenile's attorney, and the juvenile personally, the court shall determine whether there were any prior discussions involving admissions, whether the parties have entered into any arrangement with respect to the admissions and the terms thereof, and whether any improper pressure was exerted. The court may accept an admission from a juvenile only after determining that the admission is a product of informed choice.

(c) The court may accept an admission only after determining that there is a factual basis for the admission. This determination may be based upon any of the following information: a statement of the facts by the prosecutor; a written statement of the juvenile; sworn testimony which may include reliable hearsay; or a statement of facts by the juvenile's attorney. (1979, c. 815, s. 1; 1998-202, s. 6.)

§ 7B-2408. Rules of evidence.

If the juvenile denies the allegations of the petition, the court shall proceed in accordance with the rules of evidence applicable to criminal cases. In addition, no statement made by a juvenile to the juvenile court counselor during the preliminary inquiry and evaluation process shall be admissible prior to the dispositional hearing. (1979, c. 815, s. 1; 1981, ch. 469, s. 17; 1998-202, s. 6; 2001-490, s. 2.17.)

§ 7B-2409. Quantum of proof in adjudicatory hearing.

The allegations of a petition alleging the juvenile is delinquent shall be proved beyond a reasonable doubt. The allegations in a petition alleging undisciplined behavior shall be proved by clear and convincing evidence. (1979, c. 815, s. 1; 1998-202, s. 6.)

§ 7B-2410. Record of proceedings.

All adjudicatory and dispositional hearings and hearings on probable cause and transfer to superior court shall be recorded by stenographic notes or by electronic or mechanical means. Records shall be reduced to a written transcript only when timely notice of appeal has been given. The court may order that other hearings be recorded. (1979, c. 815, s. 1; 1998-202, s. 6.)

§ 7B-2411. Adjudication.

If the court finds that the allegations in the petition have been proved as provided in G.S. 7B-2409, the court shall so state in a written order of adjudication, which shall include, but not be limited to, the date of the offense, the misdemeanor or felony classification of the offense, and the date of adjudication. If the court finds that the allegations have not been proved, the court shall dismiss the petition with prejudice and the juvenile shall be released from secure or nonsecure custody if the juvenile is in custody. (1979, c. 815, s. 1; 1998-202, s. 6; 2009-545, s. 4.)

§ 7B-2412. Legal effect of adjudication of delinquency.

An adjudication that a juvenile is delinquent or commitment of a juvenile to the Division for placement in a youth development center shall neither be considered conviction of any criminal offense nor cause the juvenile to forfeit any citizenship rights. (1979, c. 815, s. 1; 1998-202, s. 6; 2000-137, s. 3; 2001-95, s. 5; 2011-145, s. 19.1(l).)

§ 7B-2413. Predisposition investigation and report.

The court shall proceed to the dispositional hearing upon receipt of the predisposition report. A risk and needs assessment, containing information regarding the juvenile's social, medical, psychiatric, psychological, and educational history, as well as any factors indicating the probability of the juvenile committing further delinquent acts, shall be conducted for the juvenile and shall be attached to the predisposition report. In cases where no predisposition report is available and the court makes a written finding that a report is not needed, the court may proceed with the dispositional hearing. No predisposition report or risk and needs assessment of any child alleged to be delinquent or undisciplined shall be made prior to an adjudication that the juvenile is within the juvenile jurisdiction of the court unless the juvenile, the juvenile's parent, guardian, or custodian, or the juvenile's attorney files a written statement with the juvenile court counselor granting permission and giving consent to the predisposition report or risk and needs assessment. No predisposition report shall be submitted to or considered by the court prior to the completion of the adjudicatory hearing. The court shall permit the juvenile to inspect any predisposition report, including any attached risk and needs assessment, to be considered by the court in making the disposition unless the court determines that disclosure would seriously harm the juvenile's treatment or rehabilitation or would violate a promise of confidentiality. Opportunity to offer evidence in rebuttal shall be afforded the juvenile and the juvenile's parent, guardian, or custodian at the dispositional hearing. The court may order counsel not to disclose parts of the report to the juvenile or the juvenile's parent, guardian, or custodian if the court finds that disclosure would seriously harm the treatment or rehabilitation of the juvenile or would violate a promise of confidentiality given to a source of information. (1979, c. 815, s. 1; 1998-202, s. 6; 1999-423, s. 13; 2001-490, s. 2.18.)

§ 7B-2414. When jeopardy attaches.

Jeopardy attaches in an adjudicatory hearing when the court begins to hear evidence. (1979, c. 815, s. 1; 1998-202, s. 6.)

Article 25.

Dispositions.

§ 7B-2500. Purpose.

The purpose of dispositions in juvenile actions is to design an appropriate plan to meet the needs of the juvenile and to achieve the objectives of the State in exercising jurisdiction, including the protection of the public. The court should develop a disposition in each case that:

(1)     Promotes public safety;

(2)     Emphasizes accountability and responsibility of both the parent, guardian, or custodian and the juvenile for the juvenile's conduct; and

(3)     Provides the appropriate consequences, treatment, training, and rehabilitation to assist the juvenile toward becoming a nonoffending, responsible, and productive member of the community. (1979, c. 815, s. 1; 1995 (Reg. Sess., 1996), c. 609, s. 1; 1998-202, s. 6.)

§ 7B-2501. Dispositional hearing.

(a) The dispositional hearing may be informal, and the court may consider written reports or other evidence concerning the needs of the juvenile. The court may consider any evidence, including hearsay evidence as defined in G.S. 8C-1, Rule 801, that the court finds to be relevant, reliable, and necessary to determine the needs of the juvenile and the most appropriate disposition.

(b) The juvenile and the juvenile's parent, guardian, or custodian shall have an opportunity to present evidence, and they may advise the court concerning the disposition they believe to be in the best interests of the juvenile.

(c) In choosing among statutorily permissible dispositions, the court shall select the most appropriate disposition both in terms of kind and duration for the delinquent juvenile. Within the guidelines set forth in G.S. 7B-2508, the court shall select a disposition that is designed to protect the public and to meet the needs and best interests of the juvenile, based upon:

(1) The seriousness of the offense;

(2) The need to hold the juvenile accountable;

(3) The importance of protecting the public safety;

(4) The degree of culpability indicated by the circumstances of the particular case; and

(5) The rehabilitative and treatment needs of the juvenile indicated by a risk and needs assessment.

(d) The court may dismiss the case, or continue the case for no more than six months in order to allow the family an opportunity to meet the needs of the juvenile through more adequate home supervision, through placement in a private or specialized school or agency, through placement with a relative, or through some other plan approved by the court. (1979, c. 815, s. 1; 1981, c. 469, s. 18; 1998-202, s. 6; 2003-62, s. 5.)

§ 7B-2502. Evaluation and treatment of undisciplined and delinquent juveniles.

(a) In any case, the court may order that the juvenile be examined by a physician, psychiatrist, psychologist, or other qualified expert as may be needed for the court to determine the needs of the juvenile. In the case of a juvenile adjudicated delinquent for committing an offense that involves the possession, use, sale, or delivery of alcohol or a controlled substance, the court shall require the juvenile to be tested for the use of controlled substances or alcohol within 30 days of the adjudication. In the case of any juvenile adjudicated delinquent, the court may, if it deems it necessary, require the juvenile to be tested for the use of controlled substances or alcohol. The results of these initial tests conducted pursuant to this subsection shall be used for evaluation and treatment purposes only. In placing a juvenile in out-of-home care under this section, the court shall also consider whether it is in the juvenile's best interest to remain in the juvenile's community of residence.

(b)     Upon completion of the examination, the court shall conduct a hearing to determine whether the juvenile is in need of medical, surgical, psychiatric, psychological, or other evaluation or treatment and who should pay the cost of the evaluation or treatment. The county manager, or any other person who is designated by the chair of the board of county commissioners, of the county of the juvenile's residence shall be notified of the hearing, and allowed to be heard. If the court finds the juvenile to be in need of medical, surgical, psychiatric, psychological, or other evaluation or treatment, the court shall permit the parent, guardian, custodian, or other responsible persons to arrange for evaluation or treatment. If the parent, guardian, or custodian declines or is unable to make necessary arrangements, the court may order the needed evaluation or treatment, surgery, or care, and the court may order the parent to pay the cost of the care pursuant to Article 27 of this Chapter. If the court finds the parent is unable to pay the cost of evaluation or treatment, the court shall order the county to arrange for evaluation or treatment of the juvenile and to pay for the cost of the evaluation or treatment. The county department of social services shall recommend the facility that will provide the juvenile with evaluation or treatment.

(c)     If the court believes, or if there is evidence presented to the effect that the juvenile is mentally ill or is developmentally disabled, the court shall refer the juvenile to the area mental health, developmental disabilities, and substance abuse services director for appropriate action. A juvenile shall not be committed directly to a State hospital or mental retardation center; and orders purporting to commit a juvenile directly to a State hospital or mental retardation center except for an examination to determine capacity to proceed shall be void and of no effect. The area mental health, developmental disabilities, and substance abuse director shall be responsible for arranging an interdisciplinary evaluation of the juvenile and mobilizing resources to meet the juvenile's needs. If institutionalization is determined to be the best service for the juvenile, admission shall be with the voluntary consent of the parent, guardian, or custodian. If the parent, guardian, or custodian refuses to consent to a mental hospital or retardation center admission after such institutionalization is recommended by the area mental health, developmental disabilities, and substance abuse director, the signature and consent of the court may be substituted for that purpose. In all cases in which a regional mental hospital refuses admission to a juvenile referred for admission by the court and an area mental health, developmental disabilities, and substance abuse director or discharges a juvenile previously admitted on court referral prior to completion of the juvenile's treatment, the hospital shall submit to the court a written report setting out the reasons for denial of admission or discharge and setting out the juvenile's diagnosis, indications of mental illness, indications of need for treatment, and a statement as to the location of any facility known to have a treatment program for the juvenile in question. (1979, c. 815, s. 1; 1981, c. 469, s. 19; 1985, c. 589, s. 5; c. 777, s. 1; 1985 (Reg. Sess., 1986), c. 863, s. 2; 1991, c. 636, s. 19(a); 1995 (Reg. Sess., 1996), c. 609, s. 3; 1997-516, s. 1A; 1998-202, s. 6; 1998-229, s. 6; 2002-164, s. 4.9.)

§ 7B-2503. Dispositional alternatives for undisciplined juveniles.

The following alternatives for disposition shall be available to the court exercising jurisdiction over a juvenile who has been adjudicated undisciplined. In placing a juvenile in out-of-home care under this section, the court shall also consider whether it is in the juvenile's best interest to remain in the juvenile's community of residence. The court may combine any of the applicable alternatives when the court finds it to be in the best interests of the juvenile:

(1) In the case of any juvenile who needs more adequate care or supervision or who needs placement, the judge may:

a. Require that the juvenile be supervised in the juvenile's own home by a department of social services in the juvenile's county of residence, a juvenile court counselor, or other personnel as may be available to the court, subject to conditions applicable to the parent, guardian, or custodian or the juvenile as the judge may specify; or

b. Place the juvenile in the custody of a parent, guardian, custodian, relative, private agency offering placement services, or some other suitable person; or

c. If the director of the department of social services has received notice and an opportunity to be heard, place the juvenile in the custody of a department of social services in the county of the juvenile's residence, or in the case of a juvenile who has legal residence outside the State, in the physical custody of a department of social services in the county where the juvenile is found so that agency may return the juvenile to the responsible authorities in the juvenile's home state. An order placing a juvenile in the custody or placement responsibility of a county department of social services shall contain a finding that the juvenile's continuation in the juvenile's own home would be contrary to the juvenile's best interest. This placement shall be reviewed in accordance with G.S. 7B-906.1. The director may, unless otherwise ordered by the judge, arrange for, provide, or consent to, needed routine or emergency medical or surgical care or treatment. In the case where the parent is unknown, unavailable, or unable to act on behalf of the juvenile or juveniles, the director may, unless otherwise ordered by the judge, arrange for, provide or consent to any psychiatric, psychological, educational, or other remedial evaluations or treatment for the juvenile placed by a judge or the judge's designee in the custody or physical custody of a county department of social services under the authority of this or any other Chapter of the General Statutes. Prior to exercising this authority, the director shall make reasonable efforts to obtain consent from a parent, guardian, or custodian of the affected juvenile. If the director cannot obtain consent, the director shall promptly notify the parent, guardian, or custodian that care or treatment has been provided and shall give the parent, guardian, or custodian frequent status reports on the circumstances of the juvenile. Upon request of a parent, guardian, or custodian of the affected juvenile, the results or records of the aforementioned evaluations, findings, or treatment shall be made available to the parent, guardian, or custodian by the director unless prohibited by G.S. 122C-53(d).

(2) Place the juvenile under the protective supervision of a juvenile court counselor for a period of up to three months, with an extension of an additional three months in the discretion of the court.

(3) Excuse the juvenile from compliance with the compulsory school attendance law when the court finds that suitable alternative plans can be arranged by the family through other community resources for one of the following:

a. An education related to the needs or abilities of the juvenile including vocational education or special education;

b.   A suitable plan of supervision or placement; or

c.   Some other plan that the court finds to be in the best interests of the juvenile. (1979, c. 815, s. 1; 1981, c. 469, s. 19; 1985, c. 589, s. 5; c. 777, s. 1; 1985 (Reg. Sess., 1986), c. 863, s. 2; 1991, c. 636, s. 19(a); 1995 (Reg. Sess., 1996), c. 609, s. 3; 1997-516, s. 1A; 1998-202, s. 6; 1998-229, s. 6; 2001-208, s. 8; 2001-487, s. 101; 2001-490, s. 2.19; 2002-164, s. 4.10; 2009-311, s. 16; 2013-129, s. 39.)

§ 7B-2504. Conditions of protective supervision for undisciplined juveniles.

The court may place a juvenile on protective supervision pursuant to G.S. 7B-2503 so that the juvenile court counselor may (i) assist the juvenile in securing social, medical, and educational services and (ii) visit and work with the family as a unit to ensure the juvenile is provided proper supervision and care. The court may impose any combination of the following conditions of protective supervision that are related to the needs of the juvenile, including:

(1)   That the juvenile shall remain on good behavior and not violate any laws;

(2)   That the juvenile attend school regularly;

(3)   That the juvenile maintain passing grades in up to four courses during each grading period and meet with the juvenile court counselor and a representative of the school to make a plan for how to maintain those passing grades;

(4)   That the juvenile not associate with specified persons or be in specified places;

(5)   That the juvenile abide by a prescribed curfew;

(6)   That the juvenile report to a juvenile court counselor as often as required by a juvenile court counselor;

(7)   That the juvenile be employed regularly if not attending school; and

(8)   That the juvenile satisfy any other conditions determined appropriate by the court. (1979, c. 815, s. 1; 1998-202, s. 6; 2001-490, s. 2.20.)

§ 7B-2505. Violation of protective supervision by undisciplined juvenile.

(a) On motion of the juvenile court counselor or the juvenile, or on the court's own motion, the court may review the progress of any juvenile on protective supervision at any time during the period of protective supervision. When the motion is filed during the period of protective supervision and either alleges a violation of protective supervision or seeks an extension of protective supervision as permitted by G.S. 7B-2503(2), the court's review may occur within a reasonable time after the period of protective supervision ends, and the court shall have jurisdiction to enter an order under this section. The conditions or duration of protective supervision may be modified only as provided in this Subchapter and only after notice and a hearing.

(b) If the court, after notice and a hearing, finds by the greater weight of the evidence that the juvenile has violated the conditions of protective supervision set by the court, the court may do one or more of the following:

(1) Continue or modify the conditions of protective supervision.

(2) Order any disposition authorized by G.S. 7B-2503.

(3) Notwithstanding the time limitation in G.S. 7B-2503(2), extend the period of protective supervision for up to three months. (1998-202, s. 6; 2001-490, s. 2.21; 2012-172, s. 5.)

§ 7B-2506. Dispositional alternatives for delinquent juveniles.

The court exercising jurisdiction over a juvenile who has been adjudicated delinquent may use the following alternatives in accordance with the dispositional structure set forth in G.S. 7B-2508:

(1) In the case of any juvenile who needs more adequate care or supervision or who needs placement, the judge may:

a. Require that a juvenile be supervised in the juvenile's own home by the department of social services in the juvenile's county, a juvenile court counselor, or other personnel as may be available to the court, subject to conditions applicable to the parent, guardian, or custodian or the juvenile as the judge may specify; or

b. Place the juvenile in the custody of a parent, guardian, custodian, relative, private agency offering placement services, or some other suitable person; or

c. If the director of the county department of social services has received notice and an opportunity to be heard, place the juvenile in the custody of the department of social services in the county of his residence, or in the case of a juvenile who has legal residence outside the State, in the physical custody of a department of social services in the county where the juvenile is found so that agency may return the juvenile to the responsible authorities in the juvenile's home state. An order placing a juvenile in the custody or placement responsibility of a county department of social services shall contain a finding that the juvenile's continuation in the juvenile's own home would be contrary to the juvenile's best interest. This placement shall be reviewed in accordance with G.S. 7B-906.1. The director may, unless otherwise ordered by the judge, arrange for, provide, or consent to, needed routine or emergency medical or surgical care or treatment. In the case where the parent is unknown, unavailable, or unable to act on behalf of the juvenile or juveniles, the director may, unless otherwise ordered by the judge, arrange for, provide, or consent to any psychiatric, psychological, educational, or other remedial evaluations or treatment for the juvenile placed by a judge or his designee in the custody or physical custody of a county department of social services under the authority of this or any other Chapter of the General Statutes. Prior to exercising this authority, the director shall make reasonable efforts to obtain consent from a parent, guardian, or custodian of the affected juvenile. If the director cannot obtain consent, the director shall promptly notify the parent, guardian, or custodian that care or treatment has been provided and shall give the parent, guardian, or custodian frequent status reports on the circumstances of the juvenile. Upon request of a parent, guardian, or custodian of the affected juvenile, the results or records of the aforementioned evaluations, findings, or treatment shall be made available to the parent, guardian, or custodian by the director unless prohibited by G.S. 122C-53(d).

(2) Excuse the juvenile from compliance with the compulsory school attendance law when the court finds that suitable alternative plans can be arranged by the family through other community resources for one of the following:

a. An education related to the needs or abilities of the juvenile including vocational education or special education;

b.  A suitable plan of supervision or placement; or

c.  Some other plan that the court finds to be in the best interests of the juvenile.

(3)  Order the juvenile to cooperate with a community-based program, an intensive substance abuse treatment program, or a residential or nonresidential treatment program. Participation in the programs shall not exceed 12 months.

(4)  Require restitution, full or partial, up to five hundred dollars ($500.00), payable within a 12-month period to any person who has suffered loss or damage as a result of the offense committed by the juvenile. The court may determine the amount, terms, and conditions of the restitution. If the juvenile participated with another person or persons, all participants should be jointly and severally responsible for the payment of restitution; however, the court shall not require the juvenile to make restitution if the juvenile satisfies the court that the juvenile does not have, and could not reasonably acquire, the means to make restitution.

(5)  Impose a fine related to the seriousness of the juvenile's offense. If the juvenile has the ability to pay the fine, it shall not exceed the maximum fine for the offense if committed by an adult.

(6)  Order the juvenile to perform up to 100 hours supervised community service consistent with the juvenile's age, skill, and ability, specifying the nature of the work and the number of hours required. The work shall be related to the seriousness of the juvenile's offense and in no event may the obligation to work exceed 12 months.

(7)  Order the juvenile to participate in the victim-offender reconciliation program.

(8)  Place the juvenile on probation under the supervision of a juvenile court counselor, as specified in G.S. 7B-2510.

(9)  Order that the juvenile shall not be licensed to operate a motor vehicle in the State of North Carolina for as long as the court retains jurisdiction over the juvenile or for any shorter period of time. The clerk of court shall notify the Division of Motor Vehicles of that order.

(10)  Impose a curfew upon the juvenile.

(11) Order that the juvenile not associate with specified persons or be in specified places.

(12) Impose confinement on an intermittent basis in an approved detention facility. Confinement shall be limited to not more than five 24-hour periods, the timing of which is determined by the court in its discretion.

(13) Order the juvenile to cooperate with placement in a wilderness program.

(14) Order the juvenile to cooperate with placement in a residential treatment facility, an intensive nonresidential treatment program, an intensive substance abuse program, or in a group home other than a multipurpose group home operated by a State agency.

(15) Place the juvenile on intensive probation under the supervision of a juvenile court counselor.

(16) Order the juvenile to cooperate with a supervised day program requiring the juvenile to be present at a specified place for all or part of every day or of certain days. In determining whether to order a juvenile to a particular supervised day program, the court shall consider the structure and operations of the program and whether that program will meet the needs of the juvenile. The court also may require the juvenile to comply with any other reasonable conditions specified in the dispositional order that are designed to facilitate supervision.

(17) Order the juvenile to participate in a regimented training program.

(18) Order the juvenile to submit to house arrest.

(19) Suspend imposition of a more severe, statutorily permissible disposition with the provision that the juvenile meet certain conditions agreed to by the juvenile and specified in the dispositional order. The conditions shall not exceed the allowable dispositions for the level under which disposition is being imposed.

(20) Order that the juvenile be confined in an approved juvenile detention facility for a term of up to 14 24-hour periods, which confinement shall not be imposed consecutively with intermittent confinement pursuant to subdivision (12) of this section at the same dispositional hearing. The timing of this confinement shall be determined by the court in its discretion.

(21)   Order the residential placement of a juvenile in a multipurpose group home operated by a State agency.

(22)   Require restitution of more than five hundred dollars ($500.00), full or partial, payable within a 12-month period to any person who has suffered loss or damage as a result of an offense committed by the juvenile. The court may determine the amount, terms, and conditions of restitution. If the juvenile participated with another person or persons, all participants should be jointly and severally responsible for the payment of the restitution; however, the court shall not require the juvenile to make restitution if the juvenile satisfies the court that the juvenile does not have, and could not reasonably acquire, the means to make restitution.

(23)   Order the juvenile to perform up to 200 hours supervised community service consistent with the juvenile's age, skill, and ability, specifying the nature of work and the number of hours required. The work shall be related to the seriousness of the juvenile's offense.

(24)   Commit the juvenile to the Division for placement in a youth development center in accordance with G.S. 7B-2513 for a period of not less than six months. (1979, c. 815, s. 1; 1981, c. 469, ss. 19, 20; 1985, c. 589, s. 5; c. 777, s. 1; 1985 (Reg. Sess., 1986), c. 863, s. 2; 1991, c. 353, s. 1; 636, s. 19(a); 1991 (Reg. Sess., 1992), c. 1030, s. 4; 1993, c. 369, s. 1; c. 462, s. 1; 1995 (Reg. Sess., 1996), c. 609, s. 3; 1997-516, s. 1A; 1998-202, s. 6; 1998-229, s. 6; 1999-444, s. 1; 2000-137, s. 3; 2001-95, s. 5; 2001-179, s. 2; 2001-208, s. 9; 2001-487, s. 101; 2001-490, s. 2.22; 2009-311, s. 17; 2011-145, s. 19.1(l); 2013-129, s. 40.)


§ 7B-2507.  Delinquency history levels.

(a)   Generally. - The delinquency history level for a delinquent juvenile is determined by calculating the sum of the points assigned to each of the juvenile's prior adjudications and to the juvenile's probation status, if any, that the court finds to have been proved in accordance with this section.

(b)   Points. - Points are assigned as follows:

(1)   For each prior adjudication of a Class A through E felony offense, 4 points.

(2) For each prior adjudication of a Class F through I felony offense or Class A1 misdemeanor offense, 2 points.

(3) For each prior adjudication of a Class 1, 2, or 3 misdemeanor offense, 1 point.

(4) If the juvenile was on probation at the time of offense, 2 points.

No points shall be assigned for a prior adjudication that a juvenile is in direct contempt of court or indirect contempt of court.

(c) Delinquency History Levels. - The delinquency history levels are:

(1) Low - No more than 1 point.

(2) Medium - At least 2, but not more than 3 points.

(3) High - At least 4 points.

In determining the delinquency history level, the classification of a prior offense is the classification assigned to that offense at the time the juvenile committed the offense for which disposition is being ordered.

(d) Multiple Prior Adjudications Obtained in One Court Session. - For purposes of determining the delinquency history level, if a juvenile is adjudicated delinquent for more than one offense in a single session of district court, only the adjudication for the offense with the highest point total is used.

(e) Classification of Prior Adjudications From Other Jurisdictions. - Except as otherwise provided in this subsection, an adjudication occurring in a jurisdiction other than North Carolina is classified as a Class I felony if the jurisdiction in which the offense occurred classifies the offense as a felony, or is classified as a Class 3 misdemeanor if the jurisdiction in which the offense occurred classifies the offense as a misdemeanor. If the juvenile proves by the preponderance of the evidence that an offense classified as a felony in the other jurisdiction is substantially similar to an offense that is a misdemeanor in North Carolina, the conviction is treated as that class of misdemeanor for assigning delinquency history level points. If the State proves by the preponderance of the evidence that an offense classified as either a misdemeanor or a felony in the other jurisdiction is substantially similar to an offense in North Carolina that is classified as a Class I felony or higher, the conviction is treated as that class of felony for assigning delinquency history level points. If the State proves by the preponderance of the evidence that an offense classified as a misdemeanor in the other jurisdiction is substantially similar to an offense classified as a Class A1 misdemeanor in North Carolina, the adjudication is treated as a Class A1 misdemeanor for assigning delinquency history level points.

(f) Proof of Prior Adjudications. - A prior adjudication shall be proved by any of the following methods:

(1) Stipulation of the parties.

(2) An original or copy of the court record of the prior adjudication.

(3) A copy of records maintained by the Division of Criminal Information or by the Division.

(4) Any other method found by the court to be reliable.

The State bears the burden of proving, by a preponderance of the evidence, that a prior adjudication exists and that the juvenile before the court is the same person as the juvenile named in the prior adjudication. The original or a copy of the court records or a copy of the records maintained by the Division of Criminal Information or of the Division, bearing the same name as that by which the juvenile is charged, is prima facie evidence that the juvenile named is the same person as the juvenile before the court, and that the facts set out in the record are true. For purposes of this subsection, "a copy" includes a paper writing containing a reproduction of a record maintained electronically on a computer or other data processing equipment, and a document produced by a facsimile machine. The prosecutor shall make all feasible efforts to obtain and present to the court the juvenile's full record. Evidence presented by either party at trial may be utilized to prove prior adjudications. If asked by the juvenile, the prosecutor shall furnish the juvenile's prior adjudications to the juvenile within a reasonable time sufficient to allow the juvenile to determine if the record available to the prosecutor is accurate. (1998-202, s. 6; 2000-137, s. 3; 2007-168, s. 5; 2011-145, s. 19.1(l).)

§ 7B-2508. Dispositional limits for each class of offense and delinquency history level.

(a) Offense Classification. - The offense classifications are as follows:

(1) Violent - Adjudication of a Class A through E felony offense;

(2) Serious - Adjudication of a Class F through I felony offense or a Class A1 misdemeanor;

(3) Minor - Adjudication of a Class 1, 2, or 3 misdemeanor or adjudication of indirect contempt by a juvenile.

(b) Delinquency History Levels. - A delinquency history level shall be determined for each delinquent juvenile as provided in G.S. 7B-2507.

(c) Level 1 - Community Disposition. - A court exercising jurisdiction over a juvenile who has been adjudicated delinquent and for whom the dispositional chart in subsection (f) of this section prescribes a Level 1 disposition may provide for evaluation and treatment under G.S. 7B-2502 and for any of the dispositional alternatives contained in subdivisions (1) through (13) and (16) of G.S. 7B-2506. In determining which dispositional alternative is appropriate, the court shall consider the needs of the juvenile as indicated by the risk and needs assessment contained in the predisposition report, the appropriate community resources available to meet those needs, and the protection of the public.

(d) Level 2 - Intermediate Disposition. - A court exercising jurisdiction over a juvenile who has been adjudicated delinquent and for whom the dispositional chart in subsection (f) of this section prescribes a Level 2 disposition may provide for evaluation and treatment under G.S. 7B-2502 and for any of the dispositional alternatives contained in subdivisions (1) through (23) of G.S. 7B-2506, but shall provide for at least one of the intermediate dispositions authorized in subdivisions (13) through (23) of G.S. 7B-2506. However, notwithstanding any other provision of this section, a court may impose a Level 3 disposition if the juvenile has previously received a Level 3 disposition in a prior juvenile action. In determining which dispositional alternative is appropriate, the court shall consider the needs of the juvenile as indicated by the risk and needs assessment contained in the predisposition report, the appropriate community resources available to meet those needs, and the protection of the public.

(e) Level 3 - Commitment. - A court exercising jurisdiction over a juvenile who has been adjudicated delinquent and for whom the dispositional chart in subsection (f) of this section prescribes a Level 3 disposition shall commit the juvenile to the Division for placement in a youth development center in accordance with G.S. 7B-2506(24). However, a court may impose a Level 2 disposition rather than a Level 3 disposition if the court submits written findings on the record that substantiate extraordinary needs on the part of the offending juvenile.

(f)   Dispositions for Each Class of Offense and Delinquency History Level; Disposition Chart Described. - The authorized disposition for each class of offense and delinquency history level is as specified in the chart below. Delinquency history levels are indicated horizontally on the top of the chart. Classes of offense are indicated vertically on the left side of the chart. Each cell on the chart indicates which of the dispositional levels described in subsections (c) through (e) of this section are prescribed for that combination of offense classification and delinquency history level:

DELINQUENCY HISTORY OFFENSE

|  | LOW | MEDIUM | HIGH |
|---|---|---|---|
| VIOLENT | Level 2 or 3 | Level 3 | Level 3 |
| SERIOUS | Level 1 or 2 | Level 2 | Level 2 or 3 |
| MINOR | Level 1 | Level 1 or 2 | Level 2. |

(g)   Notwithstanding subsection (f) of this section, a juvenile who has been adjudicated for a minor offense may be committed to a Level 3 disposition if the juvenile has been adjudicated of four or more prior offenses. For purposes of determining the number of prior offenses under this subsection, each successive offense is one that was committed after adjudication of the preceding offense.

(h)   If a juvenile is adjudicated of more than one offense during a session of juvenile court, the court shall consolidate the offenses for disposition and impose a single disposition for the consolidated offenses. The disposition shall be specified for the class of offense and delinquency history level of the most serious offense. (1998-202, s. 6; 2000-137, s. 3; 2001-95, s. 5; 2001-179, s. 1; 2007-168, s. 6; 2011-145, s. 19.1(l).)

§ 7B-2509. Registration of certain delinquent juveniles.

In any case in which a juvenile, who was at least 11 years of age at the time of the offense, is adjudicated delinquent for committing a violation of G.S. 14-27.2 (first-degree rape), G.S. 14-27.3 (second degree rape), G.S. 14-27.4 (first-degree sexual offense), G.S. 14-27.5 (second degree sexual offense), or G.S. 14-27.6 (attempted rape or sexual offense), the judge, upon a finding that the juvenile is a danger to the community, may order that the juvenile register in accordance with Part 4 of Article 27A of Chapter 14 of the General Statutes. (1997-516, s. 1A; 1998-202, s. 11.)

§ 7B-2510. Conditions of probation; violation of probation.

(a) In any case where a juvenile is placed on probation pursuant to G.S. 7B-2506(8), the juvenile court counselor shall have the authority to visit the juvenile where the juvenile resides. The court may impose conditions of probation that are related to the needs of the juvenile and that are reasonably necessary to ensure that the juvenile will lead a law-abiding life, including:

(1) That the juvenile shall remain on good behavior.

(2) That the juvenile shall not violate any laws.

(3) That the juvenile shall not violate any reasonable and lawful rules of a parent, guardian, or custodian.

(4) That the juvenile attend school regularly.

(5) That the juvenile maintain passing grades in up to four courses during each grading period and meet with the juvenile court counselor and a representative of the school to make a plan for how to maintain those passing grades.

(6) That the juvenile not associate with specified persons or be in specified places.

(7) That the juvenile:

a. Refrain from use or possession of any controlled substance included in any schedule of Article 5 of Chapter 90 of the General Statutes, the Controlled Substances Act;

b. Refrain from use or possession of any alcoholic beverage regulated under Chapter 18B of the General Statutes; and

c. Submit to random drug testing.

(8) That the juvenile abide by a prescribed curfew.

(9) That the juvenile submit to a warrantless search at reasonable times.

(10) That the juvenile possess no firearm, explosive device, or other deadly weapon.

(11) That the juvenile report to a juvenile court counselor as often as required by the juvenile court counselor.

(12) That the juvenile make specified financial restitution or pay a fine in accordance with G.S. 7B-2506(4), (5), and (22).

(13) That the juvenile be employed regularly if not attending school.

(14) That the juvenile satisfy any other conditions determined appropriate by the court.

(b) In addition to the regular conditions of probation specified in subsection (a) of this section, the court may, at a dispositional hearing or any subsequent hearing, order the juvenile to comply, if directed to comply by the chief court counselor, with one or more of the following conditions:

(1) Perform up to 20 hours of community service;

(2) Submit to substance abuse monitoring and treatment;

(3) Participate in a life skills or an educational skills program administered by the Division;

(4) Cooperate with electronic monitoring; and

(5) Cooperate with intensive supervision.

However, the court shall not give the chief court counselor discretion to impose the conditions of either subsection (4) or (5) of this section unless the juvenile is subject to Level 2 dispositions pursuant to G.S. 7B-2508 or subsection (d) of this section.

(c) An order of probation shall remain in force for a period not to exceed one year from the date entered. Prior to expiration of an order of probation, the court may extend it for an additional period of one year after a hearing, if the court finds that the extension is necessary to protect the community or to safeguard the welfare of the juvenile.

(d) On motion of the juvenile court counselor or the juvenile, or on the court's own motion, the court may review the progress of any juvenile on probation at any time during the period of probation or at the end of probation. The conditions or duration of probation may be modified only as provided in this Subchapter and only after notice and a hearing.

(e) If the court, after notice and a hearing, finds by the greater weight of the evidence that the juvenile has violated the conditions of probation set by the court, the court may continue the original conditions of probation, modify the conditions of probation, or, except as provided in subsection (f) of this section, order a new disposition at the next higher level on the disposition chart in G.S. 7B-2508. In the court's discretion, part of the new disposition may include an order of confinement in a secure juvenile detention facility for up to twice the term authorized by G.S. 7B-2508.

(f) A court shall not order a Level 3 disposition for violation of the conditions of probation by a juvenile adjudicated delinquent for an offense classified as minor under G.S. 7B-2508. (1979, c. 815, s. 1; 1981, c. 469, s. 20; 1991, c. 353, s. 1; 1991 (Reg. Sess., 1992), c. 1030, s. 4; 1993, c. 369, s. 1; c. 462, s. 1; 1998-202, s. 6; 2000-137, s. 3; 2001-490, ss. 2.23, 2.24; 2011-145, s. 19.1(l).)

§ 7B-2511. Termination of probation.

At the end of or at any time during probation, the court may terminate probation by written order upon finding that there is no further need for supervision. The finding and order terminating probation may be entered in chambers in the absence of the juvenile and may be based on a report from the juvenile court counselor or, at the election of the court, the order may be entered with the juvenile present after notice and a hearing. (1979, c. 815, s. 1; 1998-202, s. 6; 2001-490, s. 2.25.)

§ 7B-2512. Dispositional order.

The dispositional order shall be in writing and shall contain appropriate findings of fact and conclusions of law. The court shall state with particularity, both orally and in the written order of disposition, the precise terms of the disposition including the kind, duration, and the person who is responsible for carrying out the disposition and the person or agency in whom custody is vested. (1979, c. 815, s. 1; 1987 (Reg. Sess., 1988), c. 1090, s. 10; 1991, c. 434, s. 1; 1997-390, s. 8; 1998-202, s. 6; 1998-229, s. 7.)

§ 7B-2513. Commitment of delinquent juvenile to Division.

(a) Pursuant to G.S. 7B-2506 and G.S. 7B-2508, the court may commit a delinquent juvenile who is at least 10 years of age to the Division for placement in a youth development center. Commitment shall be for an indefinite term of at least six months. In no event shall the term exceed:

(1) The twenty-first birthday of the juvenile if the juvenile has been committed to the Division for an offense that would be first-degree murder pursuant to G.S. 14-17, first-degree rape pursuant to G.S. 14-27.2, or first-degree sexual offense pursuant to G.S. 14-27.4 if committed by an adult;

(2) The nineteenth birthday of the juvenile if the juvenile has been committed to the Division for an offense that would be a Class B1, B2, C, D, or E felony if committed by an adult, other than an offense set forth in subdivision (1) of this subsection; or

(3) The eighteenth birthday of the juvenile if the juvenile has been committed to the Division for an offense other than an offense that would be a Class A, B1, B2, C, D, or E felony if committed by an adult.

No juvenile shall be committed to a youth development center beyond the minimum six-month commitment for a period of time in excess of the maximum term of imprisonment for which an adult in prior record level VI for felonies or in prior conviction level III for misdemeanors could be sentenced for the same offense, except when the Division pursuant to G.S. 7B-2515 determines that the juvenile's commitment needs to be continued for an additional period of time to continue care or treatment under the plan of care or treatment developed under subsection (f) of this section. At the time of commitment to a youth development center, the court shall determine the maximum period of time the juvenile may remain committed before a determination must be made by the Division pursuant to G.S. 7B-2515 and shall notify the juvenile of that determination.

(b)     The court may commit a juvenile to a definite term of not less than six months and not more than two years if the court finds that the juvenile is 14 years of age or older, has been previously adjudicated delinquent for two or more felony offenses, and has been previously committed to a youth development center.

(c)     The chief court counselor shall have the responsibility for transporting the juvenile to the youth development center designated by the Division. The juvenile shall be accompanied to the youth development center by a person of the same sex.

(d)     The chief court counselor shall ensure that the records requested by the Division accompany the juvenile upon transportation for admittance to a youth development center or, if not obtainable at the time of admission, are sent to the youth development center within 15 days of the admission. If records requested by the Division for admission do not exist, to the best knowledge of the chief court counselor, the chief court counselor shall so stipulate in writing to the youth development center. If such records do exist, but the chief court counselor is unable to obtain copies of them, a district court may order that the records from public agencies be made available to the youth development center. Records that are confidential by law shall remain confidential and the Division shall be bound by the specific laws governing the confidentiality of these records. All records shall be used in a manner consistent with the best interests of the juvenile.

(e)     A commitment order accompanied by information requested by the Division shall be forwarded to the Division. The Division shall place the juvenile in the youth development center that would best provide for the juvenile's needs and shall notify the committing court. The Division may assign a juvenile committed for delinquency to any institution of the Division or licensed by the Division, which program is appropriate to the needs of the juvenile.

The Division, after assessment of the juvenile, may provide commitment services to the juvenile in a program not located in a youth development center or detention facility. If the Division recommends that commitment services for the juvenile are to be provided in a setting that is not located in a youth development center or detention facility, the Division shall file a motion, along with information about the recommended services for the juvenile, with the committing court prior to placing the juvenile in the identified commitment program. The Division shall send notice of the motion to the District Attorney, the juvenile, and the juvenile's attorney. Upon receipt of the motion filed by the Division, the court may enter an order without the appearance of witnesses and without hearing if the court determines that the identified commitment program is appropriate and a hearing is not necessary. The court must hold a hearing if the juvenile or the juvenile's attorney requests a hearing. If the court notifies the Division of its intent to hold a hearing, the date for that hearing shall be set by the court and the Division shall place the juvenile in a youth development center or detention facility until the determination of the court at that hearing.

(f)     When the court commits a juvenile to the Division for placement in a youth development center, the Division shall prepare a plan for care or treatment within 30 days after assuming custody of the juvenile.

(g)     Commitment of a juvenile to the Division for placement in a youth development center does not terminate the court's continuing jurisdiction over the juvenile and the juvenile's parent, guardian, or custodian. Commitment of a juvenile to the Division for placement in a youth development center transfers only physical custody of the juvenile. Legal custody remains with the parent, guardian, custodian, agency, or institution in whom it was vested.

(h)     Pending placement of a juvenile with the Division, the court may house a juvenile who has been adjudicated delinquent for an offense that would be a Class A, B1, B2, C, D, or E felony if committed by an adult in a holdover facility up to 72 hours if the court, based on the information provided by the juvenile court counselor, determines that no acceptable alternative placement is available and the protection of the public requires that the juvenile be housed in a holdover facility.

(i)     A juvenile who is committed to the Division for placement in a youth development center shall be tested for the use of controlled substances or alcohol. The results of this initial test shall be incorporated into the plan of care as provided in subsection (f) of this section and used for evaluation and treatment purposes only.

(j)     When a juvenile is committed to the Division for placement in a youth development center for an offense that would have been a Class A or B1 felony if committed by an adult, the chief court counselor shall notify the victim and members of the victim's immediate family that the victim, or the victim's immediate family members may request in writing to be notified in advance of the juvenile's scheduled release date in accordance with G.S. 7B-2514(d). (1979, c. 815, s. 1; 1983, c. 133, s. 2; 1987, c. 100; c. 372; 1991, c. 434, ss. 2, 3; 1995 (Reg. Sess., 1996), c. 609, s. 2; 1997-443, s. 11A.118(a); 1998-202, s. 6; 1999-423, s. 1; 2000-137, s. 3; 2001-95, s. 5; 2001-490, s. 2.26; 2003-53, s. 1; 2011-145, s. 19.1(l).)

§ 7B-2514. Post-release supervision planning; release.

(a) The Division shall be responsible for evaluation of the progress of each juvenile at least once every six months as long as the juvenile remains in the care of the Division. Any determination that the juvenile should remain in the care of the Division for an additional period of time shall be based on the Division's determination that the juvenile requires additional treatment or rehabilitation pursuant to G.S. 7B-2515. If the Division determines that a juvenile is ready for release, the Division shall initiate a post-release supervision planning process. The post-release supervision planning process shall be defined by rules and regulations of the Division, but shall include the following:

(1) Written notification shall be given to the court that ordered commitment.

(2) A post-release supervision planning conference shall be held involving as many as possible of the following: the juvenile, the juvenile's parent, guardian, or custodian, juvenile court counselors who have supervised the juvenile on probation or will supervise the juvenile on post-release supervision, and staff of the facility that found the juvenile ready for release. The planning conference shall include personal contact and evaluation rather than telephonic notification.

(3) The planning conference participants shall consider, based on the individual needs of the juvenile and pursuant to rules adopted by the Division, placement of the juvenile in any program under the auspices of the Division, including the juvenile court services programs that, in the judgment of the Division, would be appropriate transitional placement, pending release under G.S. 7B-2513.

(b) The Division shall develop the plan in writing and base the terms on the needs of the juvenile and the protection of the public. Every plan shall require the juvenile to complete at least 90 days, but not more than one year, of post-release supervision.

(c) The Division shall release a juvenile under a plan of post-release supervision at least 90 days prior to:

(1) Completion of the juvenile's definite term of commitment; or

(2) The juvenile's twenty-first birthday if the juvenile has been committed to the Division for an offense that would be first-degree murder pursuant to G.S. 14-17, first-degree rape pursuant to G.S. 14-27.2, or first-degree sexual offense pursuant to G.S. 14-27.4 if committed by an adult.

(3) The juvenile's nineteenth birthday if the juvenile has been committed to the Division for an offense that would be a Class B1, B2, C, D, or E felony if committed by an adult, other than an offense set forth in G.S. 7B-1602(a).

(4) The juvenile's eighteenth birthday if the juvenile has been committed to the Division for an offense other than an offense that would be a Class A, B1, B2, C, D, or E felony if committed by an adult.

(d) Notwithstanding Articles 30 and 31 of Subchapter III of this Chapter, at least 45 days before releasing to post-release supervision a juvenile who was committed for a Class A or B1 felony, the Division shall notify, by first-class mail at the last known address:

(1) The juvenile;

(2) The juvenile's parent, guardian, or custodian;

(3) The district attorney of the district where the juvenile was adjudicated;

(4) The head of the enforcement agency that took the juvenile into custody; and

(5) The victim and any of the victim's immediate family members who have requested in writing to be notified.

The notification shall include only the juvenile's name, offense, date of commitment, and date proposed for release. A copy of the notice shall be sent to the appropriate clerk of superior court for placement in the juvenile's court file.

(e) The Division may release a juvenile under an indefinite commitment to post-release supervision only after the juvenile has been committed to the

Division for placement in a youth development center for a period of at least six months.

(f) A juvenile committed to the Division for placement in a youth development center for a definite term shall receive credit toward that term for the time the juvenile spends on post-release supervision.

(g) A juvenile on post-release supervision shall be supervised by a juvenile court counselor. Post-release supervision shall be terminated by order of the court. (1979, c. 815, s. 1; 1983, c. 133, s. 1; c. 276, s. 1; 1989, c. 235; 1996, 2nd Ex. Sess., c. 18, s. 23.2(e); 1998-202, s. 6; 2000-137, s. 3; 2001-95, s. 5; 2001-490, ss. 2.27, 2.28; 2011-145, s. 19(l).)

§ 7B-2515. Notification of extended commitment; plan of treatment.

(a) In determining whether a juvenile should be released before the juvenile's 18th birthday, the Division shall consider the protection of the public and the likelihood that continued placement will lead to further rehabilitation. If the Division does not intend to release the juvenile prior to the juvenile's eighteenth birthday, or if the Division determines that the juvenile's commitment should be continued beyond the maximum commitment period as set forth in G.S. 7B-2513(a), the Division shall notify the juvenile and the juvenile's parent, guardian, or custodian in writing at least 30 days in advance of the juvenile's eighteenth birthday or the end of the maximum commitment period, of the additional specific commitment period proposed by the Division, the basis for extending the commitment period, and the plan for future care or treatment.

(b) The Division shall modify the plan of care or treatment developed pursuant to G.S. 7B-2513(f) to specify (i) the specific goals and outcomes that require additional time for care or treatment of the juvenile; (ii) the specific course of treatment or care that will be implemented to achieve the established goals and outcomes; and (iii) the efforts that will be taken to assist the juvenile's family in creating an environment that will increase the likelihood that the efforts to treat and rehabilitate the juvenile will be successful upon release. If appropriate, the Division may place the juvenile in a setting other than a youth development center.

(c) The juvenile and the juvenile's parent, guardian, or custodian may request a review by the court of the Division's decision to extend the juvenile's commitment beyond the juvenile's eighteenth birthday or maximum commitment period, in which case the court shall conduct a review hearing. The court may modify the Division's decision and the juvenile's maximum commitment period. If the juvenile or the juvenile's parent, guardian, or custodian does not request a review of the Division's decision, the Division's decision shall become the juvenile's new maximum commitment period. (1998-202, s. 6; 1998-217, s. 57(1); 2000-137, s. 3; 2001-95, s. 5; 2011-145, s. 19.1(l).)

§ 7B-2516. Revocation of post-release supervision.

(a) On motion of the juvenile court counselor providing post-release supervision or motion of the juvenile, or on the court's own motion, and after notice, the court may hold a hearing to review the progress of any juvenile on post-release supervision at any time during the period of post-release supervision. With respect to any hearing involving allegations that the juvenile has violated the terms of post-release supervision, the juvenile:

(1) Shall have reasonable notice in writing of the nature and content of the allegations in the motion, including notice that the purpose of the hearing is to determine whether the juvenile has violated the terms of post-release supervision to the extent that post-release supervision should be revoked;

(2) Shall be represented by an attorney at the hearing;

(3) Shall have the right to confront and cross-examine witnesses; and

(4) May admit, deny, or explain the violation alleged and may present proof, including affidavits or other evidence, in support of the juvenile's contentions. A record of the proceeding shall be made and preserved in the juvenile's record.

(b) If the court determines by the greater weight of the evidence that the juvenile has violated the terms of post-release supervision, the court may revoke the post-release supervision or make any other disposition authorized by this Subchapter.

(c) If the court revokes post-release supervision, the juvenile shall be returned to the Division for placement in a youth development center for an indefinite term of at least 90 days, provided, however, that no juvenile shall remain committed to the Division for placement in a youth development center past:

(1) The juvenile's twenty-first birthday if the juvenile has been committed to the Division for an offense that would be first-degree murder pursuant to G.S. 14-17, first-degree rape pursuant to G.S. 14-27.2, or first-degree sexual offense pursuant to G.S. 14-27.4 if committed by an adult.

(2) The juvenile's nineteenth birthday if the juvenile has been committed to the Division for an offense that would be a Class B1, B2, C, D, or E felony if committed by an adult, other than an offense set forth in G.S. 7B-1602(a).

(3) The juvenile's eighteenth birthday if the juvenile has been committed to the Division for an offense other than an offense that would be a Class A, B1, B2, C, D, or E felony if committed by an adult. (1979, c. 815, s. 1; 1998-202, s. 6; 2000-137, s.3; 2001-95, s. 5; 2001-490, s. 2.29; 2011-145, s. 19.1(l).)

§ 7B-2517. Transfer authority of Governor.

The Governor may order transfer of any person less than 18 years of age from any jail or penal facility of the State to one of the residential facilities operated by the Division in appropriate circumstances, provided the Governor shall consult with the Division concerning the feasibility of the transfer in terms of available space, staff, and suitability of program.

When an inmate, committed to the Division of Adult Correction of the Department of Public Safety, is transferred by the Governor to a residential program operated by the Division, the Division may release the juvenile based on the needs of the juvenile and the best interests of the State. Transfer shall not divest the probation or parole officer of the officer's responsibility to supervise the inmate on release. (1979, c. 815, s. 1; 1997-443, s. 11A.118(a); 1998-202, s. 6; 2000-137, s. 3; 2011-145, ss. 19.1(h), (l).)

Article 26.

Modification and Enforcement of Dispositional Orders; Appeals.

§ 7B-2600. Authority to modify or vacate.

(a) Upon motion in the cause or petition, and after notice, the court may conduct a review hearing to determine whether the order of the court is in the best interests of the juvenile, and the court may modify or vacate the order in light of changes in circumstances or the needs of the juvenile.

(b) In a case of delinquency, the court may reduce the nature or the duration of the disposition on the basis that it was imposed in an illegal manner or is unduly severe with reference to the seriousness of the offense, the culpability of the juvenile, or the dispositions given to juveniles convicted of similar offenses.

(c) In any case where the court finds the juvenile to be delinquent or undisciplined, the jurisdiction of the court to modify any order or disposition made in the case shall continue (i) during the minority of the juvenile, (ii) until the juvenile reaches the age of 19 years if the juvenile has been adjudicated delinquent and committed to the Division for an offense that would be a Class B1, B2, C, D, or E felony if committed by an adult, other than an offense set forth in G.S. 7B-1602(a), (iii) until the juvenile reaches the age of 21 years if the juvenile has been adjudicated delinquent and committed for an offense that would be first-degree murder pursuant to G.S. 14-17, first-degree rape pursuant to G.S. 14-27.2, or first-degree sexual offense pursuant to G.S. 14-27.4 if committed by an adult, or (iv) until terminated by order of the court. (1979, c. 815, s. 1; 1998-202, s. 6; 2000-137, s. 3; 2011-145, s. 19.1(l).)

§ 7B-2601. Request for modification for lack of suitable services.

If the Division finds that any juvenile committed to the Division's care is not suitable for its program, the Division may make a motion in the cause so that the court may make an alternative disposition that is consistent with G.S. 7B-2508. (1979, c. 815, s. 1; 1998-202, s. 6; 2000-137, s. 3; 2011-145, s. 19.1(l).)

§ 7B-2602. Right to appeal.

Upon motion of a proper party as defined in G.S. 7B-2604, review of any final order of the court in a juvenile matter under this Article shall be before the Court of Appeals. Notice of appeal shall be given in open court at the time of the hearing or in writing within 10 days after entry of the order. However, if no disposition is made within 60 days after entry of the order, written notice of appeal may be given within 70 days after such entry. A final order shall include:

(1) Any order finding absence of jurisdiction;

(2) Any order which in effect determines the action and prevents a judgment from which appeal might be taken;

(3) Any order of disposition after an adjudication that a juvenile is delinquent or undisciplined; or

(4) Any order modifying custodial rights. (1979, c. 815, s. 1; 1998-202, s. 6.)

§ 7B-2603. Right to appeal transfer decision.

(a) Notwithstanding G.S. 7B-2602, any order transferring jurisdiction of the district court in a juvenile matter to the superior court may be appealed to the superior court for a hearing on the record. Notice of the appeal must be given in open court or in writing within 10 days after entry of the order of transfer in district court. Entry of an order shall be treated in the same manner as entry of a judgment under G.S. 1A-1, Rule 58 of the North Carolina Rules of Civil Procedure. The clerk of superior court shall provide the district attorney with a copy of any written notice of appeal filed by the attorney for the juvenile. Upon expiration of the 10 day period in which an appeal may be entered, if an appeal has been entered and not withdrawn, the clerk shall transfer the case to the superior court docket. The superior court shall, within a reasonable time, review the record of the transfer hearing for abuse of discretion by the juvenile court in the issue of transfer. The superior court shall not review the findings as to probable cause for the underlying offense.

(b) Once an order of transfer has been entered by the district court, the juvenile has the right to be considered for pretrial release as provided in G.S. 15A-533 and G.S. 15A-534. The release order shall specify the person or persons to whom the juvenile may be released. Pending release, the court shall order that the juvenile be detained in a detention facility while awaiting trial. The court may order the juvenile to be held in a holdover facility as defined by G.S. 7B-1501 at any time the presence of the juvenile is required in court for pretrial hearings or trial, if the court finds that it would be inconvenient to return the juvenile to the detention facility.

(c) If an appeal of the transfer order is taken, the superior court shall enter an order either (i) remanding the case to the juvenile court for adjudication or (ii) upholding the transfer order. If the superior court remands the case to juvenile court for adjudication and the juvenile has been granted pretrial release provided in G.S 15A-533 and G.S. 15A-534, the obligor shall be released from the juvenile's bond upon the district court's review of whether the juvenile shall be placed in secure or nonsecure custody as provided in G.S. 7B-1903.

(d) The superior court order shall be an interlocutory order, and the issue of transfer may be appealed to the Court of Appeals only after the juvenile has been convicted in superior court. (1979, c. 815, s. 1; 1998-202, s. 6; 1999-309, s. 2; 1999-423, s. 2.)

§ 7B-2604. Proper parties for appeal.

(a) An appeal may be taken by the juvenile, the juvenile's parent, guardian, or custodian, a county, or the State.

(b) The State's appeal is limited to the following orders in delinquency or undisciplined cases:

(1) An order finding a State statute to be unconstitutional; and

(2) Any order which terminates the prosecution of a petition by upholding the defense of double jeopardy, by holding that a cause of action is not stated under a statute, or by granting a motion to suppress.

(c) A county's appeal is limited to orders in which the county has been ordered to pay for medical, surgical, psychiatric, psychological, or other evaluation or treatment of a juvenile pursuant to G.S. 7B-2502, or other medical, psychiatric, psychological, or other evaluation or treatment of a parent pursuant to G.S. 7B-2702. (1979, c. 815, s. 1; 1998-202, s. 6; 2003-171, s. 1.)

§ 7B-2605. Disposition pending appeal.

Pending disposition of an appeal, the release of the juvenile, with or without conditions, should issue in every case unless the court orders otherwise. For compelling reasons which must be stated in writing, the court may enter a temporary order affecting the custody or placement of the juvenile as the court finds to be in the best interests of the juvenile or the State. (1979, c. 815, s. 1; 1987 (Reg. Sess., 1988), c. 1090, s. 12; 1998-202, s. 6.)

§ 7B-2606. Disposition after appeal.

Upon the affirmation of the order of adjudication or disposition of the court by the Court of Appeals or by the Supreme Court in the event of an appeal, the court shall have authority to modify or alter the original order of adjudication or disposition as the court finds to be in the best interests of the juvenile to reflect any adjustment made by the juvenile or change in circumstances during the period of time the appeal was pending. If the modifying order is entered ex parte, the court shall give notice to interested parties to show cause within 10 days thereafter as to why the modifying order should be vacated or altered. (1979, c. 815, s. 1; 1998-202, s. 6.)

Article 27.

Authority over Parents of Juveniles Adjudicated Delinquent or Undisciplined.

§ 7B-2700. Appearance in court.

The parent, guardian, or custodian of a juvenile under the jurisdiction of the juvenile court shall attend the hearings of which the parent, guardian, or custodian receives notice. The court may excuse the appearance of either or both parents or the guardian or custodian at a particular hearing or all hearings. Unless so excused, the willful failure of a parent, guardian, or custodian to attend a hearing of which the parent, guardian, or custodian has notice shall be grounds for contempt. (1998-202, s. 6.)

§ 7B-2701. Parental responsibility classes.

The court may order the parent, guardian, or custodian of a juvenile who has been adjudicated undisciplined or delinquent to attend parental responsibility classes if those classes are available in the judicial district in which the parent, guardian, or custodian resides. (1998-202, s. 6.)

§ 7B-2702. Medical, surgical, psychiatric, or psychological evaluation or treatment of juvenile or parent.

(a)     If the court orders medical, surgical, psychiatric, psychological, or other evaluation or treatment pursuant to G.S. 7B-2502, the court may order the parent or other responsible parties to pay the cost of the treatment or care ordered.

(b) At the dispositional hearing or a subsequent hearing, if the court finds that it is in the best interests of the juvenile for the parent to be directly involved in the juvenile's evaluation or treatment, the court may order that person to participate in medical, psychiatric, psychological, or other evaluation or treatment of the juvenile. The cost of the evaluation or treatment shall be paid pursuant to G.S. 7B-2502.

(c) At the dispositional hearing or a subsequent hearing, the court may determine whether the best interests of the juvenile require that the parent undergo psychiatric, psychological, or other evaluation or treatment or counseling directed toward remedying behaviors or conditions that led to or contributed to the juvenile's adjudication or to the court's decision to remove custody of the juvenile from the parent. If the court finds that the best interests of the juvenile require the parent undergo evaluation or treatment, it may order that person to comply with a plan of evaluation or treatment approved by the court or condition legal custody or physical placement of the juvenile with the parent upon that person's compliance with the plan of evaluation or treatment.

(d) In cases in which the court has ordered the parent of the juvenile to comply with or undergo evaluation or treatment, the court may order the parent to pay the cost of evaluation or treatment ordered pursuant to this subsection. In cases in which the court has conditioned legal custody or physical placement of the juvenile with the parent upon the parent's compliance with a plan of evaluation or treatment, the court may charge the cost of the evaluation or treatment to the county of the juvenile's residence if the court finds the parent is unable to pay the cost of the evaluation or treatment. In all other cases, if the court finds the parent is unable to pay the cost of the evaluation or treatment ordered pursuant to this subsection, the court may order the parent to receive evaluation or treatment currently available from the area mental health program that serves the parent's catchment area. (1979, c. 815, s. 1; 1981, c. 469, s. 19; 1983, c. 837, ss. 2, 3; 1985, c. 589, s. 5; c. 777, s. 1; 1985 (Reg. Sess., 1986), c. 863, s. 2; 1987, c. 598, s. 2; 1989, c. 218; c. 529, s. 7; 1991, c. 636, s. 19(a); 1995, c. 328, s. 2; 1995 (Reg. Sess., 1996), c. 609, ss. 3, 4; 1997-456, s. 1; 1997-516, s. 1A; 1998-202, s. 6; 1998-229, s. 6.)

§ 7B-2703. Compliance with orders of court.

(a) The court may order the parent, guardian, or custodian, to the extent that person is able to do so, to provide transportation for a juvenile to keep an appointment with a juvenile court counselor or to comply with other orders of the court.

(b) The court may order a parent, guardian, or custodian to cooperate with and assist the juvenile in complying with the terms and conditions of probation or other orders of the court. (1998-202, s. 6; 2001-490, s. 2.30.)

§ 7B-2704. Payment of support or other expenses; assignment of insurance coverage.

At the dispositional hearing or a subsequent hearing, if the court finds that the parent is able to do so, the court may order the parent to:

(1) Pay a reasonable sum that will cover in whole or in part the support of the juvenile. If the court requires the payment of child support, the amount of the payments shall be determined as provided in G.S. 50-13.4;

(2) Pay a fee for probation supervision or residential facility costs;

(3) Assign private insurance coverage to cover medical costs while the juvenile is in secure detention, youth development center, or other out-of-home placement; and

(4) Pay appointed attorneys' fees.

All money paid by a parent pursuant to this section shall be paid into the office of the clerk of superior court.

If the court places a juvenile in the custody of a county department of social services and if the court finds that the parent is unable to pay the cost of the support required by the juvenile, the cost shall be paid by the county department of social services in whose custody the juvenile is placed, provided the juvenile is not receiving care in an institution owned or operated by the State or federal government or any subdivision thereof. (1979, c. 815, s. 1; 1981, c. 469, s. 19; 1983, c. 837, ss. 2, 3; 1985, c. 589, s. 5; c. 777, s. 1; 1985 (Reg. Sess., 1986), c. 863, s. 2; 1987, c. 598, s. 2; 1989, c. 218; c. 529, s. 7; 1991, c. 636, s. 19(a); 1995, c. 328, s. 2; 1995 (Reg. Sess., 1996), c. 609, ss. 3, 4; 1997-456, s. 1; 1997-516, s. 1A; 1998-202, s. 6; 1998-229, s. 6; 2000-144, s. 24; 2001-95, s. 5.)

§ 7B-2705. Employment discrimination unlawful.

No employer may discharge, demote, or deny a promotion or other benefit of employment to any employee because the employee complies with the provisions of this Article. The Commissioner of Labor shall enforce the provisions of this section according to Article 21 of Chapter 95 of the General Statutes, including the rules and regulations issued pursuant to that Article. (1998-202, s. 6.)

§ 7B-2706. Contempt for failure to comply.

Upon motion of the juvenile court counselor or prosecutor or upon the court's own motion, the court may issue an order directing the parent, guardian, or custodian to appear and show cause why the parent, guardian, or custodian should not be found or held in civil or criminal contempt for willfully failing to comply with an order of the court. Chapter 5A of the General Statutes shall govern contempt proceedings initiated pursuant to this Article. (1998-202, s. 6; 2001-490, s. 2.31.)

Article 28.

Interstate Compact on Juveniles.

§ 7B-2800. (For contingent repeal - see note) Execution of Compact.

The Governor is hereby authorized and directed to execute a Compact on behalf of this State with any other state or states legally joining therein in the form substantially as follows: The contracting states solemnly agree. (1963, c. 910, s. 1; 1965, c. 925, s. 1; 1979, c. 815, s. 1; 1998-202, s. 6.)

§ 7B-2801. (For contingent repeal - see note) Findings and purposes.

Juveniles who are not under proper supervision and control, or who have absconded, escaped, or run away, are likely to endanger their own health, morals, and welfare, and the health, morals, and welfare of others. The cooperation of the states party to this Compact is therefore necessary to provide for the welfare and protection of juveniles and of the public with respect to:

(1) Cooperative supervision of delinquent juveniles on probation or parole;

(2) The return, from one state to another, of delinquent juveniles who have escaped or absconded;

(3) The return, from one state to another, of nondelinquent juveniles who have run away from home; and

(4) Additional measures for the protection of juveniles and of the public, which any two or more of the party states may find desirable to undertake cooperatively.

In carrying out the provisions of this Compact, the party states shall be guided by the noncriminal, reformative, and protective policies which guide their laws concerning delinquent, neglected, or dependent juveniles generally. It shall be the policy of the states party to this Compact to cooperate and observe their respective responsibilities for the prompt return and acceptance of juveniles and delinquent juveniles who become subject to the provisions of this Compact. The provisions of this Compact shall be reasonably and liberally construed to accomplish the foregoing purposes. (1963, c. 910, s. 1; 1965, c. 925, s. 1; 1979, c. 815, s. 1; 1998-202, s. 6.)

§ 7B-2802. (For contingent repeal - see note) Existing rights and remedies.

All remedies and procedures provided by this Compact are in addition to and not in substitution for other rights, remedies, and procedures and are not in derogation of parental rights and responsibilities. (1963, c. 910, s. 1; 1965, c. 925, s. 1; 1979, c. 815, s. 1; 1998-202, s. 6.)

§ 7B-2803. (For contingent repeal - see note) Definitions.

For the purposes of this Compact, "delinquent juvenile" means any juvenile who has been adjudged delinquent and who, at the time the provisions of this Compact are invoked, is still subject to the jurisdiction of the court that has made adjudication or to the jurisdiction or supervision of an agency or institution pursuant to an order of the court; "probation or parole" means any kind of post-release supervision of juveniles authorized under the laws of the states party hereto; "court" means any court having jurisdiction over delinquent, neglected, or dependent juveniles; "state" means any state, territory, or possession of the

United States, the District of Columbia, and the Commonwealth of Puerto Rico; and "residence" or any variant thereof means a place at which a home or regular place of abode is maintained. (1963, c. 910, s. 1; 1965, c. 925, s. 1; 1979, c. 815, s. 1; 1998-202, s. 6.)

§ 7B-2804. (For contingent repeal - see note) Return of runaways.

(a) The parent, guardian, person, or agency entitled to legal custody of a juvenile who has not been adjudged delinquent but who has run away without the consent of the parent, guardian, person, or agency may petition the appropriate court in the demanding state for the issuance of a requisition for the juvenile's return. The petition shall state the name and age of the juvenile, the name of the petitioner, and the basis of entitlement to the juvenile's custody, the circumstances of the running away, the juvenile's location if known at the time application is made, and any other facts that may tend to show that the juvenile who has run away is endangering the juvenile's own welfare or the welfare of others and is not an emancipated minor. The petition shall be verified by affidavit, shall be executed in duplicate, and shall be accompanied by two certified copies of the document or documents on which the petitioner's entitlement to the juvenile's custody is based, such as birth certificates, letters of guardianship, or custody decrees. Any further affidavits and other documents as may be deemed proper may be submitted with the petition. The judge of the court to which this application is made may hold a hearing thereon to determine whether for the purposes of this Compact the petitioner is entitled to the legal custody of the juvenile, whether or not it appears that the juvenile has in fact run away without consent, whether or not the juvenile is an emancipated minor, and whether or not it is in the best interests of the juvenile to compel the juvenile's return to the state. If the judge determines, either with or without a hearing, that the juvenile should be returned, the judge shall present to the appropriate court or to the executive authority of the state where the juvenile is alleged to be located a written requisition for the return of the juvenile. The requisition shall set forth the name and age of the juvenile, the determination of the court that the juvenile has run away without the consent of a parent, guardian, person, or agency entitled to legal custody, and that it is in the best interests and for the protection of the juvenile that the juvenile be returned. In the event that a proceeding for the adjudication of the juvenile as a delinquent, neglected, or dependent juvenile is pending in the court at the time when the juvenile runs away, the court may issue a requisition for the return of the juvenile upon its own motion, regardless of the consent of the parent, guardian, person, or agency entitled to legal custody, reciting therein the nature and circumstances of the pending proceeding. The requisition shall in every case be executed in duplicate and shall be signed by the judge. One copy of the requisition shall be filed with the Compact Administrator of the demanding state, there to remain on file subject to the provisions of law governing records of the court. Upon the receipt of a requisition demanding the return of a juvenile who has run away, the court or the executive authority to whom the requisition is addressed shall issue an order to any peace officer or other appropriate person directing that person to take into custody and detain the juvenile. The detention order must substantially recite the facts necessary to the validity of its issuance hereunder. No juvenile detained upon the order shall be delivered over to the officer whom the court has appointed to receive the juvenile unless the juvenile first is taken before a judge of a court in the state, who shall inform the juvenile of the demand made for the juvenile's return, and who may determine that counsel or guardian ad litem for the juvenile should be appointed. If the court finds that the requisition is in order, the court shall deliver the juvenile over to the officer appointed to receive the juvenile by the court demanding the juvenile. The court, however, may fix a reasonable time to be allowed for the purpose of testing the legality of the proceeding.

Upon reasonable information that a person is a juvenile who has run away from another state party to this Compact without the consent of a parent, guardian, person, or agency entitled to legal custody, the juvenile may be taken into custody without a requisition and brought before a judge of the appropriate court who may determine that counsel or guardian ad litem for the juvenile should be appointed and who shall determine after a hearing whether sufficient cause exists to hold the person, subject to the order of the court, for the juvenile's own protection and welfare, for such a time not exceeding 90 days as will enable the return of the juvenile to another state party to this Compact pursuant to a requisition for return from a court of that state. In cases in which the court determines that counsel or guardian ad litem should be provided for the juvenile, appointment shall be in accordance with rules adopted by the Office of Indigent Defense Services. If, at the time when a state seeks the return of a juvenile who has run away, there is pending in the state wherein the juvenile is found, any criminal charge, or any proceeding to have the juvenile adjudicated a delinquent juvenile for an act committed in the state, or if the juvenile is suspected of having committed within the state a criminal offense or an act of juvenile delinquency, the juvenile shall not be returned without the consent of the state until discharged from prosecution or other form of proceeding, imprisonment, detention, or supervision for the offense or juvenile delinquency. The duly accredited officers of any state party to this Compact, upon the establishment of their authority and the identity of the juvenile being returned, shall be permitted to transport the juvenile through any and all states party to this Compact, without interference. Upon return of the juvenile to the state from which the juvenile ran away, the juvenile shall be subject to such further proceedings as may be appropriate under the laws of that state.

(b) The state to which the juvenile is returned under this Article shall be responsible for payment of the transportation costs of return.

(c) The term "juvenile" as used in this Article means any person who is a minor under the law of the state of residence of the parent, guardian, person, or agency entitled to the legal custody of the minor. (1963, c. 910, s. 1; c. 1965, c. 925, s. 1; 1979, c. 815, s. 1; 1998-202, s. 6; 2000-144, s. 25.)

§ 7B-2805. (For contingent repeal - see note) Return of escapees and absconders.

(a) The appropriate person or authority from whose probation or parole supervision a delinquent juvenile has absconded or from whose institutional custody a delinquent juvenile has escaped shall present to the appropriate court or to the executive authority of the state where the delinquent juvenile is alleged to be located a written requisition for the return of the delinquent juvenile. The requisition shall state the name and age of the delinquent juvenile, the particulars of the juvenile's adjudication as a delinquent juvenile, the circumstances of the breach of the terms of probation or parole or of the juvenile's escape from an institution or agency vested with legal custody or supervision, and the location of the delinquent juvenile, if known, at the time the requisition is made. The requisition shall be verified by affidavit, shall be executed in duplicate, and shall be accompanied by two certified copies of the judgment, formal adjudication, or order of commitment which subjects the delinquent juvenile to probation or parole or to the legal custody of the institution or agency concerned. Any further affidavits and documents as may be deemed proper may be submitted with the requisition. One copy of the requisition shall be filed with the Compact Administrator of the demanding state, there to remain on file subject to the provisions of the law governing records of the appropriate court. Upon the receipt of a requisition demanding the return of a delinquent juvenile who has absconded or escaped, the court or the executive authority to whom the requisition is addressed shall issue an order to any peace officer or other appropriate person directing the person to take into custody and detain such delinquent juvenile. The detention order must substantially recite the facts necessary to the validity of its issuance hereunder. No delinquent juvenile detained upon the order shall be delivered over to the officer whom the appropriate person or authority demanding the juvenile has appointed to receive the juvenile, unless the juvenile is first taken forthwith before a judge of an appropriate court in the state, who shall inform the juvenile of the demand made for the return, and who may determine that counsel or guardian ad litem for the juvenile should be appointed. If the judge of the court finds that the requisition is in order, the judge shall deliver the delinquent juvenile over to the officer whom the appropriate person or authority demanding the juvenile appointed to receive the juvenile. The judge, however, may fix a reasonable time to be allowed for the purpose of testing the legality of the proceeding.

Upon reasonable information that a person is a delinquent juvenile who has absconded while on probation or parole, or escaped from an institution or agency vested with legal custody or supervision in any state party to this Compact, the person may be taken into custody in any other state party to this Compact without a requisition. But in that event, the juvenile shall be taken forthwith before a judge of the appropriate court, who may determine that counsel or guardian ad litem for the person should be appointed and who shall determine after a hearing, whether sufficient cause exists to hold the person subject to the order of the court for a length of time, not exceeding 90 days, as will enable detention of the juvenile under a detention order issued on a requisition pursuant to this Article. If, at the time when a state seeks the return of a delinquent who has either absconded while on probation or parole or escaped from an institution or agency vested with legal custody or supervision, there is pending in the state wherein the juvenile is detained any criminal charge or any proceeding to have the juvenile adjudicated a delinquent juvenile for an act committed in the state, or if the juvenile is suspected of having committed a criminal offense or an act of juvenile delinquency within the state, the juvenile shall not be returned without the consent of the state until discharged from prosecution or other form of proceeding, imprisonment, detention, or supervision for the offense or juvenile delinquency. The duly accredited officers of any state party to this Compact, upon the establishment of their authority and the identity of the delinquent juvenile being returned, shall be permitted to transport the delinquent juvenile through any and all states party to this Compact, without interference. Upon return to the state from which the juvenile escaped or absconded, the delinquent juvenile shall be subject to any further proceedings appropriate under the laws of that state.

(b) The state to which a delinquent juvenile is returned under this Article shall be responsible for the payment of transportation costs of the return.

(c) If the court determines that counsel or guardian ad litem should be provided under this section, appointment shall be in accordance with rules adopted by the Office of Indigent Defense Services. (1963, c. 910, s. 1; 1965, c. 925, s. 1; 1979, c. 815, s. 1; 1998-202, s. 6; 2000-144, s. 26.)

§ 7B-2806. (For contingent repeal - see note) Voluntary return procedure.

Any delinquent juvenile who has absconded while on probation or parole, or escaped from an institution or agency vested with legal custody or supervision in any state party to this Compact, and any juvenile who has run away from any state party to this Compact, who is taken into custody without a requisition in another state party to this Compact under the provisions of G.S. 7B-2804(a) or G.S. 7B-2805(a), may consent to the immediate return of the juvenile to the state from which the juvenile absconded, escaped, or ran away. Consent shall be given by the juvenile or delinquent juvenile and the juvenile's counsel or guardian ad litem, if any, by executing or subscribing a writing in the presence of a judge of the appropriate court, which states that the juvenile or delinquent juvenile and the juvenile's counsel or guardian ad litem, if any, consent to return of the juvenile to the demanding state. Before consent is executed or subscribed, however, the judge, in the presence of counsel or guardian ad litem, if any, shall inform the juvenile or delinquent juvenile of the juvenile's rights under this Compact. When the consent has been duly executed, it shall be forwarded to and filed with the Compact Administrator of the state in which the court is located, and the judge shall direct the officer having the juvenile or delinquent juvenile in custody to deliver the juvenile to the duly accredited officer or officers of the state demanding return of the juvenile and shall cause to be delivered to the officer or officers a copy of the consent. The court may, however, upon the request of the state to which the juvenile or delinquent juvenile is being returned, order the juvenile to return unaccompanied to the state and shall provide the juvenile with a copy of the court order; in that event a copy of the consent shall be forwarded to the Compact Administrator of the state to which the juvenile or delinquent juvenile is ordered to return. (1963, c. 910, s. 1; 1965, c. 925, s. 1; 1979, c. 815, s. 1; 1998-202, s. 6.)

§ 7B-2807. (For contingent repeal - see note) Cooperative supervision of probationers and parolees.

(a) That the duly constituted judicial and administrative authorities of a state party to this Compact (herein called "sending state") may permit any delinquent juvenile within such state, placed on probation or parole, to reside in any other state party to this Compact (herein called "receiving state") while on probation or parole, and the receiving state shall accept the delinquent juvenile, if the parent, guardian, or person entitled to the legal custody of the delinquent juvenile is residing or undertakes to reside within the receiving state. Before granting permission, opportunity shall be given to the receiving state to make investigations as it deems necessary. The authorities of the sending state shall send to the authorities of the receiving state copies of pertinent court orders, social case studies, and all other available information which may be of value to and assist the receiving state in supervising a probationer or parolee under this Compact. A receiving state, in its discretion, may agree to accept supervision of a probationer or parolee in cases where the parent, guardian, or person entitled to the legal custody of the delinquent juvenile is not a resident of the receiving state, and if so accepted, the sending state may transfer the supervision accordingly.

(b)     That each receiving state will assume the duties of visitation and of supervision over any delinquent juvenile and in the exercise of those duties will be governed by the same standards of visitation and supervision that prevail for its own delinquent juveniles released on probation or parole.

(c)     That, after consultation between the appropriate authorities of the sending state and of the receiving state as to the desirability and necessity of returning the delinquent juvenile, the duly accredited officers of a sending state may enter a receiving state and there apprehend and retake any delinquent juvenile on probation or parole. For that purpose, no formalities will be required other than establishing the authority of the officer and the identity of the delinquent juvenile to be retaken and returned. The decision of the sending state to retake a delinquent juvenile on probation or parole shall be conclusive upon and not reviewable within the receiving state, but if, at the time the sending state seeks to retake a delinquent juvenile on probation or parole, there is pending against the juvenile within the receiving state any criminal charge or any proceeding to have the juvenile adjudicated a delinquent juvenile for any act committed in the state or if the juvenile is suspected of having committed within the state a criminal offense or an act of juvenile delinquency, the juvenile shall not be returned without the consent of the receiving state until discharged from prosecution or other form of proceeding, imprisonment, detention, or supervision for the offense or juvenile delinquency. The duly accredited officers of the sending state shall be permitted to transport delinquent juveniles being so returned through any and all states party to this Compact without interference.

(d) The sending state shall be responsible under this Article for paying the costs of transporting any delinquent juvenile to the receiving state or of returning any delinquent juvenile to the sending state. (1963, c. 910, s. 1; 1965, c. 925, s. 1; 1979, c. 815, s. 1; 1998-202, s. 6.)

§ 7B-2808. (For contingent repeal - see note) Responsibility for costs.

(a) The provisions of G.S. 7B-2804(b), 7B-2805(b), and 7B-2807(d) shall not be construed to alter or affect any internal relationship among the departments, agencies, and officers of and in the government of a party state, or between a party state and its subdivisions, as to the payment of costs or responsibilities therefor.

(b) Nothing in this Compact shall be construed to prevent any party state or subdivision thereof from asserting any right against any person, agency, or other entity in regard to costs for which such party state or subdivision thereof may be responsible pursuant to G.S. 7B-2804(b), 7B-2805(b), and 7B-2807(d). (1963, c. 910, s. 1; 1965, c. 925, s. 1; 1979, c. 815, s. 1; 1998-202, s. 6.)

§ 7B-2809. (For contingent repeal - see note) Detention practices.

To every extent possible, it shall be the policy of states party to this Compact that no juvenile or delinquent juvenile shall be placed or detained in any prison, jail, or lockup, nor be detained or transported in association with criminal, vicious, or dissolute persons. (1963, c. 910, s. 1; 1965, c. 925, s. 1; 1979, c. 815, s. 1; 1998-202, s. 6.)

§ 7B-2810. (For contingent repeal - see note) Supplementary agreements.

The duly constituted administrative authorities of a state party to this Compact may enter into supplementary agreements with any other state or states party hereto for the cooperative care, treatment, and rehabilitation of delinquent juveniles whenever they find that the agreements will improve the facilities or programs available for care, treatment, and rehabilitation. Care, treatment, and rehabilitation may be provided in an institution located within any state entering into a supplementary agreement. Supplementary agreements shall:

(1) Provide the rates to be paid for the care, treatment, and custody of delinquent juveniles taking into consideration the character of facilities, services, and subsistence furnished;

(2) Provide that the delinquent juvenile shall be given a court hearing prior to the juvenile being sent to another state for care, treatment, and custody;

(3) Provide that the state receiving a delinquent juvenile in one of its institutions shall act solely as agent for the state sending the delinquent juvenile;

(4) Provide that the sending state shall at all times retain jurisdiction over delinquent juveniles sent to an institution in another state;

(5) Provide for reasonable inspection of the institutions by the sending state;

(6) Provide that the consent of the parent, guardian, person, or agency entitled to the legal custody of the delinquent juvenile shall be secured prior to the juvenile being sent to another state; and

(7) Make provisions for any other matters and details as shall be necessary to protect the rights and equities of delinquent juveniles and of the cooperating states. (1963, c. 910, s. 1; 1965, c. 925, s. 1; 1979, c. 815, s. 1; 1998-202, s. 6.)

§ 7B-2811. (For contingent repeal - see note) Acceptance of federal and other aid.

Any state party to this Compact may accept any and all donations, gifts, and grants of money, equipment, and services from the federal or any local government, or any agency thereof and from any person, firm, or corporation, for any of the purposes and functions of this Compact, and may receive and utilize, the same subject to the terms, conditions, and regulations governing such donations, gifts, and grants. (1963, c. 910, s. 1; 1965, c. 925, s. 1; 1979, c. 815, s. 1; 1998-202, s. 6.)

§ 7B-2812. (For contingent repeal - see note) Compact administrators.

The governor of each state party to this Compact shall designate an officer who, acting jointly with like officers of other party states, shall promulgate rules and regulations to carry out more efficiently the terms and provisions of this Compact. (1963, c. 910, s. 1; 1965, c. 925, s. 1; 1979, c. 815, s. 1; 1998-202, s. 6.)

§ 7B-2813. (For contingent repeal - see note) Execution of Compact.

This Compact shall become operative immediately upon its execution by any state as between it and any other state or states so executing. When executed it shall have the full force and effect of law within the state, the form of execution to be in accordance with the laws of the executing state. (1963, c. 910, s. 1; 1965, c. 925, s. 1; 1979, c. 815, s. 1; 1998-202, s. 6.)

§ 7B-2814. (For contingent repeal - see note) Renunciation.

This Compact shall continue in force and remain binding upon each executing state until renounced by it. Renunciation of this Compact shall be by the same authority which executed it, by sending six months' notice in writing of its intention to withdraw from the Compact to the other states party hereto. The duties and obligations of a renouncing state under G.S. 7B-2807 hereof shall continue as to parolees and probationers residing therein at the time of withdrawal until retaken or finally discharged. Supplementary agreements entered into under G.S. 7B-2810 hereof shall be subject to renunciation as provided by supplementary agreements and shall not be subject to the six months' renunciation notice of the present section. (1963, c. 910, s. 1; 1965, c. 925, s. 1; 1979, c. 815, s. 1; 1998-202, s. 6.)

§ 7B-2815. (For contingent repeal - see note) Severability.

The provisions of this Compact shall be severable and, if any phrase, clause, sentence, or provision of this Compact is declared to be contrary to the constitution of any participating state or of the United States or the applicability thereof to any government, agency, person, or circumstances is held invalid, the validity of the remainder of this Compact and the applicability thereof to any government, agency, person, or circumstances shall not be affected thereby. If this Compact shall be held contrary to the constitution of any state participating therein, the Compact shall remain in full force and effect as to the remaining states and in full force and effect as to the state affected as to all severable matters. (1963, c. 910, s. 1; 1965, c. 925, s. 1; 1979, c. 815, s. 1; 1998-202, s. 6.)

§ 7B-2816. (For contingent repeal - see note) Authority of Governor to designate Compact Administrator.

Pursuant to said Compact, the Governor is hereby authorized and empowered to designate an officer who shall be the Compact Administrator and who, acting jointly with like officers of other party states, shall adopt rules and regulations to carry out more effectively the terms of the Compact. The Compact Administrator shall serve subject to the pleasure of the Governor. The Compact Administrator is hereby authorized, empowered, and directed to cooperate with all departments, agencies, and officers of and in the government of this State and its subdivisions in facilitating the proper administration of the Compact or of any supplementary agreement or agreements entered into by this State hereunder. (1963, c. 910, s. 2; 1979, c. 815, s. 1; 1998-202, s. 6.)

§ 7B-2817. (For contingent repeal - see note) Authority of Compact Administrator to enter into supplementary agreements.

The Compact Administrator is hereby authorized and empowered to enter into supplementary agreements with appropriate officials of other states pursuant to the Compact. In the event that the supplementary agreement shall require or contemplate the use of any institution or facility of this State or require or contemplate the provision of any service by this State, the supplementary agreement shall have no force or effect until approved by the head of the department or agency under whose jurisdiction said institution or facility is operated or whose department or agency will be charged with the rendering of the service. (1963, c. 910, s. 3; 1979, c. 815, s. 1; 1998-202, s. 6.)

§ 7B-2818. (For contingent repeal - see note) Discharging financial obligations imposed by Compact or agreement.

The Compact Administrator, subject to the approval of the Director of the Budget, may make or arrange for any payments necessary to discharge any financial obligations imposed upon this State by the Compact or by any supplementary agreement entered into thereunder. (1963, c. 910, s. 4; 1979, c. 815, s. 1; 1998-202, s. 6.)

§ 7B-2819. (For contingent repeal - see note) Enforcement of Compact.

The courts, departments, agencies, and officers of this State and subdivisions shall enforce this Compact and shall do all things appropriate to the effectuation of its purposes and intent which may be within their respective jurisdictions. (1963, c. 910, s. 5; 1979, c. 815, s. 1; 1998-202, s. 6.)

§ 7B-2820. (For contingent repeal - see note) Additional procedure for returning runaways not precluded.

In addition to any procedure provided in G.S. 7B-2804 and G.S. 7B-2806 of the Compact for the return of any runaway juvenile, the particular states, the juvenile or the juvenile's parents, the courts, or other legal custodian involved may agree upon and adopt any other plan or procedure legally authorized under the laws of this State and the other respective party states for the return of any runaway juvenile. (1963, c. 910, s. 6; 1979, c. 815, s. 1; 1998-202, s. 6.)

§ 7B-2821. (For contingent repeal - see note) Proceedings for return of runaways under G.S. 7B-2804 of Compact; "juvenile" construed.

The judge of any court in North Carolina to which an application is made for the return of a runaway under the provisions of G.S. 7B-2804 of the Interstate Compact on Juveniles shall hold a hearing thereon to determine whether for the purposes of the Compact the petitioner is entitled to the legal custody of the juvenile, whether or not it appears that the juvenile has in fact run away without consent, whether or not the juvenile is an emancipated minor, and whether or not it is in the best interests of the juvenile to compel the return of the juvenile to the state. The judge of any court in North Carolina, finding that a requisition for the return of a juvenile under the provisions of G.S. 7B-2804 of the Compact is in order, shall upon request fix a reasonable time to be allowed for the purpose of testing the legality of the proceeding. The period of time for holding a juvenile in custody under the provisions of G.S. 7B-2804 of the Compact for the protection and welfare of the juvenile, subject to the order of a court of this State, to enable the juvenile's return to another state party to the Compact pursuant to a requisition for return from a court of that state, shall not exceed 30 days. In applying the provisions of G.S. 7B-2804 of the Compact to secure the return of a runaway from North Carolina, the courts of this State shall construe the word "juvenile" as used in this Article to mean any person who has not reached the person's eighteenth birthday. (1965, c. 925, s. 2; 1971, c. 1231, s. 2; 1977, c. 552; 1979, c. 815, s. 1; 1998-202, s. 6.)

§ 7B-2822. (For contingent repeal - see note) Interstate parole and probation hearing procedures for juveniles.

Where supervision of a parolee or probationer is being administered pursuant to the Interstate Compact on Juveniles, the appropriate judicial or administrative authorities in this State shall notify the Compact Administrator of the sending state whenever, in their view, consideration should be given to retaking or reincarceration for a parole or a probation violation. Prior to giving of notification, a hearing shall be held in accordance with this Article within a reasonable time, unless the hearing is waived by the parolee or probationer. The appropriate officer or officers of this State shall, as soon as practicable, following termination of any hearing, report to the sending state, furnish a copy of the hearing record, and make recommendations regarding the disposition to be made of the parolee or probationer by the sending state. Pending any proceeding pursuant to this section, the appropriate officers of this State may take custody of and detain the parolee or probationer involved for a period not to exceed 10 days prior to the hearing and, if it appears to the hearing officer or officers that retaking or reincarceration is likely to follow, for a reasonable period after the hearing or waiver as may be necessary to arrange for retaking or the reincarceration. (1979, c. 815, s. 1; 1998-202, s. 6.)

§ 7B-2823. (For contingent repeal - see note) Hearing officers.

Any hearing pursuant to this Article may be before the Administrator of the Interstate Compact on Juveniles, a deputy of the Administrator, or any other person authorized pursuant to the juvenile laws of this State to hear cases of alleged juvenile parole or probation violations, except that no hearing officer shall be the person making the allegation of violation. (1979, c. 815, s. 1; 1998-202, s. 6.)

§ 7B-2824. (For contingent repeal - see note) Due process at parole or probation violation hearing.

With respect to any hearing pursuant to this Article, the parolee or probationer:

(1) Shall have reasonable notice in writing of the nature and content of the allegations to be made, including notice that the purpose of the hearing is to determine whether there is probable cause to believe that the parolee or probationer has committed a violation that may lead to a revocation of parole or probation;

(2) Shall be permitted to advise with any persons whose assistance the parolee or probationer reasonably desires, prior to the hearing;

(3) Shall have the right to confront and examine any persons who have made allegations against the parolee or probationer, unless the hearing officer determines that confrontation would present a substantial present or subsequent danger of harm to the person or persons; and

(4) May admit, deny, or explain the violation alleged and may present proof, including affidavits and other evidence, in support of the parolee's or probationer's contentions.

A record of the proceedings shall be made and preserved. (1979, c. 815, s. 1; 1998-202, s. 6.)

§ 7B-2825. (For contingent repeal - see note) Effect of parole or probation violation hearing outside State.

In any case of alleged parole or probation violation by a person being supervised in another state pursuant to the Interstate Compact on Juveniles, any appropriate judicial or administrative officer or agency in another state is authorized to hold a hearing on the alleged violation. Upon receipt of the record of a parole or probation violation hearing held in another state pursuant to a statute substantially similar to this Article, such record shall have the same standing and effect as though the proceeding of which it is a record was had before the appropriate officer or officers in this State, and any recommendations contained in or accompanying the record shall be fully considered by the appropriate officer or officers of this State in making disposition of the matter. (1979, c. 815, s. 1; 1998-202, s. 6.)

§ 7B-2826. (For contingent repeal - see note) Amendment to Interstate Compact on Juveniles concerning interstate rendition of juveniles alleged to be delinquent.

(a) This amendment shall provide additional remedies and shall be binding only as among and between those party states which specifically execute the same.

(b) All provisions and procedures of G.S. 7B-2805 and G.S. 7B-2806 of the Interstate Compact on Juveniles shall be construed to apply to any juvenile charged with being a delinquent by reason of a violation of any criminal law. Any juvenile, charged with being a delinquent by reason of violating any criminal law, shall be returned to the requesting state upon a requisition to the state where the juvenile may be found. A petition in the case shall be filed in a court of competent jurisdiction in the requesting state where the violation of criminal law is alleged to have been committed. The petition may be filed regardless of whether the juvenile has left the state before or after the filing of the petition. The requisition described in G.S. 7B-2805 of the Compact shall be forwarded by the judge of the court in which the petition has been filed. (1979, c. 815, s. 1; 1998-202, s. 6.)

§ 7B-2827. (For contingent repeal - see note) Out-of-State Confinement Amendment.

(a) The Out-of-State Confinement Amendment to the Interstate Compact on Juveniles is hereby enacted into law and entered into by this State with all other states legally joining therein in the form substantially as follows:

(1) Whenever the fully constituted judicial or administrative authorities in a sending state shall determine that confinement of a probationer or reconfinement of a parolee is necessary or desirable, the officials may direct that the confinement or reconfinement be in an appropriate institution for delinquent juveniles within the territory of the receiving state, the receiving state to act in that regard solely as agent for the sending state.

(2) Escapees and absconders who would otherwise be returned pursuant to G.S. 7B-2805 of the Compact may be confined or reconfined in the receiving state pursuant to this amendment. In any case in which the information and allegations are required to be made and furnished in a requisition pursuant to G.S. 7B-2805, the sending state shall request confinement or reconfinement in

the receiving state. Whenever applicable, detention orders, as provided in G.S. 7B-2805, may be employed pursuant to this paragraph preliminary to disposition of the escapee or absconder.

(3) The confinement or reconfinement of a parolee, probationer, escapee, or absconder pursuant to this amendment shall require the concurrence of the appropriate judicial or administrative authorities of the receiving state.

(4) As used in this amendment: (i) "sending state" means a sending state as that term is used in G.S. 7B-2807 of the Compact or the state from which a delinquent juvenile has escaped or absconded within the meaning of G.S. 7B-2805 of the Compact; (ii) "receiving state" means any state, other than the sending state, in which a parolee, probationer, escapee, or absconder may be found, provided that the state is a party to this amendment.

(5) Every state which adopts this amendment shall designate at least one of its institutions for delinquent juveniles as a "Compact Institution" and shall confine persons therein as provided in subdivision (1) of this subsection unless the sending and receiving state in question shall make specific contractual arrangements to the contrary. All states party to this amendment shall have access to "Compact Institutions" at all reasonable hours for the purpose of inspecting the facilities thereof and for the purpose of visiting such of the State's delinquents as may be confined in the institution.

(6) Persons confined in "Compact Institutions" pursuant to the terms of this Compact shall at all times be subject to the jurisdiction of the sending state and may at any time be removed from the "Compact Institution" for transfer to an appropriate institution within the sending state, for return to probation or parole, for discharge, or for any purpose permitted by the laws of the sending state.

(7) All persons who may be confined in a "Compact Institution" pursuant to the provisions of this amendment shall be treated in a reasonable and humane manner. The fact of confinement or reconfinement in a receiving state shall not deprive any person so confined or reconfined of any rights which the person would have had if confined or reconfined in an appropriate institution of the sending state. No agreement to submit to confinement or reconfinement pursuant to the terms of this amendment may be construed as a waiver of any rights which the delinquent would have had if the person had been confined or reconfined in any appropriate institution of the sending state, except that the hearing or hearings, if any, to which a parolee, probationer, escapee, or absconder may be entitled (prior to confinement or reconfinement) by the laws

of the sending state may be had before the appropriate judicial or administrative officers of the receiving state. In this event, said judicial and administrative officers shall act as agents of the sending state after consultation with appropriate officers of the sending state.

(8)     Any receiving state incurring costs or other expenses under this amendment shall be reimbursed in the amount of the costs or other expenses by the sending state unless the states concerned shall specifically otherwise agree. Any two or more states party to this amendment may enter into supplementary agreements determining a different allocation of costs as among themselves.

(9)     This amendment shall take initial effect when entered into by any two or more states party to the Compact and shall be effective as to those states which have specifically enacted this amendment. Rules and regulations necessary to effectuate the terms of this amendment may be adopted by the appropriate officers of those states which have enacted this amendment.

(b)     In addition to any institution in which the authorities of this State may otherwise confine or order the confinement of a delinquent juvenile, the authorities may, pursuant to the Out-of-State Confinement Amendment to the Interstate Compact on Juveniles, confine or order the confinement of a delinquent juvenile in a Compact Institution within another party state. (1979, c. 815, s. 1; 1998-202, s. 6.)


§§ 7B-2828 through 7B-2899: Reserved for future codification purposes.


SUBCHAPTER III. JUVENILE RECORDS.

Article 29.

Records and Social Reports of Cases of Abuse, Neglect, and Dependency.

§ 7B-2900. Definitions.

The definitions of G.S. 7B-101 and G.S. 7B-1501 apply to this Subchapter. (1998-202, s. 6.)

§ 7B-2901.  Confidentiality of records.

(a)     The clerk shall maintain a complete record of all juvenile cases filed in the clerk's office alleging abuse, neglect, or dependency. The records shall be withheld from public inspection and, except as provided in this subsection, may be examined only by order of the court. The record shall include the summons, petition, custody order, court order, written motions, the electronic or mechanical recording of the hearing, and other papers filed in the proceeding. The recording of the hearing shall be reduced to a written transcript only when notice of appeal has been timely given. After the time for appeal has expired with no appeal having been filed, the recording of the hearing may be erased or destroyed upon the written order of the court.

The following persons may examine the juvenile's record maintained pursuant to this subsection and obtain copies of written parts of the record without an order of the court:

(1)     The person named in the petition as the juvenile;

(2)     The guardian ad litem;

(3)     The county department of social services; and

(4)     The juvenile's parent, guardian, or custodian, or the attorney for the juvenile or the juvenile's parent, guardian, or custodian.

(b)     The Director of the Department of Social Services shall maintain a record of the cases of juveniles under protective custody by the Department or under placement by the court, which shall include family background information; reports of social, medical, psychiatric, or psychological information concerning a juvenile or the juvenile's family; interviews with the juvenile's family; or other information which the court finds should be protected from public inspection in the best interests of the juvenile. The records maintained pursuant to this subsection may be examined only in the following circumstances:

(1)     The juvenile's guardian ad litem or the juvenile, including a juvenile who has reached age 18 or been emancipated, may examine the records.

(2)     A district or superior court judge of this State presiding over a civil matter in which the department is not a party may order the department to release confidential information, after providing the department with reasonable

notice and an opportunity to be heard and then determining that the information is relevant and necessary to the trial of the matter before the court and unavailable from any other source. This subsection shall not be construed to relieve any court of its duty to conduct hearings and make findings required under relevant federal law before ordering the release of any private medical or mental health information or records related to substance abuse or HIV status or treatment. The department may surrender the requested records to the court, for in camera review, if surrender is necessary to make the required determinations.

(3)     A district or superior court judge of this State presiding over a criminal or delinquency matter shall conduct an in camera review before releasing to the defendant or juvenile any confidential records maintained by the department of social services, except those records the defendant or juvenile is entitled to pursuant to subdivision (1) of this subsection.

(4)     The department may disclose confidential information to a parent, guardian, custodian, or caretaker in accordance with G.S. 7B-700.

(c)     In the case of a child victim, the court may order the sharing of information among such public agencies as the court deems necessary to reduce the trauma to the victim.

(d)     The court's entire record of a proceeding involving consent for an abortion on an unemancipated minor under Article 1A, Part 2 of Chapter 90 of the General Statutes is not a matter of public record, shall be maintained separately from any juvenile record, shall be withheld from public inspection, and may be examined only by order of the court, by the unemancipated minor, or by the unemancipated minor's attorney or guardian ad litem. (1979, c. 815, s. 1; 1987, c. 297; 1994, Ex. Sess., c. 7, s. 1; 1995, c. 462, s. 4; c. 509, s. 5; 1997-459, s. 2; 1998-202, s. 6; 2001-208, s. 10; 2001-487, s. 101; 2009-311, s. 18.)

§ 7B-2902. Disclosure in child fatality or near fatality cases.

(a)     The following definitions apply in this section:

(1)     Child fatality. - The death of a child from suspected abuse, neglect, or maltreatment.

(2) Findings and information. - A written summary, as allowed by subsections (c) through (f) of this section, of actions taken or services rendered by a public agency following receipt of information that a child might be in need of protection. The written summary shall include any of the following information the agency is able to provide:

a. The dates, outcomes, and results of any actions taken or services rendered.

b. The results of any review by the State Child Fatality Prevention Team, a local child fatality prevention team, a local community child protection team, the Child Fatality Task Force, or any public agency.

c. Confirmation of the receipt of all reports, accepted or not accepted by the county department of social services, for investigation of suspected child abuse, neglect, or maltreatment, including confirmation that investigations were conducted, the results of the investigations, a description of the conduct of the most recent investigation and the services rendered, and a statement of basis for the department's decision.

(3) Near fatality. - A case in which a physician determines that a child is in serious or critical condition as the result of sickness or injury caused by suspected abuse, neglect, or maltreatment.

(4) Public agency. - Any agency of State government or its subdivisions as defined in G.S. 132-1(a).

(b) Notwithstanding any other provision of law and subject to the provisions of subsections (c) through (f) of this section, a public agency shall disclose to the public, upon request, the findings and information related to a child fatality or near fatality if:

(1) A person is criminally charged with having caused the child fatality or near fatality; or

(2) The district attorney has certified that a person would be charged with having caused the child fatality or near fatality but for that person's prior death.

(c) Nothing herein shall be deemed to authorize access to the confidential records in the custody of a public agency, or the disclosure to the public of the substance or content of any psychiatric, psychological, or therapeutic evaluations or like materials or information pertaining to the child or the child's family unless directly related to the cause of the child fatality or near fatality, or the disclosure of information that would reveal the identities of persons who provided information related to the suspected abuse, neglect, or maltreatment of the child.

(d) Within five working days from the receipt of a request for findings and information related to a child fatality or near fatality, a public agency shall consult with the appropriate district attorney and provide the findings and information unless the agency has a reasonable belief that release of the information:

(1) Is not authorized by subsections (a) and (b) of this section;

(2) Is likely to cause mental or physical harm or danger to a minor child residing in the deceased or injured child's household;

(3) Is likely to jeopardize the State's ability to prosecute the defendant;

(4) Is likely to jeopardize the defendant's right to a fair trial;

(5) Is likely to undermine an ongoing or future criminal investigation; or

(6) Is not authorized by federal law and regulations.

(e) Any person whose request is denied may apply to the appropriate superior court for an order compelling disclosure of the findings and information of the public agency. The application shall set forth, with reasonable particularity, factors supporting the application. The superior court shall have jurisdiction to issue such orders. Actions brought pursuant to this section shall be set down for immediate hearing, and subsequent proceedings in such actions shall be accorded priority by the appellate courts. After the court has reviewed the specific findings and information, in camera, the court shall issue an order compelling disclosure unless the court finds that one or more of the circumstances in subsection (d) of this section exist.

(f) Access to criminal investigative reports and criminal intelligence information of public law enforcement agencies and confidential information in the possession of the State Child Fatality Prevention Team, the local teams, and the Child Fatality Task Force, shall be governed by G.S. 132-1.4 and G.S. 7B-

1413 respectively. Nothing herein shall be deemed to require the disclosure or release of any information in the possession of a district attorney.

(g)     Any public agency or its employees acting in good faith in disclosing or declining to disclose information pursuant to this section shall be immune from any criminal or civil liability that might otherwise be incurred or imposed for such action.

(h)     Nothing herein shall be deemed to narrow or limit the definition of "public records" as set forth in G.S. 132-1(a). (1997-459, s. 1; 1998-202, s. 6.)

Article 30.

Juvenile Records and Social Reports of Delinquency and Undisciplined Cases.

§ 7B-3000.  Juvenile court records.

(a)     The clerk shall maintain a complete record of all juvenile cases filed in the clerk's office to be known as the juvenile record. The record shall include the summons and petition, any secure or nonsecure custody order, any electronic or mechanical recording of hearings, and any written motions, orders, or papers filed in the proceeding.

(b)     All juvenile records shall be withheld from public inspection and, except as provided in this subsection, may be examined only by order of the court. Except as provided in subsection (c) of this section, the following persons may examine the juvenile's record and obtain copies of written parts of the record without an order of the court:

(1)     The juvenile or the juvenile's attorney;

(2)     The juvenile's parent, guardian, or custodian, or the authorized representative of the juvenile's parent, guardian, or custodian;

(3)     The prosecutor;

(4)     Court counselors; and

(5)     Probation officers in the Section of Community Corrections of the Division of Adult Correction of the Department of Public Safety, as provided in subsection (e1) of this section and in G.S. 15A-1341(e).

Except as provided in subsection (c) of this section, the prosecutor may, in the prosecutor's discretion, share information obtained from a juvenile's record with magistrates and law enforcement officers sworn in this State, but may not allow a magistrate or law enforcement officer to photocopy any part of the record.

(c)     The court may direct the clerk to "seal" any portion of a juvenile's record. The clerk shall secure any sealed portion of a juvenile's record in an envelope clearly marked "SEALED: MAY BE EXAMINED ONLY BY ORDER OF THE COURT", or with similar notice, and shall permit examination or copying of sealed portions of a juvenile's record only pursuant to a court order specifically authorizing inspection or copying.

(d)     Any portion of a juvenile's record consisting of an electronic or mechanical recording of a hearing shall be transcribed only when notice of appeal has been timely given and shall be copied electronically or mechanically, only by order of the court. After the time for appeal has expired with no appeal having been filed, the court may enter a written order directing the clerk to destroy the recording of the hearing.

(e)     Notwithstanding any other provision of law, if the defendant in a criminal proceeding involving a Class A1 misdemeanor or a felony was less than 21 years of age at the time of the offense, information obtained pursuant to subsection (b) of this section regarding the juvenile's record of an adjudication of delinquency for an offense that would be a Class A1 misdemeanor or a felony if committed by an adult, where the adjudication occurred after the defendant reached 13 years of age, may be used by law enforcement, the magistrate, the courts, and the prosecutor for pretrial release, plea negotiating decisions, and plea acceptance decisions. Information obtained regarding any juvenile record shall remain confidential and shall not be placed in any public record.

(e1)    When a person is subject to probation supervision under Article 82 of Chapter 15A of the General Statutes, for an offense that was committed while the person was less than 25 years of age, that person's juvenile record of an adjudication of delinquency for an offense that would be a felony if committed by an adult may be examined without a court order by the probation officer in the Section of Community Corrections of the Division of Adult Correction assigned to supervise the person for the purpose of assessing risk related to supervision.

Each judicial district manager in the Section of Community Corrections of the Division of Adult Correction shall designate a staff person in each county to obtain from the clerk, at the request of the probation officer assigned to supervise the person, any juvenile records authorized to be examined under this subsection. The judicial district manager shall inform the clerk in each county, in writing, of the designated staff person in the county. The designated staff person shall transfer any juvenile records obtained to the probation officer assigned to supervise the person.

Any copies of juvenile records obtained pursuant to this subsection shall continue to be withheld from public inspection and shall not become part of the public record in any criminal proceeding. Any copies of juvenile records shall be destroyed within 30 days of termination of the person's period of probation supervision. Any other information in the Section of Community Corrections of the Division of Adult Correction records, relating to a person's juvenile record, shall remain confidential and shall be maintained or destroyed pursuant to guidelines established by the Department of Cultural Resources for the maintenance and destruction of Section of Community Corrections of the Division of Adult Correction records.

(f) The juvenile's record of an adjudication of delinquency for an offense that would be a Class A, B1, B2, C, D, or E felony if committed by an adult may be used in a subsequent criminal proceeding against the juvenile either under G.S. 8C-1, Rule 404(b), or to prove an aggravating factor at sentencing under G.S. 15A-1340.4(a), 15A-1340.16(d), or 15A-2000(e). The record may be so used only by order of the court in the subsequent criminal proceeding, upon motion of the prosecutor, after an in camera hearing to determine whether the record in question is admissible.

(g) Except as provided in subsection (d) of this section, a juvenile's record shall be destroyed only as authorized by G.S. 7B-3200 or by rules adopted by the Administrative Office of the Courts. (1979, c. 815, s. 1; 1987, c. 297; 1994, Ex. Sess., c. 7, s. 1; 1995, c. 462, s. 4; c. 509, s. 5; 1997-459, s. 2; 1998-202, s. 6; 2000-137, s. 3; 2002-159, s. 26; 2009-372, s. 1; 2009-545, s. 2; 2011-145, s. 19.1(h), (k); 2011-277, s. 1; 2012-83, s. 17.)

§ 7B-3001. Other records relating to juveniles.

(a) The chief court counselor shall maintain a record of all cases of juveniles under supervision of juvenile court counselors, to be known as the juvenile court counselor's record. The juvenile court counselor's record shall include family background information; reports of social, medical, psychiatric, or psychological information concerning a juvenile or the juvenile's family; probation reports; interviews with the juvenile's family; or other information the court finds should be protected from public inspection in the best interests of the juvenile.

(b) Unless jurisdiction of the juvenile has been transferred to superior court, all law enforcement records and files concerning a juvenile shall be kept separate from the records and files of adults and shall be withheld from public inspection. The following persons may examine and obtain copies of law enforcement records and files concerning a juvenile without an order of the court:

(1) The juvenile or the juvenile's attorney;

(2) The juvenile's parent, guardian, custodian, or the authorized representative of the juvenile's parent, guardian, or custodian;

(3) The prosecutor;

(4) Juvenile court counselors; and

(5) Law enforcement officers sworn in this State.

Otherwise, the records and files may be examined or copied only by order of the court.

(c) All records and files maintained by the Division pursuant to this Chapter shall be withheld from public inspection. The following persons may examine and obtain copies of the Division records and files concerning a juvenile without an order of the court:

(1) The juvenile and the juvenile's attorney;

(2) The juvenile's parent, guardian, custodian, or the authorized representative of the juvenile's parent, guardian, or custodian;

(3) Professionals in the agency who are directly involved in the juvenile's case; and

(4) Juvenile court counselors.

Otherwise, the records and files may be examined or copied only by order of the court. The court may inspect and order the release of records maintained by the Division.

(d) When the Section of Community Corrections of the Division of Adult Correction of the Department of Public Safety is authorized to access a juvenile record pursuant to G.S. 7B-3000(e1), the Division may, at the request of the Section of Community Corrections of the Division of Adult Correction, notify the Section of Community Corrections of the Division of Adult Correction that there is a juvenile record of an adjudication of delinquency for an offense that would be a felony if committed by an adult for a person subject to probation supervision under Article 82 of Chapter 15A of the General Statutes and may notify the Section of Community Corrections of the Division of Adult Correction of the county or counties where the adjudication of delinquency occurred. (1979, c. 815, s. 1; 1987, c. 297; 1994, Ex. Sess., c. 7, s. 1; 1995, c. 462, s. 4; c. 509, s. 5; 1997-459, s. 2; 1998-202, s. 6; 2000-137, s. 3; 2001-490, s. 2.32; 2009-372, s. 2; 2009-545, s. 3; 2011-145, s. 19.1(h), (k), (l).)


Article 31.

Disclosure of Juvenile Information.

§ 7B-3100. Disclosure of information about juveniles.

(a) The Division, after consultation with the Conference of Chief District Court Judges, shall adopt rules designating certain local agencies that are authorized to share information concerning juveniles in accordance with the provisions of this section. Agencies so designated shall share with one another, upon request and to the extent permitted by federal law and regulations, information that is in their possession that is relevant to any assessment of a report of child abuse, neglect, or dependency or the provision or arrangement of protective services in a child abuse, neglect, or dependency case by a local department of social services pursuant to the authority granted under Chapter 7B of the General Statutes or to any case in which a petition is filed alleging that a juvenile is abused, neglected, dependent, undisciplined, or delinquent and shall continue to do so until the protective services case is closed by the local department of social services, or if a petition is filed when the juvenile is no longer subject to the jurisdiction of juvenile court. Agencies that may be designated as "agencies authorized to share information" include local mental health facilities, local health departments, local departments of social services, local law enforcement agencies, local school administrative units, the district's district attorney's office, the Division of Juvenile Justice of the Department of Public Safety, and the Office of Guardian ad Litem Services of the Administrative Office of the Courts, and, pursuant to the provisions of G.S. 7B-3000(e1), the Section of Community Corrections of the Division of Adult Correction of the Department of Public Safety. Any information shared among agencies pursuant to this section shall remain confidential, shall be withheld from public inspection, and shall be used only for the protection of the juvenile and others or to improve the educational opportunities of the juvenile, and shall be released in accordance with the provisions of the Family Educational and Privacy Rights Act as set forth in 20 U.S.C. § 1232g. Nothing in this section or any other provision of law shall preclude any other necessary sharing of information among agencies. Nothing herein shall be deemed to require the disclosure or release of any information in the possession of a district attorney.

(b) Disclosure of information concerning any juvenile under investigation or alleged to be within the jurisdiction of the court that would reveal the identity of that juvenile is prohibited except that publication of pictures of runaways is permitted with the permission of the parents and except as provided in G.S. 7B-3102. (1979, c. 815, s. 1; 1987, c. 297; 1994, Ex. Sess., c. 7, s. 1; 1995, c. 462, s. 4; c. 509, s. 5; 1997-459, s. 2; 1998-202, s. 6; 2000-137, s. 3; 2006-205, s. 2; 2007-458, s. 4; 2009-372, s. 3; 2011-145, s. 19.1(h), (k), (l).)


§ 7B-3101. Notification of schools when juveniles are alleged or found to be delinquent.

(a) Notwithstanding G.S. 7B-3000, the juvenile court counselor shall deliver verbal and written notification of the following actions to the principal of the school that the juvenile attends:

(1) A petition is filed under G.S. 7B-1802 that alleges delinquency for an offense that would be a felony if committed by an adult;

(2) The court transfers jurisdiction over a juvenile to superior court under G.S. 7B-2200;

(3) The court dismisses under G.S. 7B-2411 the petition that alleges delinquency for an offense that would be a felony if committed by an adult;

(4) The court issues a dispositional order under Article 25 of Chapter 7B of the General Statutes including, but not limited to, an order of probation that requires school attendance, concerning a juvenile alleged or found delinquent for an offense that would be a felony if committed by an adult; or

(5) The court modifies or vacates any order or disposition under G.S. 7B-2600 concerning a juvenile alleged or found delinquent for an offense that would be a felony if committed by an adult.

Notification of the school principal in person or by telephone shall be made before the beginning of the next school day. Delivery shall be made as soon as practicable but at least within five days of the action. Delivery shall be made in person or by certified mail. Notification that a petition has been filed shall describe the nature of the offense. Notification of a dispositional order, a modified or vacated order, or a transfer to superior court shall describe the court's action and any applicable disposition requirements. As used in this subsection, the term "offense" shall not include any offense under Chapter 20 of the General Statutes.

(b) If the principal of the school the juvenile attends returns any notification as required by G.S. 115C-404, and if the juvenile court counselor learns that the juvenile is transferring to another school, the juvenile court counselor shall deliver the notification to the principal of the school to which the juvenile is transferring. Delivery shall be made as soon as practicable and shall be made in person or by certified mail.

(c) Principals shall handle any notification delivered under this section in accordance with G.S. 115C-404.

(d) For the purpose of this section, "school" means any public or private school in the State that is authorized under Chapter 115C of the General Statutes. (1997-443, s. 8.29(e); 1998-202, s. 6.)

§ 7B-3102. Disclosure of information about juveniles who escape.

(a) Notwithstanding G.S. 7B-2102(d) or any other law to the contrary, within 24 hours of the time a juvenile escapes from custody the Division shall release to the public the juvenile's first name, last initial, and photograph; the name and location of the institution from which the juvenile escaped, or if the juvenile's escape was not from an institution, the circumstances and location of the escape; and a statement, based on the juvenile's record, of the level of concern of the Division as to the juvenile's threat to self or to others, if the juvenile escapes from a detention facility, secure custody, or a youth development center and the juvenile has been adjudicated delinquent.

(b)     When a juvenile escapes from a detention facility or secure custody, the Division may release to the public within 24 hours the juvenile's first name, last initial, and photograph; the name and location of the institution from which the juvenile escaped, or if the juvenile's escape was not from an institution, the circumstances and location of the escape; and a statement, based on the juvenile's record, of the level of concern of the Division as to the juvenile's threat to self or to others if both of the following apply:

(1)     The juvenile is alleged to have committed an offense that would be a felony if committed by an adult.

(2)     The Division determines, based on the juvenile's record, that the juvenile presents a danger to self or others.

(c)     If a juvenile subject to subsection (a) or (b) of this section is returned to custody before the disclosure required or permitted is made, the Division shall not make the disclosure.

(d)     The Division shall maintain a photograph of every juvenile in its custody.

(e)     Before information is released to the public under this section, the Division shall make a reasonable effort to notify a parent, legal guardian, or custodian of the juvenile. (2007-458, s. 2; 2008-169, s. 1; 2011-145, s. 19.1(l).)

Article 32.

Expunction of Juvenile Records.

§ 7B-3200.  Expunction of records of juveniles alleged or adjudicated delinquent and undisciplined.

(a)     Any person who has attained the age of 18 years may file a petition in the court where the person was adjudicated undisciplined for expunction of all records of that adjudication.

(b) Any person who has attained the age of 18 years may file a petition in the court where the person was adjudicated delinquent for expunction of all records of that adjudication provided:

(1) The offense for which the person was adjudicated would have been a crime other than a Class A, B1, B2, C, D, or E felony if committed by an adult.

(2) At least 18 months have elapsed since the person was released from juvenile court jurisdiction, and the person has not subsequently been adjudicated delinquent or convicted as an adult of any felony or misdemeanor other than a traffic violation under the laws of the United States or the laws of this State or any other state.

Records relating to an adjudication for an offense that would be a Class A, B1, B2, C, D, or E felony if committed by an adult shall not be expunged.

(c) The petition shall contain, but not be limited to, the following:

(1) An affidavit by the petitioner that the petitioner has been of good behavior since the adjudication and, in the case of a petition based on a delinquency adjudication, that the petitioner has not subsequently been adjudicated delinquent or convicted as an adult of any felony or misdemeanor other than a traffic violation under the laws of the United States, or the laws of this State or any other state;

(2) Verified affidavits of two persons, who are not related to the petitioner or to each other by blood or marriage, that they know the character and reputation of the petitioner in the community in which the petitioner lives and that the petitioner's character and reputation are good; and

(3) A statement that the petition is a motion in the cause in the case wherein the petitioner was adjudicated delinquent or undisciplined.

The petition shall be served upon the district attorney in the district wherein adjudication occurred. The district attorney shall have 10 days thereafter in which to file any objection thereto and shall be duly notified as to the date of the hearing on the petition.

(d) If the court, after hearing, finds that the petitioner satisfies the conditions set out in subsections (a) or (b) of this section, the court shall order and direct the clerk and all law enforcement agencies to expunge their records of the adjudication including all references to arrests, complaints, referrals, petitions, and orders.

(e) The clerk shall forward a certified copy of the order to the sheriff, chief of police, or other law enforcement agency.

(f) Records of a juvenile adjudicated delinquent or undisciplined being maintained by the chief court counselor, an intake counselor, or a juvenile court counselor shall be retained or disposed of as provided by the Division, except that no records shall be destroyed before the juvenile reaches the age of 18 or 18 months have elapsed since the person was released from juvenile court jurisdiction, whichever occurs last.

(g) Records of a juvenile adjudicated delinquent or undisciplined being maintained by personnel at a residential facility operated by the Division, shall be retained or disposed of as provided by the Division, except that no records shall be destroyed before the juvenile reaches the age of 18 or 18 months have elapsed since the person was released from juvenile court jurisdiction, whichever occurs last.

(h) Any person who was alleged to be delinquent as a juvenile and has attained the age of 16 years, or was alleged to be undisciplined as a juvenile and has attained the age of 18 years, may file a petition in the court in which the person was alleged to be delinquent or undisciplined, for expunction of all juvenile records of the juvenile having been alleged to be delinquent or undisciplined if the court dismissed the juvenile petition without an adjudication that the juvenile was delinquent or undisciplined. The petition shall be served on the chief court counselor in the district where the juvenile petition was filed. The chief court counselor shall have 10 days thereafter in which to file a written objection in the court. If no objection is filed, the court may grant the petition without a hearing. If an objection is filed or the court so directs, a hearing shall be scheduled and the chief court counselor shall be notified as to the date of the hearing. If the court finds at the hearing that the petitioner satisfies the conditions specified herein, the court shall order the clerk and the appropriate law enforcement agencies to expunge their records of the allegations of delinquent or undisciplined acts including all references to arrests, complaints, referrals, juvenile petitions, and orders. The clerk shall forward a certified copy of the order of expunction to the sheriff, chief of police, or other appropriate law enforcement agency, and to the chief court counselor, and these specified officials shall immediately destroy all records relating to the allegations that the juvenile was delinquent or undisciplined.

(i)     The clerk of superior court in each county in North Carolina shall, as soon as practicable after each term of court in the clerk's county, file with the Administrative Office of the Courts, the names of those persons granted an expunction under the provisions of this section, and the Administrative Office of the Courts shall maintain a confidential file containing the names of persons granted an expunction. The information contained in such file shall be disclosed only to judges of the General Court of Justice of North Carolina for the purpose of ascertaining whether any person charged with an offense has been previously granted an expunction. (1979, c. 815, s. 1; 1989, c. 186; 1994, Ex. Sess., c. 7, s. 2; 1995, c. 509, s. 6; 1997-443, s. 11A.118(a); 1998-202, s. 6; 2000-137, s. 3; 2001-490, s. 2.33; 2011-145, s. 19.1(l).)

§ 7B-3201. Effect of expunction.

(a)     Whenever a juvenile's record is expunged, with respect to the matter in which the record was expunged, the juvenile who is the subject of the record and the juvenile's parent may not be held thereafter under any provision of any laws to be guilty of perjury or otherwise giving a false statement by reason of the person's failure to recite or acknowledge such record or response to any inquiry made of the person for any purpose.

(b)     Notwithstanding subsection (a) of this section, in any delinquency case if the juvenile is the defendant and chooses to testify or if the juvenile is not the defendant and is called as a witness, the juvenile may be ordered to testify with respect to whether the juvenile was adjudicated delinquent. (1979, c. 815, s. 1; 1983 (Reg. Sess., 1984), c. 1037, s. 7; 1998-202, s. 6.)

§ 7B-3202. Notice of expunction.

Upon expunction of a juvenile's record, the clerk shall send a written notice to the juvenile at the juvenile's last known address informing the juvenile that the record has been expunged and with respect to the matter involved, the juvenile may not be held thereafter under any provision of any laws to be guilty of perjury or otherwise giving a false statement by reason of the juvenile's failure to recite or acknowledge such record or response to any inquiry made of the juvenile for any purpose except that upon testifying in a delinquency proceeding, the juvenile may be required by a court to disclose that the juvenile was adjudicated delinquent. (1979, c. 815, s. 1; 1983 (Reg. Sess., 1984), c. 1037, s. 8; 1998-202, s. 6.)

Article 33.

Computation of Recidivism Rates.

§ 7B-3300: Repealed by Session Laws 2005-276, s. 14.19(c), effective July 1, 2005.

SUBCHAPTER IV. PARENTAL AUTHORITY; EMANCIPATION.

Article 34.

Parental Authority over Juveniles.

§ 7B-3400. Juvenile under 18 subject to parents' control.

Notwithstanding any other provision of law, any juvenile under 18 years of age, except as provided in G.S. 7B-3402 and G.S. 7B-3403, shall be subject to the supervision and control of the juvenile's parents. (1969, c. 1080, s. 1; 1998-202, s. 6.)

§ 7B-3401. Definitions.

The definitions of G.S. 7B-101 and G.S. 7B-1501 apply to this Subchapter. (1998-202, s. 6.)

§ 7B-3402. Exceptions.

This Article shall not apply to any juvenile under the age of 18 who is married or who is serving in the Armed Forces of the United States, or who has been emancipated. (1969, c. 1080, s. 2; 1998-202, s. 6; 2011-183, s. 6.)

§ 7B-3403. No criminal liability created.

This Article shall not be interpreted to place any criminal liability on a parent, guardian, or custodian for any act of the juvenile 16 years of age or older. (1969, c. 1080, s. 3; 1998-202, s. 6.)

§ 7B-3404. Enforcement.

The provisions of this Article may be enforced by the parent, guardian, custodian, or person who has assumed the status and obligation of a parent without being awarded legal custody of the juvenile by a court to the juvenile by filing a civil action in the district court of the county where the juvenile can be found or the county of the plaintiff's residence. Upon the institution of such action by a verified complaint, alleging that the defendant juvenile has left home or has left the place where the juvenile has been residing and refuses to return and comply with the direction and control of the plaintiff, the court may issue an order directing the juvenile personally to appear before the court at a specified time to be heard in answer to the allegations of the plaintiff and to comply with further orders of the court. Such orders shall be served by the sheriff upon the juvenile and upon any other person named as a party defendant in such action. At the time of the issuance of the order directing the juvenile to appear, the court may in the same order, or by separate order, order the sheriff to enter any house, building, structure, or conveyance for the purpose of searching for the juvenile and serving the order and for the purpose of taking custody of the person of the juvenile in order to bring the juvenile before the court. Any order issued at said hearing shall be treated as a mandatory injunction and shall remain in full force and effect until the juvenile reaches the age of 18, or until further orders of the court. Within 30 days after the hearing on the original order, the juvenile, or anyone acting in the juvenile's behalf, may file a verified answer to the complaint. Upon the filing of an answer by or on behalf of the juvenile, any district court judge holding court in the county or district court district as defined in G.S. 7A-133 where the action was instituted shall have jurisdiction to hear the matter, without a jury, and to make findings of fact, conclusions of law, and render judgment thereon. Appeals from the district court to the Court of Appeals shall be allowed as in civil actions generally. The district court issuing the original order or the district court hearing the matter after answer has been filed shall also have authority to order that any person named defendant in the order or judgment shall not harbor, keep, or allow the defendant juvenile to remain on the person's premises or in the person's home. Failure of any defendant to comply with the terms of said order or judgment shall be punishable as for contempt. (1969, c. 1080, s. 4; 1987 (Reg. Sess., 1988), c. 1037, s. 108; 1991 (Reg. Sess., 1992), c. 1031, s. 1; 1998-202, s. 6.)

Article 35.

Emancipation.

§ 7B-3500. Who may petition.

Any juvenile who is 16 years of age or older and who has resided in the same county in North Carolina or on federal territory within the boundaries of North Carolina for six months next preceding the filing of the petition may petition the court in that county for a judicial decree of emancipation. (1979, c. 815, s. 1; 1998-202, s. 6.)

§ 7B-3501. Petition.

The petition shall be signed and verified by the petitioner and shall contain the following information:

(1)     The full name of the petitioner and the petitioner's birth date, and state and county of birth;

(2)     A certified copy of the petitioner's birth certificate;

(3)     The name and last known address of the parent, guardian, or custodian;

(4)     The petitioner's address and length of residence at that address;

(5)     The petitioner's reasons for requesting emancipation; and

(6)     The petitioner's plan for meeting the petitioner's needs and living expenses which plan may include a statement of employment and wages earned that is verified by the petitioner's employer. (1979, c. 815, s. 1; 1998-202, s. 6.)

§ 7B-3502. Summons.

A copy of the filed petition along with a summons shall be served upon the petitioner's parent, guardian, or custodian who shall be named as respondents. The summons shall include the time and place of the hearing and shall notify the respondents to file written answer within 30 days after service of the summons and petition. In the event that personal service cannot be obtained, service shall be in accordance with G.S. 1A-1, Rule 4(j). (1979, c. 815, s. 1; 1998-202, s. 6.)

§ 7B-3503. Hearing.

The court, sitting without a jury, shall permit all parties to present evidence and to cross-examine witnesses. The petitioner has the burden of showing by a preponderance of the evidence that emancipation is in the petitioner's best interests. Upon finding that reasonable cause exists, the court may order the juvenile to be examined by a psychiatrist, a licensed clinical psychologist, a physician, or any other expert to evaluate the juvenile's mental or physical condition. The court may continue the hearing and order investigation by a juvenile court counselor or by the county department of social services to substantiate allegations of the petitioner or respondents.

No husband-wife or physician-patient privilege shall be grounds for excluding any evidence in the hearing. (1979, c. 815, s. 1; 1998-202, s. 6; 2001-490, s. 2.34.)

§ 7B-3504. Considerations for emancipation.

In determining the best interests of the petitioner and the need for emancipation, the court shall review the following considerations:

(1)     The parental need for the earnings of the petitioner;

(2)     The petitioner's ability to function as an adult;

(3)     The petitioner's need to contract as an adult or to marry;

(4)     The employment status of the petitioner and the stability of the petitioner's living arrangements;

(5)     The extent of family discord which may threaten reconciliation of the petitioner with the petitioner's family;

(6)     The petitioner's rejection of parental supervision or support; and

(7)     The quality of parental supervision or support. (1979, c. 815, s. 1; 1998-202, s. 6.)


§ 7B-3505.  Final decree of emancipation.

After reviewing the considerations for emancipation, the court may enter a decree of emancipation if the court determines:

(1)     That all parties are properly before the court or were duly served and failed to appear and that time for filing an answer has expired;

(2)     That the petitioner has shown a proper and lawful plan for adequately providing for the petitioner's needs and living expenses;

(3)     That the petitioner is knowingly seeking emancipation and fully understands the ramifications of the act; and

(4)     That emancipation is in the best interests of the petitioner.

The decree shall set out the court's findings.

If the court determines that the criteria in subdivisions (1) through (4) are not met, the court shall order the proceeding dismissed. (1979, c. 815, s. 1; 1998-202, s. 6.)


§ 7B-3506.  Costs of court.

The court may tax the costs of the proceeding to any party or may, for good cause, order the costs remitted.

The clerk may collect costs for furnishing to the petitioner a certificate of emancipation which shall recite the name of the petitioner and the fact of the petitioner's emancipation by court decree and shall have the seal of the clerk affixed thereon. (1979, c. 815, s. 1; 1998-202, s. 6.)


§ 7B-3507.  Legal effect of final decree.

As of entry of the final decree of emancipation:

(1) The petitioner has the same right to make contracts and conveyances, to sue and to be sued, and to transact business as if the petitioner were an adult.

(2) The parent, guardian, or custodian is relieved of all legal duties and obligations owed to the petitioner and is divested of all rights with respect to the petitioner.

(3) The decree is irrevocable.

Notwithstanding any other provision of this section, a decree of emancipation shall not alter the application of G.S. 14-326.1 or the petitioner's right to inherit property by intestate succession. (1979, c. 815, s. 1; 1998-202, s. 6.)

§ 7B-3508. Appeals.

Any petitioner, parent, guardian, or custodian who is a party to a proceeding under this Article may appeal from any order of disposition to the Court of Appeals provided that notice of appeal is given in open court at the time of the hearing or in writing within 10 days after entry of the order. Entry of an order shall be treated in the same manner as entry of a judgment under G.S. 1A-1, Rule 58 of the North Carolina Rules of Civil Procedure. Pending disposition of an appeal, the court may enter a temporary order affecting the custody or placement of the petitioner as the court finds to be in the best interests of the petitioner or the State. (1979, c. 815, s. 1; 1998-202, s. 6; 1999-309, s. 3.)

§ 7B-3509. Application of common law.

A married juvenile is emancipated by this Article. All other common-law provisions for emancipation are superseded by this Article. (1979, c. 815, s. 1; 1998-202, s. 6.)

Article 36.

Judicial Consent for Emergency Surgical or Medical Treatment.

§ 7B-3600. Judicial authorization of emergency treatment; procedure.

A juvenile in need of emergency treatment under Article 1A of Chapter 90 of the General Statutes, whose physician is barred from rendering necessary treatment by reason of parental refusal to consent to treatment, may receive treatment with court authorization under the following procedure:

(1) The physician shall sign a written statement setting out:

a. The treatment to be rendered and the emergency need for treatment;

b. The refusal of the parent, guardian, custodian, or person who has assumed the status and obligation of a parent without being awarded legal custody of the juvenile by a court to consent to the treatment; and

c. The impossibility of contacting a second physician for a concurring opinion on the need for treatment in time to prevent immediate harm to the juvenile.

(2) Upon examining the physician's written statement prescribed in subdivision (1) of this section and finding:

a. That the statement is in accordance with this Article, and

b. That the proposed treatment is necessary to prevent immediate harm to the juvenile.

The court may issue a written authorization for the proposed treatment to be rendered.

(3) In acute emergencies in which time may not permit implementation of the written procedure set out in subdivisions (1) and (2) of this section, the court may authorize treatment in person or by telephone upon receiving the oral statement of a physician satisfying the requirements of subdivision (1) of this section and upon finding that the proposed treatment is necessary to prevent immediate harm to the juvenile.

(4) The court's authorization for treatment overriding parental refusal to consent should not be given without attempting to offer the parent an opportunity to state the reasons for refusal; however, failure of the court to hear the parent's objections shall not invalidate judicial authorization under this Article.

(5) The court's authorization for treatment under subdivisions (1) and (2) of this section shall be issued in duplicate. One copy shall be given to the treating physician and the other copy shall be attached to the physician's written statement and filed as a juvenile proceeding in the office of the clerk of court.

(6) The court's authorization for treatment undersubdivision (3) of this section shall be reduced to writing as soon as possible, supported by the physician's written statement as prescribed in subdivision (1) of this section and shall be filed as prescribed in subdivision (5) of this section.

The court's authorization for treatment under this Article shall have the same effect as parental consent for treatment.

Following the court's authorization for treatment and after giving notice to the juvenile's parent, guardian, or custodian the court shall conduct a hearing in order to provide for payment for the treatment rendered. The court may order the parent or other responsible parties to pay the cost of treatment. If the court finds the parent is unable to pay the cost of treatment, the cost shall be a charge upon the county when so ordered.

This Article shall operate as a remedy in addition to the provisions in G.S. 7B-903, 7B-2503, and 7B-2506. (1979, c. 815, s. 1; 1998-202, s. 6.)

SUBCHAPTER V. PLACEMENT OF JUVENILES.

Article 37.

Placing or Adoption of Juvenile Delinquents or Dependents.

§ 7B-3700. Consent required for bringing child into State for placement or adoption.

(a) No person, agency, association, institution, or corporation shall bring or send into the State any child for the purpose of giving custody of the child to some person in the State or procuring adoption by some person in the State without first obtaining the written consent of the Department of Health and Human Services.

(b) The person with whom a child is placed for either of the purposes set out in subsection (a) of this section shall be responsible for the child's proper care and training. The Department of Health and Human Services or its agents shall have the same right of visitation and supervision of the child and the home in which it is placed as in the case of a child placed by the Department or its agents as long as the child shall remain within the State and until the child shall have reached the age of 18 years or shall have been legally adopted. (1931, c. 226, s. 1; 1947, c. 609, s. 1; 1973, c. 476, s. 138; 1997-443, s. 11A.118(a); 1998-202, s. 6.)

§ 7B-3701. Bond required.

The Social Services Commission may, in its discretion, require of a person, agency, association, institution, or corporation which brings or sends a child into the State with the written consent of the Department of Health and Human Services, as provided by G.S. 7B-3700, a continuing bond in a penal sum not in excess of one thousand dollars ($1,000) with such conditions as may be prescribed and such sureties as may be approved by the Department of Health and Human Services. Said bond shall be made in favor of and filed with the Department of Health and Human Services with the premium prepaid by the said person, agency, association, institution, or corporation desiring to place such child in the State. (1931, c. 226, s. 2; 1947, c. 609, s. 2; 1969, c. 982; 1973, c. 476, s. 138; 1997-443, s. 11A.118(a); 1998-202, s. 6.)

§ 7B-3702. Consent required for removing child from State.

No child shall be taken or sent out of the State for the purpose of placing the child in a foster home or in a child-caring institution without first obtaining the written consent of the Department of Health and Human Services. The foster home or child-caring institution in which the child is placed shall report to the Department of Health and Human Services at such times as the Department of Health and Human Services may direct as to the location and well-being of such child until the child shall have reached the age of 18 years or shall have been legally adopted. (1931, c. 226, s. 3; 1947, c. 609, s. 3; 1973, c. 476, s. 138; 1997-443, s. 11A.118(a); 1998-202, s. 6.)

§ 7B-3703. Violation of Article a misdemeanor.

Every person acting for himself or for an agency who violates any of the provisions of this Article or who shall intentionally make any false statements to the Social Services Commission or the Secretary or an employee thereof acting for the Department of Health and Human Services in an official capacity in the placing or adoption of juvenile delinquents or dependents shall, upon conviction thereof, be guilty of a Class 2 misdemeanor. (1931, c. 226, s. 7; 1957, c. 100, s. 1; 1973, c. 476, s. 138; 1993, c. 539, s. 823; 1994, Ex. Sess., c. 24, s. 14(c); 1997-443, s. 11A.118(a); 1998-202, s. 6.)

§ 7B-3704. Definitions.

The term "Department" wherever used in this Article shall be construed to mean the Department of Health and Human Services. The term "Secretary" wherever used in this Article shall be construed to mean the Secretary of the Department of Health and Human Services. (1931, c. 226, s. 8; 1957, c. 100, s. 1; 1973, c. 476, s. 138; 1997-443, s. 11A.118(a); 1998-202, s. 6.)

§ 7B-3705. Application of Article.

None of the provisions of this Article shall apply when a child is brought into or sent into, or taken out of, or sent out of the State, by the guardian of the person of such child, or by a parent, stepparent, grandparent, uncle or aunt of such child, or by a brother, sister, half brother, or half sister of such child, if such brother, sister, half brother, or half sister is 18 years of age or older. (1947, c. 609, s. 5; 1971, c. 1231, s. 1; 1998-202, s. 6.)

Article 38.

Interstate Compact on the Placement of Children.

§ 7B-3800. Adoption of Compact.

The Interstate Compact on the Placement of Children is hereby enacted into law and entered into with all other jurisdictions legally joining therein in a form substantially as contained in this Article. It is the intent of the General Assembly that Article 37 of this Chapter shall govern interstate placements of children between North Carolina and any other jurisdictions not a party to this Compact. It is the intent of the General Assembly that Chapter 48 of the General Statutes shall govern the adoption of children within the boundaries of North Carolina.

Article I. Purpose and Policy.

It is the purpose and policy of the party states to cooperate with each other in the interstate placement of children to the end that:

(a) Each child requiring placement shall receive the maximum opportunity to be placed in a suitable environment and with persons or institutions having appropriate qualifications and facilities to provide a necessary and desirable degree and type of care.

(b) The appropriate authorities in a state where a child is to be placed may have full opportunity to ascertain the circumstances of the proposed placement, thereby promoting full compliance with applicable requirements for the protection of the child.

(c) The proper authorities of the state from which the placement is made may obtain the most complete information on the basis of which to evaluate a projected placement before it is made.

(d) Appropriate jurisdictional arrangements for the care of children will be promoted.

Article II. Definitions.

As used in this Compact:

(a) "Child" means a person who, by reason of minority, is legally subject to parental, guardianship or similar control.

(b) "Sending agency" means a party state officer or employee thereof; a subdivision of a party state, or officer or employee thereof; a court of a party state; a person, corporation, association, charitable agency or other entity which sends, brings, or causes to be sent or brought any child to another party state.

(c) "Receiving state" means the state to which a child is sent, brought, or caused to be sent or brought, whether by public authorities or private persons or agencies, and whether for placement with state or local public authorities of [or] for placement with private agencies or persons.

(d) "Placement" means the arrangement for the care of a child in a family free or boarding home or in a child-caring agency or institution but does not include any institution caring for the mentally ill, mentally defective, or epileptic or any institution primarily educational in character, and any hospital or other medical facility.

(e) "Appropriate public authorities" as used in Article III shall, with reference to this State, mean the Department of Health and Human Services and said agency shall receive and act with reference to notices required by Article III.

(f) "Appropriate authority in the receiving state" as used in paragraph (a) of Article V shall, with reference to this State, means the Secretary.

(g) "Executive head" as used in Article VII means the Governor.

Article III. Conditions for Placement.

(a) No sending agency shall send, bring, or cause to be sent or brought into any other party state any child for placement in foster care or as a preliminary to a possible adoption unless the sending agency shall comply with each and every requirement set forth in this Article and with the applicable laws of the receiving state governing the placement of children therein.

(b) Prior to sending, bringing, or causing any child to be sent or brought into a receiving state for placement in foster care or as a preliminary to a possible adoption, the sending agency shall furnish the appropriate public authorities in the receiving state written notice of the intention to send, bring, or place the child in the receiving state. The notice shall contain:

(1) The name, date, and place of birth of the child.

(2) The identity and address or addresses of the parents or legal guardian.

(3) The name and address of the person, agency or institution to or with which the sending agency proposes to send, bring, or place the child.

(4) A full statement of the reasons for such proposed action and evidence of the authority pursuant to which the placement is proposed to be made.

(c) Any public officer or agency in a receiving state which is in receipt of a notice pursuant to paragraph (b) of this Article may request of the sending agency, or any other appropriate officer or agency of or in the sending agency's state, and shall be entitled to receive therefrom, such supporting or additional information as it may deem necessary under the circumstances to carry out the purpose and policy of this Compact.

(d) The child shall not be sent, brought, or caused to be sent or brought into the receiving state until the appropriate public authorities in the receiving state shall notify the sending agency, in writing, to the effect that the proposed placement does not appear to be contrary to the interests of the child.

Article IV. Penalty for Illegal Placement.

The sending, bringing, or causing to be sent or brought into any receiving state of a child in violation of the terms of this Compact shall constitute a violation of the laws respecting the placement of children of both the state in which the sending agency is located or from which it sends or brings the child and of the receiving state. Such violation may be punished or subjected to penalty in either jurisdiction in accordance with its laws. In addition to liability for any such punishment or penalty, any such violation shall constitute full and sufficient grounds for the suspension or revocation of any license, permit, or other legal authorization held by the sending agency which empowers or allows it to place, or care for children.

Article V. Retention of Jurisdiction.

(a) The sending agency shall retain jurisdiction over the child sufficient to determine all matters in relation to the custody, supervision, care, treatment, and disposition of the child which it would have had if the child had remained in the sending agency's state, until the child is adopted, reaches majority, becomes self-supporting or is discharged with the concurrence of the appropriate authority in the receiving state. Such jurisdiction shall also include the power to effect or cause the return of the child or its transfer to another location and custody pursuant to law. The sending agency shall continue to have financial responsibility for support and maintenance of the child during the period of the placement. Nothing contained herein shall defeat a claim of jurisdiction by a receiving state sufficient to deal with an act of delinquency or crime committed therein.

(b) When the sending agency is a public agency, it may enter into an agreement with an authorized public or private agency in the receiving state providing for the performance of one or more services in respect of such case by the latter as agent for the sending agency.

(c) Nothing in this Compact shall be construed to prevent a private charitable agency authorized to place children in the receiving state from performing services or acting as agent in that state for a private charitable agency of the sending state; nor to prevent the agency in the receiving state from discharging financial responsibility for the support and maintenance of a child who has been placed on behalf of the sending agency without relieving the responsibility set forth in paragraph (a) hereof.

Article VI. Institutional Care of Delinquent Children.

A child adjudicated delinquent may be placed in an institution in another party jurisdiction pursuant to this Compact, but no such placement shall be made unless the child is given a court hearing on notice to the parent or guardian with opportunity to be heard, prior to the child's being sent to such other party jurisdiction for institutional care and the court finds that:

(1) Equivalent facilities for the child are not available in the sending agency's jurisdiction; and

(2) Institutional care in the other jurisdiction is in the best interests of the child and will not produce undue hardship.

Article VII. Compact Administrator.

The executive head of each jurisdiction party to this Compact shall designate an officer who shall be general coordinator of activities under this Compact in the officer's jurisdiction and who, acting jointly with like officers of other party jurisdictions, shall have power to promulgate rules and regulations to carry out more effectively the terms and provisions of this Compact.

Article VIII. Limitations.

This Compact shall not apply to: (a) the sending or bringing of a child into a receiving state by the child's parent, stepparent, grandparent, adult brother or sister, adult uncle or aunt, or the child's guardian and leaving the child with any such relative or nonagency guardian in the receiving state. (b) Any placement, sending or bringing of a child into a receiving state pursuant to any other interstate compact to which both the state from which the child is sent or brought and the receiving state are party, or to any other agreement between said states which has the force of law.

Article IX. Enactment and Withdrawal.

This Compact shall be open to joinder by any state, territory or possession of the United States, the District of Columbia, the Commonwealth of Puerto Rico, and, with the consent of Congress, the government of Canada or any province thereof. It shall become effective with respect to any such jurisdiction when such jurisdiction has enacted the same into law. Withdrawal from this Compact shall be by the enactment of a statute repealing the same, but shall not take effect until two years after the effective date of such statute and until written notice of the withdrawal has been given by the withdrawing state to the governor of each other party jurisdiction. Withdrawal of a party state shall not affect the rights, duties, and obligations under this Compact of any sending agency therein with respect to a placement made prior to the effective date of withdrawal.

Article X. Construction and Severability.

The provisions of this Compact shall be liberally construed to effectuate the purposes thereof. The provisions of this Compact shall be severable and if any phrase, clause, sentence, or provision of this Compact is declared to be contrary to the constitution of any party state or of the United States or the applicability thereof to any government, agency, person, or circumstance is held invalid, the validity of the remainder of this Compact and the applicability thereof to any government, agency, person, or circumstance shall not be affected thereby. If this Compact shall be held contrary to the constitution of any state party thereto, the Compact shall remain in full force and effect as to the remaining states and in full force and effect as to the state affected as to all severable matters. (1971, c. 453, s. 1; 1973, c. 476, s. 138; 1983, c. 454, s. 8; 1997-443, s. 11A.118(a); 1998-202, s. 6; 1999-423, s. 3.)

§ 7B-3801. Financial responsibility under Compact.

Financial responsibility for any child placed pursuant to the provisions of the Interstate Compact on the Placement of Children shall be determined in accordance with the provisions of Article V thereof in the first instance. However, in the event of partial or complete default of performance thereunder, the provisions of any other state laws fixing responsibility for the support of children also may be invoked. (1971, c. 453, s. 2; 1998-202, s. 6.)

§ 7B-3802. Agreements under Compact.

The officers and agencies of this State and its subdivisions having authority to place children are hereby empowered to enter into agreements with appropriate officers or agencies of or in other party states pursuant to paragraph (b) of Article V of the Interstate Compact on the Placement of Children. Any such agreement which contains a financial commitment or imposes a financial obligation on this State or subdivision or agency thereof shall not be binding unless it has the approval in writing of the Secretary of the Department of Health and Human Services in the case of the State and of the county director of social services in the case of a county or other subdivision of the State. (1971, c. 453, s. 2; 1973, c. 476, s. 138; 1997-443, s. 11A.118(a); 1998-202, s. 6.)

§ 7B-3803. Visitation, inspection or supervision.

Any requirements for visitation, inspection or supervision of children, homes, institutions or other agencies in another party state which may apply under the laws of this State shall be deemed to be met if performed pursuant to an agreement entered into by appropriate officers or agencies of this State or a subdivision thereof as contemplated by paragraph (b) of Article V of the Interstate Compact on the Placement of Children. (1971, c. 453, s. 2; 1998-202, s. 6.)

§ 7B-3804. Compact to govern between party states.

The provisions of Article 37 of this Chapter shall not apply to placements made pursuant to the Interstate Compact on the Placement of Children. (1971, c. 453, s. 2; 1998-202, s. 6.)

§ 7B-3805. Placement of delinquents.

Any court having jurisdiction to place delinquent children may place such a child in an institution or in another state pursuant to Article VI of the Interstate Compact on the Placement of Children and shall retain jurisdiction as provided in Article V thereof. (1971, c. 453, s. 2; 1998-202, s. 6.)

§ 7B-3806. Compact Administrator.

The Governor is hereby authorized to appoint a Compact Administrator in accordance with the terms of said Article VII. (1971, c. 453, s. 2; 1998-202, s. 6.)

Article 39.

Interstate Compact on Adoption and Medical Assistance.

§ 7B-3900. Legislative findings and purposes.

(a)     Finding adoptive families for children, for whom state assistance is desirable pursuant to G.S. 108A-49 and G.S. 108A-50, and assuring the protection of the interests of the children affected during the entire assistance period require special measures when the adoptive parents move to another state or are residents of another state. Additionally, the provision of medical and other necessary services for children receiving State assistance encounters special difficulties when the provision of services takes place in another state.

(b)     In recognition of the need for special measures, the General Assembly authorizes the Secretary of the Department of Health and Human Services to enter into interstate agreements with agencies of other states for the protection of children on behalf of whom adoption assistance is being provided by the Department of Health and Human Services and to provide procedures for interstate adoption assistance payments, including payments for medical services. (1999-190, s. 5.)

§ 7B-3901. Definitions.

Unless the context requires otherwise, as used in this Article:

(1) "Adoption assistance state" means the state that is a signatory to an adoption assistance agreement in a particular case.

(2) "Residence state" means the state where the child is living.

(3) "State" means a state of the United States, the District of Columbia, the Commonwealth of Puerto Rico, the Virgin Islands, Guam, the Commonwealth of the Northern Mariana Islands, or any territory or possession subject to the jurisdiction of the United States. (1999-190, s. 5.)

§ 7B-3902. Compacts authorized.

The Secretary of the Department of Health and Human Services may develop, participate in the development of, negotiate, and enter into one or more interstate compacts on behalf of this State with other states to implement this Article. When entered into, and for so long as it remains in force, such a compact shall have the full force and effect of law. (1999-190, s. 5.)

§ 7B-3903. Content of compacts.

(a) A compact under this Article shall contain all of the following provisions:

(1) A provision making it available for joinder by all states.

(2) A provision for withdrawal from the compact upon written notice to the parties, with a period of at least one year between the date of the notice and effective date of the withdrawal.

(3) A requirement that the protections afforded by or under the compact continue in force for the duration of the adoption assistance and apply to all children and their adoptive parents who, on the effective date of the withdrawal, are receiving adoption assistance from a party state other than the state in which they are a resident and have their principal place of abode.

(4) A requirement that each instance of adoption assistance to which the compact applies be covered by an adoption assistance agreement in writing between the adoptive parents and the state child welfare agency of the state which undertakes to provide the adoption assistance and that any such agreement be expressly for the benefit of the adopted child and enforceable by

the adoptive parents and the state child welfare agency providing the adoption assistance.

(5) Any other provisions appropriate to implement the proper administration of the compact.

(b) A compact entered into under this Article may contain any of the following provisions:

(1) Provisions establishing procedures and entitlement to medical and other necessary social services for the child in accordance with applicable laws, even though the child and the adoptive parents are in a state other than the one responsible for or providing the services or the funds to defray part or all of the expense thereof.

(2) Any other provisions appropriate or incidental to the proper administration of the compact. (1999-190, s. 5.)


§ 7B-3904. Medical assistance.

(a) A child with special needs who is a resident of this State who is the subject of an adoption assistance agreement with another state shall be accepted as being entitled to receive medical assistance certification from this State upon the filing in the department of social services of the county in which the child resides a certified copy of the adoption assistance agreement obtained from the adoption assistance state.

(b) The Division of Medical Assistance shall consider the holder of a medical assistance certification under this section to be entitled to the same medical benefits under the laws of this State as any other holder of a medical assistance certification and shall process and make payment on claims on account of that holder in the same manner and under the same conditions and procedures that apply to other recipients of medical assistance.

(c) The provisions of this section apply only to medical assistance for children under adoption assistance agreements from states that have entered into a compact with this State under which the other state provides medical assistance to children with special needs under adoption assistance agreements made by this State. (1999-190, s. 5.)

§ 7B-3905. Federal participation.

The Department of Health and Human Services, in connection with the administration of this Article and any compact entered into pursuant to this Article, shall include the provision of adoption assistance and medical assistance for which the federal government pays some or all of the cost in any state plan made pursuant to the Adoption Assistance and Child Welfare Act of 1980 (P.L. 96-272), Titles IV (E) and XIX of the Social Security Act and any other applicable federal laws. The Department shall apply for and administer all relevant federal aid in accordance with law. (1999-190, s. 5.)

§ 7B-3906. Compact Administrator.

The Secretary of the Department of Health and Human Services may appoint a Compact Administrator who shall be the general coordinator of activities under this Compact in this State and who, acting jointly with like officers of other party states, may promulgate rules to carry out more effectively the terms and provisions of this Compact. (1999-190, s. 5.)

Article 40.

Interstate Compact for Juveniles.

§ 7B-4000. (For effective date - see note) Short title.

This Article may be cited as "The Interstate Compact for Juveniles". (2005-194, s. 1.)

§ 7B-4001. (For effective date - see note) Governor to execute Compact; form of Compact.

The Governor of North Carolina is authorized and directed to execute a Compact on behalf of the State of North Carolina with any state of the United States legally joining therein in the form substantially as follows:

"Article I.

Purpose.

(a)     The compacting states to this Interstate Compact recognize that each state is responsible for the proper supervision or return of juveniles, delinquents, and status offenders who are on probation or parole and who have absconded, escaped, or run away from supervision and control and in so doing have endangered their own safety and the safety of others. The compacting states also recognize that each state is responsible for the safe return of juveniles who have run away from home and in doing so have left their state of residence. The compacting states also recognize that Congress, by enacting the Crime Control Act, 4 U.S.C. § 112 (1965), has authorized and encouraged compacts for cooperative efforts and mutual assistance in the prevention of crime.

(b)     It is the purpose of this Compact, through means of joint and cooperative action among the compacting states to:

(1)     Ensure that the adjudicated juveniles and status offenders subject to this Compact are provided adequate supervision and services in the receiving state as ordered by the adjudicating judge or parole authority in the sending state;

(2)     Ensure that the public safety interests of the citizens, including the victims of juvenile offenders, in both the sending and receiving states are adequately protected;

(3)     Return juveniles who have run away, absconded, or escaped from supervision or control, or have been accused of an offense to the state requesting their return;

(4)     Make contracts for the cooperative institutionalization in public facilities in member states for delinquent youth needing special services;

(5)     Provide for the effective tracking and supervision of juveniles;

(6)     Equitably allocate the costs, benefits, and obligations of the compacting states;

(7)     Establish procedures to manage the movement between states of juvenile offenders released to the community under the jurisdiction of courts, juvenile departments, or any other criminal or juvenile justice agency which has jurisdiction over juvenile offenders;

(8)     Ensure immediate notice to jurisdictions where defined offenders are authorized to travel or to relocate across state lines;

(9)     Establish procedures to resolve pending charges (detainers) against juvenile offenders prior to transfer or release to the community under the terms of this Compact;

(10)    Establish a system of uniform data collection on information pertaining to juveniles subject to this Compact that allows access by authorized juvenile justice and criminal justice officials and regular reporting of Compact activities to heads of state executive, judicial, and legislative branches and juvenile and criminal justice administrators;

(11)    Monitor compliance with rules governing interstate movement of juveniles and initiate interventions to address and correct noncompliance;

(12)    Coordinate training and education regarding the regulation of interstate movement of juveniles for officials involved in such activity; and

(13)    Coordinate the implementation and operation of the Compact with the Interstate Compact for the Placement of Children, the Interstate Compact for Adult Offender Supervision, and other compacts affecting juveniles particularly in those cases where concurrent or overlapping supervision issues arise.

(c)     It is the policy of the compacting states that the activities conducted by the Interstate Commission created herein are the formation of public policies and therefore are public business. Furthermore, the compacting states shall cooperate and observe their individual and collective duties and responsibilities for the prompt return and acceptance of juveniles subject to the provisions of this Compact. The provisions of this Compact shall be reasonably and liberally construed to accomplish the purposes and policies of the Compact.


Article II.

Definitions.


As used in this Compact, unless the context clearly requires a different construction:

(1) "Bylaws" means those bylaws established by the Interstate Commission for its governance or for directing or controlling its actions or conduct.

(2) "Compact Administrator" means the individual in each compacting state appointed pursuant to the terms of this Compact responsible for the administration and management of the state's supervision and transfer of juveniles subject to the terms of this Compact, the rules adopted by the Interstate Commission, and policies adopted by the State Council under this Compact.

(3) "Compacting State" means any state which has enacted the enabling legislation for this Compact.

(4) "Commissioner" means the voting representative of each compacting state appointed pursuant to Article III of this Compact.

(5) "Court" means any court having jurisdiction over delinquent, neglected, or dependent children.

(6) "Deputy Compact Administrator" means the individual, if any, in each compacting state appointed to act on behalf of a Compact Administrator pursuant to the terms of this Compact responsible for the administration and management of the state's supervision and transfer of juveniles subject to the terms of this compact, the rules adopted by the Interstate Commission, and policies adopted by the State Council under this Compact.

(7) "Interstate Commission" means the Interstate Commission for Juveniles created by Article III of this Compact.

(8) "Juvenile" means any person defined as a juvenile in any member state or by the rules of the Interstate Commission, including:

a. Accused Delinquent. - A person charged with an offense that, if committed by an adult, would be a criminal offense;

b. Adjudicated Delinquent. - A person found to have committed an offense that, if committed by an adult, would be a criminal offense;

c. Accused Status Offender. - A person charged with an offense that would not be a criminal offense if committed by an adult;

d.     Adjudicated Status Offender. - A person found to have committed an offense that would not be a criminal offense if committed by an adult; and

e.     Nonoffender. - A person in need of supervision who has not been accused or adjudicated a status offender or delinquent.

(9)    "Noncompacting State" means any state which has not enacted the enabling legislation for this Compact.

(10)   "Probation" or "Parole" means any kind of supervision or conditional release of juveniles authorized under the laws of the compacting states.

(11)   "Rule" means a written statement by the Interstate Commission promulgated pursuant to Article VI of this Compact that is of general applicability, implements, interprets, or prescribes a policy or provision of the Compact, or an organizational, procedural, or practice requirement of the Commission, and has the force and effect of statutory law in a compacting state, and includes the amendment, repeal, or suspension of an existing rule.

(12)   "State" means a state of the United States, the District of Columbia or its designee, the Commonwealth of Puerto Rico, the U.S. Virgin Islands, Guam, American Samoa, and the Northern Marianas Islands.

Article III.

Interstate Commission for Juveniles.

(a)    The compacting states hereby create the "Interstate Commission for Juveniles." The Commission shall be a body corporate and joint agency of the compacting states. The Commission shall have all the responsibilities, powers, and duties set forth herein, and such additional powers as may be conferred upon it by subsequent action of the respective legislatures of the compacting states in accordance with the terms of this Compact.

(b)    The Interstate Commission shall consist of commissioners appointed by the appropriate appointing authority in each state pursuant to the rules and requirements of each compacting state and in consultation with the State Council for Interstate Juvenile Supervision created hereunder. The

Commissioner shall be the compact administrator, deputy compact administrator, or designee from that state who shall serve on the Interstate Commission in such capacity under or pursuant to the applicable law of the compacting state.

(c)     In addition to the commissioners who are the voting representatives of each state, the Interstate Commission shall include individuals who are not commissioners, but who are members of interested organizations. Such noncommissioner members must include a member of the national organizations of governors, legislators, state chief justices, attorneys general, Interstate Compact for Adult Offender Supervision, Interstate Compact for the Placement of Children, juvenile justice and juvenile corrections officials, and crime victims. All noncommissioner members of the Interstate Commission shall be ex officio, nonvoting members. The Interstate Commission may provide in its bylaws for such additional ex officio, nonvoting members, including members of other national organizations, in such numbers as shall be determined by the Commission.

(d)     Each compacting state represented at any meeting of the Commission is entitled to one vote. A majority of the compacting states shall constitute a quorum for the transaction of business, unless a larger quorum is required by the bylaws of the Interstate Commission.

(e)     The Commission shall meet at least once each calendar year. The chairperson may call additional meetings and, upon the request of a simple majority of the compacting states, shall call additional meetings. Public notice shall be given of all meetings, and meetings shall be open to the public.

(f)     The Interstate Commission shall establish an executive committee, which shall include commission officers, members, and others as determined by the bylaws. The executive committee shall have the power to act on behalf of the Interstate Commission during periods when the Interstate Commission is not in session, with the exception of rule making and/or amendment to the Compact. The executive committee shall oversee the day-to-day activities of the administration of the Compact managed by an executive director and Interstate Commission staff, administer enforcement and compliance with the provisions of the Compact, its bylaws and rules, and perform other duties as directed by the Interstate Commission or set forth in the bylaws.

(g)     Each member of the Interstate Commission shall have the right and power to cast a vote to which that compacting state is entitled and to participate in the business and affairs of the Interstate Commission. A member shall vote in person and shall not delegate a vote to another compacting state. However, a commissioner, in consultation with the state council, shall appoint another authorized representative, in the absence of the commissioner from that state, to cast a vote on behalf of the compacting state at a specified meeting. The bylaws may provide for members' participation in meetings by telephone or other means of telecommunication or electronic communication.

(h) The Interstate Commission's bylaws shall establish conditions and procedures under which the Interstate Commission shall make its information and official records available to the public for inspection or copying. The Interstate Commission may exempt from disclosure any information or official records to the extent they would adversely affect personal privacy rights or proprietary interests.

(i) Public notice shall be given of all meetings, and all meetings shall be open to the public, except as set forth in the Rules or as otherwise provided in the Compact. The Interstate Commission and any of its committees may close a meeting to the public where it determines by two-thirds vote that an open meeting would be likely to:

(1) Relate solely to the Interstate Commission's internal personnel practices and procedures;

(2) Disclose matters specifically exempted from disclosure by statute;

(3) Disclose trade secrets or commercial or financial information which is privileged or confidential;

(4) Involve accusing any person of a crime or formally censuring any person;

(5) Disclose information of a personal nature where disclosure would constitute a clearly unwarranted invasion of personal privacy;

(6) Disclose investigative records compiled for law enforcement purposes;

(7) Disclose information contained in or related to examination, operating, or condition reports prepared by, or on behalf of or for the use of, the Interstate Commission with respect to a regulated person or entity for the purpose of regulation or supervision of such person or entity;

(8) Disclose information, the premature disclosure of which would significantly endanger the stability of a regulated person or entity; or

(9) Specifically relate to the Interstate Commission's issuance of a subpoena or its participation in a civil action or other legal proceeding.

(j) For every meeting closed pursuant to this provision, the Interstate Commission's legal counsel shall publicly certify that, in the legal counsel's opinion, the meeting may be closed to the public and shall reference each relevant exemptive provision. The Interstate Commission shall keep minutes which shall fully and clearly describe all matters discussed in any meeting and shall provide a full and accurate summary of any actions taken, and the reasons therefor, including a description of each of the views expressed on any item and the record of any roll call vote (reflected in the vote of each member on the question). All documents considered in connection with any action shall be identified in the minutes.

(k) The Interstate Commission shall collect standardized data concerning the interstate movement of juveniles as directed through its rules which shall specify the data to be collected, the means of collection and data exchange, and reporting requirements. Such methods of data collection, exchange, and reporting shall insofar as is reasonably possible conform to up-to-date technology and coordinate its information functions with the appropriate repository of records.

Article IV.

Powers and Duties of the Interstate Commission.

(a) The Interstate Commission shall have the following powers and duties:

(1) To provide for dispute resolution among compacting states.

(2) To promulgate rules to effect the purposes and obligations as enumerated in this Compact, which shall have the force and effect of statutory law and shall be binding in the compacting states to the extent and in the manner provided in this Compact.

(3) To oversee, supervise, and coordinate the interstate movement of juveniles subject to the terms of this Compact and any bylaws adopted and rules promulgated by the Interstate Commission.

(4) To enforce compliance with the Compact provisions, the rules promulgated by the Interstate Commission, and the bylaws, using all necessary and proper means including, but not limited to, the use of judicial process.

(5) To establish and maintain offices which shall be located within one or more of the compacting states.

(6) To purchase and maintain insurance and bonds.

(7) To borrow, accept, hire, or contract for services of personnel.

(8) To establish and appoint committees and hire staff which it deems necessary for the carrying out of its functions including, but not limited to, an executive committee as required by Article III of this Compact, which shall have the power to act on behalf of the Interstate Commission in carrying out its powers and duties hereunder.

(9) To elect or appoint such officers, attorneys, employees, agents, or consultants, and to fix their compensation, define their duties, and determine their qualifications; and to establish the Interstate Commission's personnel policies and programs relating to, inter alia, conflicts of interest, rates of compensation, and qualifications of personnel.

(10) To accept any and all donations and grants of money, equipment, supplies, materials, and services, and to receive, utilize, and dispose of them.

(11) To lease, purchase, accept contributions or donations of, or otherwise to own, hold, improve, or use any property, real, personal, or mixed.

(12) To sell, convey, mortgage, pledge, lease, exchange, abandon, or otherwise dispose of any property, real, personal, or mixed.

(13) To establish a budget and make expenditures and levy dues as provided in Article VIII of this Compact.

(14) To sue and be sued.

(15) To adopt a seal and bylaws governing the management and operation of the Interstate Commission.

(16) To perform such functions as may be necessary or appropriate to achieve the purposes of this Compact.

(17) To report annually to the legislatures, governors, judiciary, and state councils of the compacting states concerning the activities of the Interstate Commission during the preceding year. Such reports shall also include any recommendations that may have been adopted by the Interstate Commission.

(18) To coordinate education, training, and public awareness regarding the interstate movement of juveniles for officials involved in such activity.

(19) To establish uniform standards of the reporting, collecting, and exchanging of data.

(b) The Interstate Commission shall maintain its corporate books and records in accordance with the bylaws.

Article V.

Organization and Operation of the Interstate Commission.

(a) Bylaws. - The Interstate Commission shall, by a majority of the members present and voting, within 12 months after the first Interstate Commission meeting, adopt bylaws to govern its conduct as may be necessary or appropriate to carry out the purposes of the Compact, including, but not limited to:

(1) Establishing the fiscal year of the Interstate Commission;

(2) Establishing an executive committee and such other committees as may be necessary;

(3) Providing for the establishment of committees governing any general or specific delegation of any authority or function of the Interstate Commission;

(4) Providing reasonable procedures for calling and conducting meetings of the Interstate Commission and ensuring reasonable notice of each such meeting;

(5) Establishing the titles and responsibilities of the officers of the Interstate Commission;

(6) Providing a mechanism for concluding the operations of the Interstate Commission and the return of any surplus funds that may exist upon the termination of the Compact after the payment and/or reserving of all of its debts and obligations;

(7) Providing "start-up" rules for initial administration of the Compact; and

(8) Establishing standards and procedures for compliance and technical assistance in carrying out the Compact.

(b) Officers and Staff. - The Interstate Commission shall, by a majority of the members, elect annually from among its members a chairperson and a vice-chairperson, each of whom shall have such authority and duties as may be specified in the bylaws. The chairperson or, in the chairperson's absence or disability, the vice-chairperson shall preside at all meetings of the Interstate Commission. The officers so elected shall serve without compensation or remuneration from the Interstate Commission; provided that, subject to the availability of budgeted funds, the officers shall be reimbursed for any ordinary and necessary costs and expenses incurred by them in the performance of their duties and responsibilities as officers of the Interstate Commission.

The Interstate Commission shall, through its executive committee, appoint or retain an executive director for such period, upon such terms and conditions and for such compensation as the Interstate Commission may deem appropriate. The executive director shall serve as secretary to the Interstate Commission, but shall not be a member and shall hire and supervise such other staff as may be authorized by the Interstate Commission.

(c) Qualified Immunity, Defense, and Indemnification. - The Commission's executive director and employees shall be immune from suit and liability, either personally or in their official capacity, for any claim for damage to or loss of property or personal injury or other civil liability caused or arising out of or relating to any actual or alleged act, error, or omission that occurred, or that such person had a reasonable basis for believing occurred within the scope of

Commission employment, duties, or responsibilities; provided, that any such person shall not be protected from suit or liability for any damage, loss, injury, or liability caused by the intentional or willful and wanton misconduct of any such person.

The liability of any commissioner, or the employee or agent of a commissioner, acting within the scope of such person's employment or duties for acts, errors, or omissions occurring within such person's state may not exceed the limits of liability set forth under the Constitution and laws of that state for state officials, employees, and agents. Nothing in this subsection shall be construed to protect any such person from suit or liability for any damage, loss, injury, or liability caused by the intentional or willful and wanton misconduct of any such person.

The Interstate Commission shall defend the executive director or the employees or representatives of the Interstate Commission and, subject to the approval of the Attorney General of the state represented by any commissioner of a compacting state, shall defend such commissioner or the commissioner's representatives or employees in any civil action seeking to impose liability arising out of any actual or alleged act, error, or omission that occurred within the scope of Interstate Commission employment, duties, or responsibilities, or that the defendant had a reasonable basis for believing occurred within the scope of Interstate Commission employment, duties, or responsibilities, provided that the actual or alleged act, error, or omission did not result from intentional or willful and wanton misconduct on the part of such person.

The Interstate Commission shall indemnify and hold the commissioner of a compacting state, or the commissioner's representatives or employees, or the Interstate Commission's representatives or employees, harmless in the amount of any settlement or judgment obtained against such persons arising out of any actual or alleged act, error, or omission that occurred within the scope of Interstate Commission employment, duties, or responsibilities, or that such persons had a reasonable basis for believing occurred within the scope of Interstate Commission employment, duties, or responsibilities, provided that the actual or alleged act, error, or omission did not result from intentional or willful and wanton misconduct on the part of such persons.

Article VI.

Rule-Making Functions of the Interstate Commission.

(a) The Interstate Commission shall promulgate and publish rules in order to effectively and efficiently achieve the purposes of the Compact.

(b) Rule making shall occur pursuant to the criteria set forth in this Article and the bylaws and rules adopted pursuant thereto. Such rule making shall substantially conform to the principles of the "Model State Administrative Procedures Act," 1981 Act, Uniform Laws Annotated, Vol. 16, p. 1 (2000), or such other administrative procedures acts, as the Interstate Commission deems appropriate consistent with due process requirements under the United States Constitution as now or hereafter interpreted by the United States Supreme Court. All rules and amendments shall become binding as of the date specified, as published with the final version of the rule as approved by the Commission.

(c) When promulgating a rule, the Interstate Commission shall, at a minimum:

(1) Publish the proposed rule's entire text stating the reason for that proposed rule;

(2) Allow and invite any and all persons to submit written data, facts, opinions, and arguments, which information shall be added to the record and be made publicly available;

(3) Provide an opportunity for an informal hearing if petitioned by 10 or more persons;

(4) Promulgate a final rule and its effective date, if appropriate, based on input from state or local officials, or interested parties; and

(5) Allow, not later than 60 days after a rule is promulgated, any interested person to file a petition in the United States District Court for the District of Columbia or in the Federal District Court where the Interstate Commission's principal office is located for judicial review of such rule.

(d) If the court finds that the Interstate Commission's action is not supported by substantial evidence in the rule-making record, the court shall hold the rule unlawful and set it aside. For purposes of this subsection, evidence is substantial if it would be considered substantial evidence under the Model State Administrative Procedures Act.

(e) If a majority of the legislatures of the compacting states rejects a rule, those states may, by enactment of a statute or resolution in the same manner used to adopt the Compact, cause that rule to have no further force and effect in any compacting state.

(f) The existing rules governing the operation of the Interstate Compact on Juveniles superseded by this act shall be null and void when all states, as defined in the Compact, have adopted The Interstate Compact for Juveniles.

(g) Upon determination by the Interstate Commission that a state of emergency exists, it may promulgate an emergency rule which shall become effective immediately upon adoption, provided that the usual rule-making procedures provided hereunder shall be retroactively applied to said rule as soon as reasonably possible but no later than 90 days after the effective date of the emergency rule.

Article VII.

Oversight, Enforcement, and Dispute Resolution by the Interstate Commission.

(a) Oversight. - The Interstate Commission shall oversee the administration and operations of the interstate movement of juveniles subject to this Compact in the compacting states and shall monitor such activities being administered in noncompacting states which may significantly affect compacting states.

The courts and executive agencies in each compacting state shall enforce this Compact and shall take all actions necessary and appropriate to effectuate the Compact's purposes and intent. The provisions of this Compact and the rules promulgated hereunder shall be received by all the judges, public officers, commissions, and departments of the state government as evidence of the authorized statute and administrative rules, and all courts shall take judicial notice of the Compact and the rules. In any judicial or administrative proceeding in a compacting state pertaining to the subject matter of this Compact which may affect the powers, responsibilities, or actions of the Interstate Commission, it shall be entitled to receive all service of process in any such proceeding and shall have standing to intervene in the proceeding for all purposes.

(b) Dispute Resolution. - The compacting states shall report to the Interstate Commission on all issues and activities necessary for the administration of the

Compact as well as issues and activities pertaining to compliance with the provisions of the Compact and its bylaws and rules.

The Interstate Commission shall attempt, upon the request of a compacting state, to resolve any disputes or other issues which are subject to the Compact and which may arise among compacting states and between compacting and noncompacting states. The Commission shall promulgate a rule providing for both mediation and binding dispute resolution for disputes among the compacting states.

The Interstate Commission, in the reasonable exercise of its discretion, shall enforce the provisions and rules of this Compact using any or all means set forth in Article XI of this Compact.

Article VIII.

Finance.

(a) The Interstate Commission shall pay or provide for the payment of the reasonable expenses of its establishment, organization, and ongoing activities.

(b) The Interstate Commission shall levy on and collect an annual assessment from each compacting state to cover the cost of the internal operations and activities of the Interstate Commission and its staff which must be in a total amount sufficient to cover the Interstate Commission's annual budget as approved each year. The aggregate annual assessment amount shall be allocated based upon a formula to be determined by the Interstate Commission, taking into consideration the population of each compacting state and the volume of interstate movement of juveniles in each compacting state and shall promulgate a rule binding upon all compacting states which governs said assessment.

(c) The Interstate Commission shall not incur any obligations of any kind prior to securing the funds adequate to meet the same; nor shall the Interstate Commission pledge the credit of any of the compacting states, except by and with the authority of the compacting state.

(d) The Interstate Commission shall keep accurate accounts of all receipts and disbursements. The receipts and disbursements of the Interstate

Commission shall be subject to the audit and accounting procedures established under its bylaws. However, all receipts and disbursements of funds handled by the Interstate Commission shall be audited yearly by a certified or licensed public accountant, and the report of the audit shall be included in and become part of the annual report of the Interstate Commission.

Article IX.

The State Council.

Each member state shall create a State Council for Interstate Juvenile Supervision. While each state may determine the membership of its own state council, its membership must include at least one representative from the legislative, judicial, and executive branches of government, victims groups, and the compact administrator, deputy compact administrator, or designee. Each compacting state retains the right to determine the qualifications of the compact administrator or deputy compact administrator. Each state council will advise and may exercise oversight and advocacy concerning that state's participation in Interstate Commission activities and other duties as may be determined by that state, including, but not limited to, development of policy concerning operations and procedures of the Compact within that state.

Article X.

Compacting States, Effective Date, and Amendment.

(a)    Any state, the District of Columbia or its designee, the Commonwealth of Puerto Rico, the U.S. Virgin Islands, Guam, American Samoa, and the Northern Marianas Islands, as defined in Article II of this Compact, is eligible to become a compacting state.

(b)    The Compact shall become effective and binding upon legislative enactment of the Compact into law by no less than 35 of the states. The initial effective date shall be the later of July 1, 2004, or upon enactment into law by the 35th jurisdiction. Thereafter, it shall become effective and binding as to any other compacting state upon enactment of the Compact into law by that state. The governors of nonmember states or their designees shall be invited to participate in the activities of the Interstate Commission on a nonvoting basis prior to adoption of the Compact by all states and territories of the United States.

(c) The Interstate Commission may propose amendments to the Compact for enactment by the compacting states. No amendment shall become effective and binding upon the Interstate Commission and the compacting states unless and until it is enacted into law by unanimous consent of the compacting states.

Article XI.

Withdrawal, Default, Termination, and Judicial Enforcement.

(a) Withdrawal. - Once effective, the Compact shall continue in force and remain binding upon each and every compacting state; provided that a compacting state may withdraw from the Compact by specifically repealing the statute which enacted the Compact into law.

The effective date of withdrawal is the effective date of the repeal.

The withdrawing state shall immediately notify the chairperson of the Interstate Commission in writing upon the introduction of legislation repealing this Compact in the withdrawing state. The Interstate Commission shall notify the other compacting states of the withdrawing state's intent to withdraw within 60 days of its receipt thereof.

The withdrawing state is responsible for all assessments, obligations, and liabilities incurred through the effective date of withdrawal, including any obligations, the performance of which extend beyond the effective date of withdrawal.

Reinstatement following withdrawal of any compacting state shall occur upon the withdrawing state reenacting the Compact or upon such later date as determined by the Interstate Commission.

(b) Technical Assistance, Fines, Suspension, Termination, and Default. - If the Interstate Commission determines that any compacting state has at any time defaulted in the performance of any of its obligations or responsibilities under this Compact, or the bylaws or duly promulgated rules, the Interstate Commission may impose any or all of the following penalties:

(1) Remedial training and technical assistance as directed by the Interstate Commission;

(2) Alternative Dispute Resolution;

(3) Fines, fees, and costs in such amounts as are deemed to be reasonable as fixed by the Interstate Commission; and

(4) Suspension or termination of membership in the Compact, which shall be imposed only after all other reasonable means of securing compliance under the bylaws and rules have been exhausted, and the Interstate Commission has therefore determined that the offending state is in default. Immediate notice of suspension shall be given by the Interstate Commission to the Governor, the Chief Justice, or the Chief Judicial Officer of the state, the majority and minority leaders of the defaulting state's legislature, and the state council.

The grounds for default include, but are not limited to, failure of a compacting state to perform such obligations or responsibilities imposed upon it by this Compact, the bylaws, or duly promulgated rules, and any other grounds designated in Commission bylaws and rules. The Interstate Commission shall immediately notify the defaulting state in writing of the penalty imposed by the Interstate Commission and of the default pending a cure of the default. The Commission shall stipulate the conditions and the time period within which the defaulting state must cure its default. If the defaulting state fails to cure the default within the time period specified by the Commission, the defaulting state shall be terminated from the Compact upon an affirmative vote of a majority of the compacting states, and all rights, privileges, and benefits conferred by this Compact shall be terminated from the effective date of termination.

Within 60 days of the effective date of termination of a defaulting state, the Commission shall notify the Governor, the Chief Justice or Chief Judicial Officer, the majority and minority leaders of the defaulting state's legislature, and the state council of the termination.

The defaulting state is responsible for all assessments, obligations, and liabilities incurred through the effective date of termination, including any obligations, the performance of which extends beyond the effective date of termination.

The Interstate Commission shall not bear any costs relating to the defaulting state unless otherwise mutually agreed upon in writing between the Interstate Commission and the defaulting state.

Reinstatement following termination of any compacting state requires both a reenactment of the Compact by the defaulting state and the approval of the Interstate Commission pursuant to the rules.

(c) Judicial Enforcement. - The Interstate Commission may, by majority vote of the members, initiate legal action in the United States District Court for the District of Columbia or, at the discretion of the Interstate Commission, in the federal district where the Interstate Commission has its offices to enforce compliance with the provisions of the Compact and its duly promulgated rules and bylaws, against any compacting state in default. In the event judicial enforcement is necessary, the prevailing party shall be awarded all costs of such litigation, including reasonable attorneys' fees.

(d) Dissolution of Compact. - The Compact dissolves effective upon the date of the withdrawal or default of the compacting state, which reduces membership in the Compact to one compacting state.

Upon the dissolution of this Compact, the Compact becomes null and void and shall be of no further force or effect, and the business and affairs of the Interstate Commission shall be concluded, and any surplus funds shall be distributed in accordance with the bylaws.

Article XII.

Severability and Construction.

(a) The provisions of this Compact shall be severable, and if any phrase, clause, sentence, or provision is deemed unenforceable, the remaining provisions of the Compact shall be enforceable.

(b) The provisions of this Compact shall be liberally construed to effectuate its purposes.

Article XIII.

Binding Effect of Compact and Other Laws.

(a) Other Laws. - Nothing herein prevents the enforcement of any other law of a compacting state that is not inconsistent with this Compact.

All compacting states' laws, other than state Constitutions and other interstate compacts, conflicting with this Compact are superseded to the extent of the conflict.

(b) Binding Effect of the Compact. - All lawful actions of the Interstate Commission, including all rules and bylaws promulgated by the Interstate Commission, are binding upon the compacting states.

All agreements between the Interstate Commission and the compacting states are binding in accordance with their terms.

Upon the request of a party to a conflict over meaning or interpretation of Interstate Commission actions, and upon a majority vote of the compacting states, the Interstate Commission may issue advisory opinions regarding such meaning or interpretation.

In the event any provision of this Compact exceeds the constitutional limits imposed on the legislature of any compacting state, the obligations, duties, powers, or jurisdiction sought to be conferred by such provision upon the Interstate Commission shall be ineffective, and such obligations, duties, powers, or jurisdiction shall remain in the compacting state and shall be exercised by the agency thereof to which such obligations, duties, powers, or jurisdiction are delegated by law in effect at the time this Compact becomes effective." (2005-194, s. 1.)

§ 7B-4002. Implementation of the Compact.

(a) The North Carolina State Council for Interstate Juvenile Supervision is hereby established. The Secretary of Public Safety, or the Secretary's designee, shall serve as the Compact Administrator for the State of North Carolina and as North Carolina's Commissioner to the Interstate Commission. The Secretary of Public Safety, or the Secretary's designee, is a member of the State Council and serves as chairperson of the State Council. In addition to the chairperson, the State Council shall consist of 10 members as follows:

(1)     One member representing the executive branch, to be appointed by the Governor;

(2)     One member from a victim's assistance group, to be appointed by the Governor;

(3)     One at-large member, to be appointed by the Governor;

(4)     One member of the Senate, to be appointed by the President Pro Tempore of the Senate;

(5)     One member of the House of Representatives, to be appointed by the Speaker of the House of Representatives;

(6)     A district court judge, to be appointed by the Chief Justice of the Supreme Court; and

(7)     Four members representing the juvenile court counselors, to be appointed by the Secretary of Public Safety.

(b)     The State Council shall meet at least twice a year and may also hold special meetings at the call of the chairperson. All terms are for three years.

(c)     The State Council may advise the Compact Administrator on participation in the Interstate Commission activities and administration of the Compact.

(d)     The members of the State Council shall serve without compensation but shall be reimbursed for necessary travel and subsistence expenses in accordance with the policies of the Office of State Budget and Management.

(e)     The State Council shall act in an advisory capacity to the Secretary of Public Safety concerning this State's participation in Interstate Commission activities and other duties as may be determined by each member state, including recommendations for policy concerning the operations and procedures of the Compact within this State.

(f) The Governor shall by executive order provide for any other matters necessary for implementation of the Compact at the time that it becomes effective, and, except as otherwise provided for in this section, the State Council may promulgate rules or regulations necessary to implement and administer the Compact. (2005-194, s. 1; 2012-194, s. 3.)

# Vision Books Order Form

Fax Orders:        1-980-299-5965

Phone Orders:      1-704-898-0770

E-mail Orders:     www.visionbooks.org

Mail Orders:       Vision Books, LLC
                   P.O. Box 42406
                   Charlotte, NC 28215

---

Shipp To:
Name_____
Address_____
City_____State_____Zip_____
Phone_____Fax_____
Email_____@_____

---

Bill To: We can bill a third party on your behalf.
Name_____
Address_____
City_____State_____Zip_____
Phone____(_____)_____Fax_____
Email_____@_____

---

| Pamphlet Number ($15.00 Each) | Qty | Total Cost |
|---|---|---|
| _____ | _____ | _____ |
| _____ | _____ | _____ |
| _____ | _____ | _____ |
| _____ | _____ | _____ |
| _____ | _____ | _____ |
| _____ | _____ | _____ |
| _____ | _____ | _____ |
| **Full Volume Set 1-92** | **92 Pamphlets** | **1,380.00** |

Free Shipping Shipping & Handling on Full Volume Orders
Add $1.00 Shipping & Handling per pamphlet          $_____

Total Cost                                          $_____

Thank You for Your Support. Management!

DID YOU ENJOY THIS BOOK?

Vision Books, LLC would like to hear from you! If you or someone you know has been fasely imprisoned, we would like to hear your story. If the 'North Carolina Criminal Law and Procedure' has had an effect in your life or if you have suggestions, we would like to hear from you. Send your letters to:

Vision Books, LLC
Attn: Staff Writers
P.O. Box 42406
Charlotte, NC 28215
Email: staff@visionbooks.org

Order Additional Copies:

Fax Orders: 1-980-299-5965

Phone Orders: 1-704-898-0770

E-mail Orders: www.visionbooks.org

Mail Orders: Vision Books, LLC
P.O. Box 42406
Charlotte, NC 28215

www.ingramcontent.com/pod-product-compliance
Lightning Source LLC
Chambersburg PA
CBHW071359170526
**45165CB00001B/107**